CRITICAL EDUCAT
VOL. 2

BECOMING
A STUDENT
OF TEACHING

GARLAND REFERENCE LIBRARY
OF SOCIAL SCIENCE
VOL. 853

CRITICAL EDUCATION PRACTICE

SHIRLEY R. STEINBERG
JOE L. KINCHELOE
Series Editors

BECOMING A STUDENT OF TEACHING

Methodologies for Exploring Self and School Context

Robert V. Bullough, Jr.
Andrew Gitlin

GARLAND PUBLISHING, Inc.
New York & London / 1995

A portion of chapter one was published in the *Journal of Education for Teaching* and is here reprinted with permission.

Library of Congress Cataloging-in-Publication Data

Bullough, Robert V., 1949–
    Becoming a student of teaching : methodologies for exploring self and school context / Robert V. Bullough, Jr., Andrew Gitlin.
        p.   cm. — (Garland reference library of social science ; vol. 853. Critical education practice ; vol. 2)
    Includes bibliographical references (p.) and index.
    ISBN 0–8153–0916–3. — ISBN 0–8153–1624–0 (pbk.)
    1. Teachers—Training of—United States.   2. Education—Study and teaching (Higher)—United States.
3. Student teaching—United States.   4. Teachers—In-service training—United States.   I. Gitlin, Andrew David.   II. Title.   III. Series: Garland reference library of social science ; v. 853.   IV. Series: Garland reference library of social science. Critical education practice ; vol. 2.
LB1715.B845   1995
370.71—dc20
                                            94–28785
                                              CIP

Cover design by Patti Hefner

Printed on acid-free, 250-year-life paper
Manufactured in the United States of America

To the Memory of
Ladd Holt

Contents

Series Editors' Introduction

Becoming a Student of Teaching is an important text that grounds autobiography, history, and social theory within the context of schooling. As it transcends the prescriptions for "proper" teaching mandated by many traditional texts, *Becoming a Student of Teaching* views teaching methodology as a complex and ambiguous act. Bullough and Gitlin understand that the lived environment of the classroom cannot be reduced to a series of scientific generalizations. Traditional texts have never understood that every classroom possesses a culture of its own. Thus, the meanings of specific classroom events depend on an observer's knowledge of what happened previously—the process by which classroom conventions were negotiated. Ignoring these negotiations, traditional texts silenced our natural language of teaching as they laid out an officially approved modus operandi. Bullough and Gitlin have produced a magnum opus written for those of us who wish to experience teaching within a realm of enlightenment and, consequently, empowerment. We are placed within the personal stories, historicization, and interpretation of teachers and students. Never forgetting the human *or* the social/theoretical, this volume presents finely honed alternative methodologies that reflect what it means to be a teacher. Integrating these methodologies critically, the authors model creative, literary, and theoretical research drawn together through themes and what Bullough and Gitlin refer to as the "tension between self and context." Practitioner/advocates of qualitative inquiry may be assured that this book will add to a growing bibliography of work that redefines the personal and eclectic role of educational research.

Unlike the authors of prescriptive methods texts with their lists of right and wrong ways to teach, Bullough and Gitlin take context into account. As qualitative researchers from Paul Willis, Yvonna Lincoln, Egon Guba, and Jay MacLeod to Peter McLaren, Ivor Goodson, Michael Connelly, and Jean Clandinin have noted: our understanding of an educational situation depends on the context in which it is encountered. It would seem that this understanding should not be difficult to grasp; but, given the preponderance of methods texts and methods courses that ignore it, the concept must be more difficult than we think. John Dewey understood this in the early twentieth century, arguing that knowledge of any type could not be viewed in isolation. Indeed, Dewey was so concerned with context that he concluded that a person is reasonable in the degree to which she or he sees an event not as something isolated but in its connection to the larger experience of human beings. Here rests the importance of *Becoming a Student of Teaching* —the authors specify what exactly this contextualization, this connection, to experience might mean to teachers.

As students of teacher education, we look back at the reconceptualization of curriculum studies as introduced by William Pinar in the early 1970s. Through his notion of *currere* Pinar connected his understanding of phenomenology to psychoanalysis and aesthetics to produce a unique analytical form—a mode of inquiry that would expand our ability to contextualize the teaching act (Pinar, 1995). *Currere,* the Latin root of the word "curriculum," concerns investigating the nature of the individual's personal/public experience. Utilizing this analytical synthesis, Pinar argued that we are better prepared to approach the contents of consciousness as they appear to us in educational contexts (Pinar, 1975, 1994, 1995). Such exploration allows us, as Pinar argued, to loosen our identification with the content of consciousness so that we can gain some distance from it. From our new vantage point, we may be able to see those psychic realms that are formed by conditioning and unconscious adherence to social convention (Kincheloe, 1991).

Of course, *currere* held implications for practitioners involved in various phases of educational activity. For those of us concerned with the political and economic dimensions of schooling, *currere* taught us to guard against the tendency to allow the realm of the theoretical to overwhelm and erase the realm of the personal. As readers internalize the notion, they understand Bullough and Gitlin's attempt to extend the study of teacher education through contextualizing qualitative methodologies. The authors make these methods of inquiry and analysis accessible to a wide audience and, in the process, expand the boundaries of educational analysis. Autobiography to Bullough and Gitlin is not some abstract concept—it is autobiography-in-practice, an applied autobiography that facilitates the teacher's analysis of his or her professional activities. At this point another important dimension of *Becoming a Student of Teaching* emerges: practicality is redefined. Traditionally, practical teacher education materials were "crudely practical" in that they specified exactly what a teacher should do on Monday morning. Bullough and Gitlin have restored integrity to the notion of the "practical," as they tie various educational discourses to the realm of the classroom. In so doing, they have respected the professionality of the teacher by refusing to simply prescribe how these discourses should be applied. They refuse to lower teachers to the status of rule followers who are discouraged from engaging in interpretive acts.

Although the book engages a variety of research methodologies, "Mark's Ethnography" (Mark's discussion about an eighth-grade English class) struck a personal note. My (Shirley Steinberg) first ethnography, actually my first *real* attempt at understanding myself as a teacher/student came at my *own* recollections of *my* tenth-grade teacher. As I read Mark's descriptions, I revisited similar experiences—those that Mark related as a current student/researcher, those to which I related as a former student/researcher. We both observed the essential and the optional—the most outstanding note being the fact that time passed "quickly" in class. Returning to our investigative/interpretive modes, we redefine, rework, and once again, add to our understandings of what "makes a good teacher" (Steinberg, 1992). Here the notion of autobiography-in-practice reemerges, as Mark's observation engages my own analysis of my role as a teacher.

This type of analysis opens new possibilities for all teachers as they begin to appreciate the conditions of uncertainty, uniqueness, and conflict in which they operate. Such a context demands not a list of teaching techniques but a preparation for understanding. Such a preparation helps cultivate an art of improvisation, a form of thinking-in-action. As improvisational artists, teachers respond to unexpected situations by creating their own "rules" extemporaneously. When needs arise the improvisational teacher changes his or her lesson plan on the spot and considers new ways to connect students to the curriculum. Such teachers slowly but steadily evolve as professionals, learning more about their strengths and weaknesses and their insights and blindness. When we are able to make the professional personal and to continually re-interpret ourselves as teachers, we continue within the conversation, a conversation significantly enhanced by *Becoming a Student of Teaching.*

Shirley R. Steinberg
Joe L. Kincheloe
Penn State University

References

Kincheloe, J. (1991). *Teachers as researchers: Qualitative inquiry as a path to empowerment.* London: Falmer Press.

Pinar, W. (1975). *Curriculum theorizing: The reconceptualists.* Berkeley, CA.: McCatchan.

Pinar, W. (1994). *Autobiography, politics and sexuality: Essays in curriculum theory, 1972–1992.* New York: Peter Lang.

Pinar, W., Reynolds, W., Slattery, P., and Taubman, P., (1995). *Understanding curriculum.* New York: Peter Lang.

Steinberg, S. (1992). "Teachers under suspicion: Is it true that teachers aren't as good as they used to be?" In Kincheloe, J. and Steinberg, S. (Eds.), *Thirteen questions: Reframing education's conversation.* New York: Peter Lang.

Preparing for Postmodernity

The current changes in the economy and superstructure associated with postmodernity pose particular perils and promises for the world of teacher education. As Wolfe has argued, it is quite conceivable that it will not only be the welfare state that is dismantled in the new epoch but also aspects of the superstructure.[1] In particular, some of the median associations such as universities and schools may well be diminished and decoupled in significant ways. This means that institutional sites may no longer be the only significant sites of struggle and that methodological genres focusing on institutional analysis and institutional theorizing may be similarly diminished.

Associated with this restructuring of institutional life is an associated change in the form of knowledge, particularly the forms of workplace knowledge that will be promoted. Significantly, much of the workplace knowledge currently being promoted is context specific and personal.[2] Putting these two things together means that there will be two different sites for struggle in the postmodernist period. First, there will be the continuing struggle for the theoretical and critical mission inside the surviving (but conceivably diminished) institutional sites. Second, and probably progressively more important for the future, will be the site of the personal life and identity. It is here that perhaps the most interesting project, what Giddens calls "the reflexive project of the self," will be contested in the next epoch. Life politics, the politics of identity construction and ongoing identity maintenance, will become a major growing site of ideological and intellectual contestation and nowhere more so than in teacher education.

Bullough and Gitlin march thoughtfully into this new terrain. Their position stands close to C. Wright Mills' famous dictum that "social science deals with problems of biography, of history and of their intersections within social structures."[3] This is a profoundly honest text in a number of ways but in two that I want to stress. First, it is honest in the sense that it stands on clear, morally defined ground, it has a strongly embedded base in humanistic values. Second, it is honest in that the authors can be clearly viewed (and therefore interrogated) in the text. These are not dispassionate authors but men who are clear about where they come from and where they stand. They provide a clear genesis and genealogy for their arguments.

In a sense they are writing about what I have called elsewhere the "reinscription of the theoretical and critical mission"[4] within the new more field-based terrain of teacher education. Their search for a new biographically informed and embedded mode of theorizing is an invigorating one. It provides a textual journey guaranteed to stimulate readers to push their search for educational theory into new and fruitful domains. *Becoming a Student of Teaching* aids its readers in confronting the perils and promises of the postmodern world.

Ivor Goodson
University of Western Ontario

NOTES

1. Wolfe, A. (1989) *Whose keeper? Social science and moral obligation.* Berkeley: University of California Press.

2. Goodson, I.F. (1993). Forms of knowledge and teacher education. *Journal of Education for Teaching, JET Papers No. 1,* pp. 1–3.

3. Mills, C.W. (1970). *The sociological imagination.* London: Penguin. p. 159.

4. Goodson, I.F. (1994). *Representing teachers.* New York: Teachers College Press.

Preface

Becoming a Student of Teaching: Methodologies for Exploring Self and School Context represents the culmination of many years of work with certification students. Our approach to teacher education has evolved as our understanding of the problems associated with educating teachers has increased. It has also evolved in response to our efforts to forge institutional arrangements and develop instructional approaches consistent with our view of the nature of teaching and the role teachers are to play in a complex and ever changing school environment.

Becoming a Student of Teaching presents a challenge to the traditional and dominant view of teacher education as training, which has as its primary concern the mastery of a set of techniques or skills and privileges public theory—theory found in policy documents and educational literature—over private theory—theory grounded in personal experience (see Griffiths & Tann, 1992). Training presents an image of the beginning teacher as passive and isolated and rightfully dependent on the expertise of others. Teacher educators who espouse this view think of teaching as a politically and perhaps morally neutral act and think of learners as bits of putty to be molded into predetermined shapes.

In contrast to a training view of teacher education, *Becoming a Student of Teaching* emphasizes education. Drawing on the Latin root of education, *educere*, teacher education, in contrast to training, emphasizes the use of methods that lead or draw out, that educe. Thus, consistent with a view of knowledge as socially constructed, we understand that like other learners, the beginning teacher forges personal systems of meaning within the bounds of a particular context (see Presidential Task Force,

1993). And we believe that teacher educators must build on and help reconstruct these systems, which are grounded in biography and life experience.

Becoming a Student of Teaching places the beginning teacher at the center of teacher education. The methodologies described are intended to enable the exploration and reconstruction not only of self, when deemed necessary, but also of context, in particular the school context. We wish to bring to the forefront issues of power that are crucially important to thinking through questions about the teacher's role and the educational purposes and practices that characterize that role. But more than this, the methodologies are intended to encourage the commitment to building and extending professional communities, where teachers, administrators, and college and university faculties join together in reciprocal relationships to improve the education offered young people and the quality of life of those who work within schools. In very broad strokes, this is our orientation.

We wish to thank the many certification students who have borne the brunt of our experimentation and given us pointed criticism that has sharpened our thinking. Feedback from Professor Bullough's 1993–1994 cohort group was especially helpful. We wish also to thank David Stokes for his thoughtful and good-humored criticism and Irene Tomsic for help with chapters four, seven, and ten. Finally, we dedicate *Becoming a Student of Teaching* to the memory of our friend and colleague, Ladd Holt, who was a first-rate teacher educator. Ladd exemplified teaching as an ethical relationship. We miss him. After a courageous and painful two-year battle with cancer, he spent part of the Thursday before he died reading, thinking about, and then chatting with Professor Bullough about chapter two. We hope he likes what we did with his suggestions.

A Note to Teacher Educators
on the Use of *Becoming a Student of Teaching*

Program Description

In our secondary teacher certification program we work with our students for an entire academic year and are responsible for their curriculum and general-methods courses along with student or practice teaching. Students are organized into a cohort group of about twenty-five, which stays together throughout the year and meets during the first two quarters for three hours, twice a week. The cohort organization is the foundation upon which we seek to build an incipient professional community, an essential condition for the success of our work and the accomplishment of our aims. Context matters. All twenty-five students are placed within a few schools early first term and begin to work with teachers and, in time, help select one who will serve as a cooperating or mentoring teacher. It is within these schools, and with the permission and support of the administration and faculty, that the work described in *Becoming a Student of Teaching* is accomplished. About midway through the second quarter certification students plan and teach a "short course," a unit approximately three weeks in length, as a means for identifying strengths and working on weaknesses in anticipation of practice teaching. Full-time practice teaching takes place during the third quarter and, with some variations, runs for ten weeks. The major variation is that some of our programs, similarly organized around cohorts, run for four quarters and involve approximately five months of half-time practice teaching. Obviously, the latter arrangement allows greater opportunities to link theory with practice and for students to study their practice. Finally, along with practice teaching, the students are enrolled in a weekly, two-hour seminar that provides a setting for posing questions about practice and considering alternatives.

Book and Chapter Organization

Following the introductory chapter, the book is organized into two parts. Part one, "Preservice Teacher Education," is subdivided into three sections: "Methodologies for Exploring Self," "Methodologies for Exploring School Context," and "Integrating Methodologies," the latter emphasizing the intimate linkage of self and context. Part two, "In-service Teacher Education," contains one chapter, and presents an integrating methodology, "Educative Research." This particular organization is the result of an extended discussion and compromise. Initially we resisted separating the methodologies this way because conceptually self and context must be considered together if teachers are to understand how meanings are constructed and how some meanings gain and maintain legitimacy. However, in the end we opted to organize the chapters around "self" and "school context" for the sake of simplicity and clarity. Some methodologies emphasize self over context, while others emphasize context over self. In both instances it is important to keep in mind the dialectical and mutually generative relationship of self and context. When using a methodology that emphasizes self, then, it is important to also attend to school context, and vice versa. Otherwise the nature of making meaning is distorted.

Except for chapter one, the chapters that make up *Becoming a Student of Teaching* are meant to stand alone. We organized and wrote them this way so that the methodologies will still be useful to those of you working within programs structured quite differently from our own, and to allow for variations in program emphasis on "self" and "school context."

We have used the word *methodology*—instead of *method*, *strategy*, or *technique*—intentionally, to distinguish our viewpoint from those of others. We are not presenting prescriptions to be followed, but rather clusters of diverse approaches to becoming a student of teaching that require intelligent adaptation, adjustment, and integration. Integration is essential if the program is to have coherence, a quality typically lacking when training orientations dominate.

As you read and think about how you might want to use the various methodologies (which ones, in what ways, and in what order), undoubtedly you will wonder about time constraints. As always, a lack of sufficient time in teacher education is a serious problem. As for teachers, so with teacher educators: The battle with the calendar and clock is frustrating, and you may discover that it is not possible to use each of the methodologies or in the manner and with the intensity we suggest.

Each chapter is divided into four parts. The first part introduces the methodology and includes a brief rationale for its use. The second includes samples of student work, which illustrate some aspects of the methodology. This work is included with the permission of the students and either is representative of the kind of work we receive or is included because it is especially provocative and possesses unusual potential to stimulate interest and involvement, or illustrates a common problem encountered by students when working with the methodologies. Within the third section we explore the students' work with an eye toward identifying a few—certainly not all—of the interesting, enlightening, and in some instances, troubling issues that we believe worthy of the attention of teacher education students. Within the final section, "A Note to Teacher Educators and Students," we address practical and sometimes theoretical issues related to use of the methodology. We hope students will read these sections. They ought to know something about the thinking that is behind what they are being asked to do, and they ought to be encouraged to become part of the teacher education conversation.

Additional Materials

We should mention that you may wish to complement your use of *Becoming a Student of Teaching* with other texts, perhaps ones that place a greater emphasis on the more technical aspects of learning to teach, such as lesson and unit planning and the skills associated with classroom management. These certainly are important topics for study. If you do select an additional text, it is important to help students avoid the seductiveness of the training mentality. In the quest for technical expertise it is easy to neglect the moral, political, and personal dimensions of teaching and learning to teach. *Becoming a Student of Teaching* presents a challenge to a training mentality, but the power of such a view is considerable and ought not to be underestimated.

The methodologies we describe enable beginning teachers to become, and to understand themselves as, producers of knowledge. Saying this does not mean, however, that in the quest to become a student of teaching, there is no place for knowledge produced by others. To become a student of teaching requires that texts be compared, ones self-generated with those produced by others, usually academics. We will not often specify the exact readings we use with the methodologies because you will want to make this decision yourself based on your values, program structure, and understanding of students. We think it is important, however, that students be provided opportunities to read what others have to say that has a bearing on their own studies of teaching. Text comparison enriches the study of teaching and elevates it while having the added virtue of introducing the neophyte to the issues and concerns debated in the wider educational community.

Integrating Methodologies

We need to say a word about the integrating methodologies. Chapters two through ten focus on individual methodologies. The educational value of the methodologies, however, comes when they are linked together and integrated and when means are provided to enable students to examine their development critically. Two methodologies, Action Reseach (see chapter eight) and the "personal teaching text" (PTT; see chapter nine), seek to do just this for preservice teacher education. These "integrating" methodologies bring self and context together. We call these methodologies to your attention now because they build on the work done in each of the preceding chapters and require careful advanced planning.

The PTT (Bullough, 1993) is a case record, of sorts, of the beginning teacher's teacher education experience. All written work produced through the methodologies introduced in

Becoming a Student of Teaching (including Action Research) is organized by each student into a PTT. At predetermined points throughout the year the certification students we work with are required to review and in writing critically analyze their PTTs. Although the specific task is presented in chapter nine, at this point it is important to note that like other learners, beginning teachers are often not aware of their development and of the direction they are heading. They tend to be overwhelmed by the here and now, the press of immediate demands. By pausing from time to time to consider what they have been doing and why, and where they are heading, students we work with are encouraged to take charge of their development. Additionally, the PTT has proven to be an important means for enhancing program continuity, a quality often lacking when training dominates professional education.

Becoming
a Student
of Teaching

CHAPTER ONE

Getting Oriented

Personal Stories

We have been educators for over twenty years: first as teachers, later as teacher educators. The past thirteen years, we have worked together in teacher education programs at the University of Utah. During this time we have sought to challenge traditional approaches to teacher education as training and sought to develop programs and practices that maximize beginning teachers' control over their own professional development.

When we first began working together, the secondary teacher education program at the university was disjointed, fragmented, and confusing. Training was the program's aim: Based on a delivery conception of teaching, emphasis was placed on learning and practicing discrete skills, and programmatically public and private theories were clearly separated and public theories privileged. By "public theory" we mean expert talk—the substance of academic discourse, including concepts, generalizations, models, and ways of making meaning (see Griffiths & Tann, 1992). In contrast, private theory is grounded experientially, and is represented by personal, idiosyncratic, biographically embedded, and often implicit concepts and understandings by which individuals make life meaningful. Private theory shapes what is seen and how it is understood (see Cole, 1990).

Methods courses were disconnected from curriculum courses, and both were disconnected from practice teaching. Similarly, foundations courses, and their concern for the aims of education, were unrelated to methods courses and their

3

emphasis on means. Moreover, students were strangers to one another and dropped in and out of the program at their convenience. Who these people were was of no particular importance to the program or to teaching. Like the students, professors drifted in and out of the courses and felt little connection to them.

Students complained loudly about content duplication and superficiality; about the kind, quality, and quantity of field experiences offered; and perhaps more than anything, about not feeling cared for. No one was responsible for the individual student and for seeing that he or she was on course and making reasonable progress toward certification. What mattered was accumulating the credits needed for certification. Student complaints were hard to ignore, especially since they were frequent enough and loud enough to convince the dean's office that something was amiss and in need of fixing. But what to do about them? A change in the program would necessitate a change in faculty roles, and under the best of circumstances, this is difficult to achieve even when there is widespread dissatisfaction. After all, program fragmentation plays to professors' desires for autonomy and independence.

In response to growing dissatisfaction, the faculty began meeting to explore the problem in order to provide a solution. Some faculty members understood the problem as simply a matter of providing better integration of methods courses with fieldwork and of improving the quality of student advising; no shift in orientation was required. From this view, all that was needed was for faculty members to share course syllabi and come to some agreement about who would teach which topics and for the student-advising office to shape up and do a better job.

Others had a different view of the problem, a more structural and philosophical view. Separate courses taught by faculty who rotated through them and felt no ownership of them would inevitably give rise to problems of duplication and, perhaps, of superficiality. From this viewpoint, occasional meetings within which syllabi were shared would do little to change the situation and nothing to bridge the separation of public and private theories about teaching or educational aims from means. Moreover, when both students and faculty drop into and out of courses, it is unreasonable to expect that caring relationships would develop, and caring relationships, some thought, were central to effective advising *and* teaching. Teaching is a relationship, a way of being with and relating to others, and not merely an expression of having mastered a set of delivery skills. And advising is a matter not just of dispensing information in a timely fashion but of building trust, of talking and problem solving together. Some sort of fundamental change in program structure and orientation was needed.

Eventually, the faculty agreed to experiment with a cohort organization, an attempt to create the "shared ordeal" (Lortie, 1975) that would help students see themselves as part of the teaching profession. For a full academic year a team of two professors (later this changed to a professor and a teaching associate because of limited resources) would be responsible for planning, teaching, and coordinating a large portion of the certification work of a group of twenty-five students. This included general methods courses and curriculum courses, which met for six hours a week for the first two terms, and student teaching, which included a weekly seminar. Moreover, within the cohort organization, professors would do much of the advising that had formerly been done by the advising office. The courses leading up to practice teaching were to involve significant fieldwork, and to this end the students were to be placed in a school early in the year and continue to work within it throughout the year. Eventually, some of these schools became professional development sites (Holmes, 1990), places where practicing teachers are specially educated to serve as mentors for student and beginning teachers and study their practice, but this is getting ahead of the story.

We supported this proposal and nudged it along, although we worried about the amount of time that the change would demand of us. Training teachers is less demanding than educating them. Soon, we found ourselves assigned to our first group of students, and with this assignment we faced a daunting problem. Being responsible for such a large portion of a program, and having students for an entire academic year, meant that we would be teaching new courses that required of us the development of new areas of expertise; and even when we had previously taught the content, a different approach or organization was needed. As we discovered, our relationships to students would also dramatically change. Despite these fears, however, we realized that the structure would allow us to experiment with different approaches to teacher education. For instance, for the first time in our careers it became possible, at least in principle, to introduce a theoretical concept, such as the implicit or "hidden curriculum," have students work with the concept in a field site, return to campus for further exploration of the concept, and then, as the students gained experience, return to it later in the year and in different ways. We could, then, better link public and private theories and the study of aims and educational means.

Critical Theory and Teacher Education

At this point in the story, we need to step back for a moment and share a bit of our biographies. Although attending different graduate schools (Ohio State and Wisconsin), we were both deeply influenced by work being done in critical theory in education, a theory that directed our attention to the relationship between schools and the social priorities and inequalities that characterize capitalism. We thought of public education as an extremely important avenue for furthering social and economic justice, but believed the institution—its organization and traditions—stunted this potential. We saw schools as factories, driven by class interests and infused with the values of a technocracy: control and efficiency, the handmaidens of training. We thought of teachers as oppressed workers, trapped, victims of an oppressive and alienating system. Indeed, much of our early research reflects this view (Bullough, Goldstein & Holt, 1984; Gitlin, 1983).

Our focus, then, was primarily on critique and not on relationship. We sought to identify the ways in which schooling limited and constrained teachers' actions and student learning, not the ways in which schools could enable their development or the ways in which teachers could shape the institution to achieve their purposes and build desired relationships with students.

Not surprisingly, we often found the beginning and practicing teachers we taught interested but largely disconnected from our analysis of schooling. Our project, and the public theories we presented, was not their project; being well-trained students, they mastered our discourse to give it back to us but, apparently unaffected, left us to engage in their lives' work as though they have never been in our classes.

A Reconsideration

Reenter the cohort: Imagine yourself for a moment in our shoes, and being assigned to work with a group of twenty-five preservice teacher education students for an entire academic year, good students who genuinely wanted to become teachers. Now, imagine having as your central professional message that schools are lousy places to work, young people alienated, and the curriculum fundamentally and perhaps fatally flawed! True or not, a year is a long time to endure such fare, and perhaps even a longer time to push it. What the cohort organization did was force us to reconsider our political and professional agendas, our theories in relationship to our students' theories, and their desire to become teachers and to succeed in the short run in practice teaching and in the long run as teachers. In our work at the University, the question for us was (and still is): How could we develop encounters with teacher education content and theory that would help our students achieve their goals and simultaneously enable us to maintain our intellectual and personal integrity? Many a long and sometimes disheartening conversation addressed this topic.

Our dilemma was softened a bit by developments within critical theory as applied to education that led to an attack on correspondence theory (Apple, 1979a). Correspondence theory, representing a rather vulgar, deterministic Marxism, suggested that schooling reproduced social inequality by corresponding with the inequalities of the larger society and, by implication, persons do as contexts allow them to do; consciousness follows context as day follows night. In this view, human agency was a delusion, a liberal's foolish fantasy. The attack on correspondence theories brought with it a message of hope that rang true to our experience: persons frequently resist pressures to conform, and with their resistance comes the possibility for institutional change and, therefore, hope for school reform. This turn was reflected in our own work as we conducted studies and worked with teachers who, in various ways, resisted institutional pressures to conform and seemed to make school a better place for their students as a result (Bullough & Gitlin, 1985; Bullough, Gitlin & Goldstein, 1984). Importantly, we came to recognize that resistance is often grounded in private theory and in beliefs about self as teacher. Potentially, then, teacher education could play a part in school transformation, and critical theory could serve as a lens for focusing our work so long as it was seen in relation to the private theories held by students.

Our study of the writings of Jurgen Habermas (1971; 1975) also proved important to our development. We found compelling his vigorous critique of instrumental reason, the kind of reason that reduced human beings to numbers, the universe to a giant, grinding machine, and education to training. But unlike a good many critical theorists, Habermas moved beyond critique. He recognized in the innate ability and desire of humans to relate to one another through language a means for generating a social and political ideal worth striving for: communication without domination. He explored the conditions needed for communication to proceed fruitfully, and explicated some of the ways in which communication is distorted, often intentionally for strategic reasons as when we manipulate our friends to get our way and to set aside their own interests. His ideal—communication without domination—got us thinking about teaching in ways we had never thought of before and sharpened our awareness of the negative influence of the assumptions of training on our students' development as teachers. We recognized that as a relationship teaching always involved unequal distributions of power between teachers and students, but began to explore the ways in which we might minimize domination through dialogue (see Bullough, 1988; Gitlin, 1990). More broadly, we began to think of learning to teach in terms of engaging our students in the critical and communal study of their own thinking and practice and of linking this study to public theories about institutional power and education.

Working with the cohort groups and getting to know, respect, and enjoy our students also played an important part in nudging along our development. For the most part, they were very able and interesting people, adults, who brought with them a commitment to, as many of them often have said, "make things better." One could not work with such people and still hold strongly to the view that their actions were merely reproductive of social and economic inequalities, that they were only pawns in a cruel social charade. To incorporate our growing appreciation of the importance of agency in institutional life, we eventually organized our practice within the cohort around the dialectical and dynamic relationship of self and context. We focused on self because of its connection to knowledge production (private theories) and agency. We came to think of our students as moral-political agents about to assume positions of power and authority. We focused on context because critical theory had helped us understand how contexts often direct teacher behavior not only in ways that run counter to their intentions and aims but also in ways that prevent scrutinizing institutionally accepted roles and relationships. Later, the building of an educational community, both among teachers and in a wider sense, assumed a central place in our thinking because of its potential for furthering collective action as a means for challenging contextual limits.

As our thinking evolved, so did our practice; as our practice evolved, so did our thinking about preservice teacher education. We encountered many frustrations. Perhaps the most important frustration from the point of view of altering our thinking came as a result of watching much of our work "wash out" during student teaching and the first year of teaching. It appeared as though, once our students became "real" teachers, they forgot or simply discarded much that we had "taught" them (see Bullough, 1989; Bullough, Knowles & Crow, 1992). We wanted our students to become producers of knowledge and, through the process, students of the politics of schooling. We saw too little evidence to suggest that our aims were being met. Survival and the desire to obtain a positive evaluation or to fit into a department consumed many of them during practice teaching and during their first year of teaching, just as trainers who emphasize apprenticeships long claimed. Recognizing this problem as partially related to a student teaching format that was a holdover from our program when training was the central aim, we changed student teaching from full- to half-time teaching so that additional time was available for reflection. This helped, but the problem persisted. We came to realize that no matter how hard we worked within preservice teacher education or how many adjustments we made in practice teaching, the problem would continue until preservice teacher education was linked to in-service teacher education and both challenged training assumptions.

A serious limitation of training is that it permits the dropping off of newly certified teachers at the school's doorstep as though the knowledge about teaching that has been poured over their heads makes them a teacher. Our students, we realized, needed ongoing support after certification to continue their exploration of self and context, particularly when the results of this exploration produced tension between institutionally favored roles and relationships and personally valued ones. Thus, our initial vision of teacher education as a group enterprise defined by cohort membership expanded beyond the confines of preservice teacher education. We seek now to assist in the building of a professional community in recognition that teacher education is never ending and that the creation of a vital community is central not only to educational renewal but to individual teacher development. In this work, public theory plays an important part.

Five Propositions

For the most part, *Becoming a Student of Teaching* presents the results of a kind of informed trial-and-error approach to teacher education, but this tells only a part of the story. We have not worked within an institutional or intellectual vacuum, and in our case the institutional context has been one that has allowed experimentation. Within the cohorts we have enjoyed remarkable freedom; benign neglect has its virtues. Our students have not only tolerated our sometimes crazy ideas but—through interviews, questionnaires, and other means—have given useful feedback on our work that has greatly assisted our efforts (see Bullough with Stokes, 1994). Being students of our practice, we have taken this feedback seriously; and it is the results of this ongoing inquiry that follow.

Through the years of experimenting and of testing our hunches, along with our reading about and study of teacher education, we have come to a few conclusions about how to make teacher education educative. We stand by them, although we realize that with time and increased experience adjustments will likely be necessary. They have taken the form of five interrelated propositions that we believe *taken together* offer an alternative to teacher training and whose echoes resound on every page of *Becoming a Student of Teaching*. The first proposition is that certification signals only the beginning of teacher education, not its ending. Ultimately, preservice must be joined to ongoing in-service teacher education. The second proposition is that because work contexts either enable or limit human development, they need to be carefully studied and criticized. The third proposition is that our conceptions of ourselves as teachers are grounded biographically. If teacher education is to make a difference, it must start with biography and find ways to identify, clarify, articulate, and critique the assumptions—the personal theories—about teaching, learning, students, and education embedded within it (see Knowles, 1992). Public and private theories need to converse. The fourth proposition is that reflection, systematic inquiry, is a central and crucial element in making teacher education educational. The fifth and last proposition has two parts: (1) Given that teachers have a wealth of knowledge about teaching and are central actors in the educational community, it is vital that they be actively involved in furthering one another's development; and (2) recognizing that the context of teaching is hostile to teachers working with and assisting other teachers, institutional roles and relationships must be created that enable collegiality and community building. Altering established patterns of interaction that isolate teachers and minimize their involvement in decision making is essential to establishing a powerful and progressive profession. "Full participation" (Pateman, 1970), where individuals and groups have access to decision making and the power to act upon their decisions, ought to be our aim. A brief discussion of the basis for each proposition follows.

Certification

In 1981 Ken Zeichner and Bob Tabachnick published an article that raised a troubling question: "Are the effects of university teacher education washed out by school experience?" At the time, the widely held view was that the university experience represented a liberalizing influence on the thinking of teacher education students that was then crushed by the reality of school practice during student teaching. Teacher education students became increasingly conservative; and to many teacher educators, ourselves included, this was cause for lament. However, as Zeichner and Tabachnick pointed out in their article, it was unlikely that the university experience generally, or teacher education specifically, was ever as liberalizing as many professors assumed or claimed: There may not have been anything to "wash out" in the first place!

If teacher education is to be more influential, a different way of working with students and school faculties must be forged. Teacher educators, teachers, and administrators need to join together collaboratively, not merely cooperatively, and jointly seek to produce conditions within schools so that reflection on public and private theories about teaching, and the aims and means of education, may become commonplace and shared action becomes the norm rather than the exception. Much needs to be done if these two very different institutions and cultures, the schools and universities, are to work productively together. Resources are scarce, and becoming more so, and the potential for exploitation is very real, particularly as professors continue to seek sites to conduct their studies and to place students while distancing themselves from the school culture. Nevertheless, through sharing strengths and resources and openly exploring and accepting differences, there is the potential to develop institutional structures and relationships that break the mold of the tried and true and move us in the direction of enabling teachers to become more active participants in the remaking of their educational world. Surely, such a project promises significant benefits to teacher educators and especially to students.

Some of you reading these words may be tempted to say, "So what? Who cares if teacher education has little impact? Good subject matter knowledge and some practice teaching are all that it takes to make a good teacher. Good teachers are born, not made." This is a very common perception, and one that we find troubling. Still, it is a view not likely to go away, at least in the near future. It troubles us not only because it denies the value of a substantial and growing body of research useful for thinking about and designing encounters with content, what we would call "pedagogical knowledge" (Grimmett & MacKinnon, 1992), but also because it suggests that learning to teach is a simple matter when it is not. Quite to the contrary, excellent teaching may be among the most difficult of human accomplishments. Like any other expression of excellence, its achievement is enhanced through the study of its practice; and in good measure this is what we conceive teacher education to be. For this reason, among others, we have become increasingly involved over the years in the effort to bring schools and colleges and universities committed to teacher education together to explore ways of creating the conditions needed for beginning teachers to become students of their own thinking and practice, not just student teachers. This is fundamentally important to distinguishing our work from training.

Work Context

All social contexts, schools included, are defined and given their particular character by the accepted and evolving roles, relationships, and rules that govern interaction. There is no meaning without context, and context shapes what is perceived as valued and valuable. In a myriad of ways, most of which are subtle and generally taken for granted, newcomers to teaching are told what are and are not appropriate actions and utterances and are encouraged and enticed to comply with expectations.

School contexts press conformity on the individual, who may respond in any number of ways, including strategic compliance—doing what seems necessary (Lacey, 1977)—and open resistance. Thinking about schools as historical contexts within which meaning is made and that value some interests over others presents a pressing challenge to teachers and teacher educators. Part of the challenge is to provide assistance to beginning teachers so they can examine and perhaps reconstruct institutionally preferred roles in the quest for a place within the school that is ethically defensible, morally and politically responsible, and personally satisfying. Knowing about a context and how it defines what is reasonable and possible is crucial to successful role negotiation, as it is to changing a role when change is seen as desirable. Another part of learning about context involves assisting the beginning teacher to understand how the local school context is influenced by educational policies and practices at state and national levels.

Biography

Despite the assumptions of training, in a manner perhaps unlike that of any other profession, in teaching the medium is the message and the medium is who and what a person is (Goodson, 1992; Knowles, Cole with Presswood, 1994). As a beginning teacher it is in good measure through you—and your values, beliefs, and knowledge of young people and about content and how to teach it—that students will either engage or disengage from learning. Who you are is important in other ways as well. It is in large part through your prior experience that you will make sense of teaching and of your students' backgrounds and abilities, formulate a curriculum, frame problems for study, and ultimately negotiate a teacher role.

From our viewpoint, teacher education should start with who the beginning teacher is—or rather, who you imagine yourself to be as a teacher—and then assist you to engage in the active exploration of the private or "implicit theories" (Clark, 1988) you bring to teaching. It is through these biographically embedded theories, which are generally taken for granted and assumed to be natural, that sense is made of teacher education and, later, the world of teaching. Through them as a beginning teacher you will either screen out, accept, or adjust to what is taught. You seek first a confirmation of who you think you are as teacher, and this is to be expected. But if you are to become educated as a teacher, commonly held assumptions about teaching must be challenged and tested. Masquerading as common sense, your private theories need to be made explicit so they can be criticized and, when found wanting, reconstructed. Long ago, John Dewey characterized education as a matter of "reconstructing experience," and this is precisely the aim of teacher education: to assist you to confront and, in some ways, reconstruct your thinking. Ultimately, only you can do this, however; your teachers can only create conditions that they believe are most likely to facilitate the facing of self. The methodologies presented in *Becoming a Student of Teaching* are intended to help create these conditions.

Reflection

Currently much is being spoken and written about the value of reflection in teacher education both as an aim and a means (see Clift, Houston & Pugach, 1991)). The "good teacher," it is said, is a reflective teacher, one who inquires into his or her thinking and practice with an eye toward making improvements. We too stand on the side of the angels who are championing programs that will promote the development of reflective teachers. We also want to encourage teachers to carefully consider the consequences of their actions in the classroom and on others' development. But too often, the calls to get teachers to engage in reflection and to study their practice are only empty slogans and boil down to nothing more than a plea that they "think hard" about what they are doing and why they are doing it. To be sure, there is much to be said for "thinking hard" about something, but how does one think hard, about what, and for what purposes? Moreover, what does one do while teaching to solve a problem, when there is so little time to stop and think, when reflection takes place in action (Schon, 1987)?

Sometimes when the meaning of reflection is made explicit, one discovers the assumptions of training that are hidden away. For example, one of the most often articulated reasons for valuing reflection is that it is a means for narrowing the gap between teacher practice and educational theory and research. Theory and research provide the models of good practice. The problem with this view is that the self and the private theories beginning teachers hold get lost: it matters little who the individual is or what educational aims are valued; instead, the object is to make practice better by conforming to an external standard of some kind. Determining what makes practice better, however, involves a judgment based on contextual and personal factors too easily excluded from the equation. Accordingly, reflection may become merely a training tool, when it ought to be a process of linking means and ends so that self and context can be examined and reconstructed where necessary and public and private theories can be brought together in a dynamic and reflexive relationship.

Thus, to be reflective means more than just thinking hard about what you, as a beginning teacher, are doing and whether or not a particular practice is "working" or is consistent with a list of competencies or outcomes. To be reflective means that careful attention is given to individual experience and how meaning is made and justified, and to the analysis of the constraining and enabling influence of contexts and how they shape human relations (Bullough & Gitlin, 1989). It involves attending to how problems are framed and to the relationship between public and private theories.

Problem framing goes directly to the issue of what kinds of questions and issues you should be reflective about. In this regard, Liston and Zeichner offer some help when they assert that teachers ought to inquire into:

> (1) the pedagogical and curricular means used to attain education aims, (2) the underlying assumptions and consequences of pedagogical action, and (3) the moral implications of pedagogical actions and the structure of schooling. (Liston & Zeichner 1987:2)

We agree that these are among the issues that ought to be grappled with. We would add, however, that in addition to these you need to be involved in ongoing reflection about self and about the school context within which you are working. These ought to be primary considerations, not merely afterthoughts.

One intent of *Becoming a Student of Teaching* is to assist beginning teachers to frame problems in ways that expose the relationship between the technical concerns of teachers and the personal, ethical, and political dimensions of teaching which are so often neglected. With respect to the latter, beginning teachers need to understand that all that they do and say represents their vision of the good life—their social philosophy—and is therefore inherently political. To be sure, teachers can be reflective about many things, silly and serious; our wish is to encourage you to not forget that there is more to becoming a teacher than mastering supposedly proven techniques. Emphatically, you ought to become suspicious of the comfort that comes from the common teacher pronouncement, "It works." Many things work, but not everything that "works" is morally, socially, or educationally defensible. Thus, we seek to influence what you see as a problem.

To this end, *Becoming a Student of Teaching* presents some of the processes our students have found useful in their study of teaching and helpful in their development as teachers; they are methodologies of inquiry. Inevitably, their influence is unpredictable and indirect, however. Only trainers would claim otherwise. Put differently, their influence on your thinking and development as a teacher is what you decide it will be. Perhaps the best that teacher educators can hope for is that what they teach *and* how they teach it will influence the grounds upon which you make your decisions and assist you to frame problems usefully. It is in this way that teacher education has a bearing on reflection when it takes place in action.

Educational Community

Many of the beginning teachers we have worked with over the years have been hesitant to ask for assistance when they have needed it. They do not think of learning as a community affair and responsibility. Through the cohort we seek to provide for our students a balance between support and challenge: without support, challenge often leads to defensiveness; with it, reconstruction of private theories becomes possible. Once our students are hired as first-year teachers, however, they are often left alone by administrators and more experienced teachers to make it on their own. Beginning teachers often discover that teaching is a solitary activity, but it need not be.

Fortunately, because of a growing awareness of the problems faced by beginning teachers and of the importance to the quality of the education offered young people of a successful transition for the neophyte into teaching, the tradition of neglect is changing. A sign of change is that, increasingly, beginning teachers can expect to be assigned a mentor teacher. Not surprisingly, it appears as though the aim of mentoring tends to be one of facilitating socialization to the context of teaching and thus represents an extension of training. Getting oriented to a new context is important, but additional aims (including exploring how the work context shapes relationships and directs meaning making) should be part of mentoring. Mentoring provides the opportunity for beginning teachers to study teaching and their thinking about teaching together and to make adjustments in the context of teaching based on continual examination of the relation between articulated aims and means.

Although the quality of the mentoring offered is often uneven, such programs are inspired by the recognition that becoming a teacher is the responsibility of the entire educational community, including the university, and that the health and vitality of that community is directly dependent upon its ability to attract, induct, and nurture talented neophytes. Rosenholtz nicely captures this view:

> If teaching is collectively viewed as an inherently difficult undertaking, it is both necessary and legitimate to seek and to offer professional assistance. This is exactly what occurs in instructionally successful schools, where, because of strong administrative or faculty leadership, teaching is considered a collective rather than an individual enterprise; requests and offers of assistance among colleagues are frequent; and reasoned intentions, informed choices, and collective actions set the conditions under which teachers improve instructionally. (1989:430)

The process involved in becoming a teacher is of vital interest to the educational community in part because it is a means by which that community is sustained or reconstructed. But, not only the professional community is affected by the outcome. As fragmented as it is, the professional community has a responsibility for building and shaping our collective social being as well. Like it or not, as John Goodlad (1991) phrased it, teachers are "moral stewards" of schooling, and as such have the responsibility to be engaged actively in the "continuous renewal of the schools" for the sake of children, themselves, and our collective well-being. They are charged with creating within schools the kind and quality of life that ought to be lived without them. It was for this reason that Boyd H. Bode argued many years ago that "educational practice which avoids social theory is at best a trivial thing and at worst a serious obstruction to progress" (1937:74).

Communities are strong when there is both diversity and a shared vision. The culture of teaching, however, is one that often encourages teacher isolation and disengagement. These are coping strategies some teachers use to make the work tolerable if not enjoyable. Sikes and her colleagues make a useful distinction between "private" and "public" coping strategies. "Private strategies," they state, "are employed by individual teachers to gain their own ends or cope with whatever is in front of them" whereas public strategies "involve a group of teachers acting together to gain their aims" (1985:72, 95). One of the most powerful private strategies used by teachers, one that seriously undermines efforts to build community, is simply to close the classroom door and ignore what goes on outside of it. In contrast, teacher education needs to be thought of as a community affair, one that employs public strategies and brings with it the responsibility to reach out to others who share the quest to become effective teachers and to work with them and others to strengthen and improve our schools.

These, then, are the five propositions that underpin the methodologies and analyses presented in *Becoming a Student of Teaching*.

PART ONE

Preservice Teacher Education

The chapters that follow present methodologies that we think will further your development as a student of teaching. Unfortunately, the emphasis within many certification programs is narrowly focused on practical teaching skills devoid of theory. In contrast, our concern is to influence the grounds upon which you will make professional decisions. Accordingly, we have developed methodologies to enable you to articulate and examine the theories embedded in your thinking about teaching and your teaching practice. However, if these methodologies are to make a difference in your professional development, they need to go hand in hand with changes in your understanding of what it means to teach. The insights of one of the students who used many of the methodologies we will describe suggest how her view of what it means to teach and the importance of theory to teacher development changed during the preservice teacher education program.

> There was a lot of material there that the cohort [the teacher education program] offered, but I was too anxious to get into the classroom, and too egotistical [to pay careful attention] believing. . . . I know how to teach. There are things that I needed, I'm going back to reread now. . . . There was material that [the teacher education program] offered . . . guidance offered that I didn't take advantage of. I wish the students who were in the cohort this year would—if they would listen to anything—listen to that. Don't be too anxious to get into the classroom. Pay attention to theory. It gives you a foundation [for studying teaching].

Methodologies for Exploring Self

CHAPTER TWO

Life History/Educational Autobiography

Introduction

Years of experience as a student and perhaps in various teaching-related activities provides part of the backdrop against which teacher development takes place. From this experience the beginning teacher brings to teacher education a plethora of unarticulated and unexamined beliefs about teaching, learning, and the self as teacher that require scrutiny. Writing and exploring life histories or educational autobiographies is an important means for illuminating and beginning to confront and perhaps change these beliefs or assumptions. By making them explicit, by uncovering and exploring their biographical origins, one may reconstruct them. Thus, life history is a means for shaping one's future.

To know the past is to know oneself as an individual *and* as a representative of a socio-historical moment in time; like others each person is a victim, vehicle, and ultimately a resolution of a culture's dilemmas. We are born into a particular family, holding particular values, within a particular social, economic, and political context that brings with it specific problems and issues and ways of making meaning. Educationally, it makes a difference, then, if one is born in an urban setting to a single, unskilled, and unemployed mother or to a large, rural farm family, and these differences are expressed in how the world is made sensible and in how and what one learns. Making the past explicit, finding themes, and identifying continuities and discontinuities sharpen and darken the lines around self and, simultaneously, the other. As lines darken, contexts and the roles and relationships that define them are illuminated. Made explicit, and then competently articulated, the past as a story of self forms the basis for powerfully entering negotiation with new situations, like a first teaching job, and the roles and subtexts that characterize them self-confidently and self-consciously. From this grounding educational judgements can be made and justified, and criticism can be directed toward those elements of a school context that are seen as miseducative. This is so because to say who one is is to say what one stands for.

To be able to say who one is as teacher and what one stands for, however, does not mean that what one stands for is "right" or morally and educationally responsible. Rather, it is part of an ongoing process of challenging and *perhaps* reconfiguring elements of self. We say "perhaps reconfiguring self" because much of what life history reveals about self will be self-confirming, representing values and beliefs that are central to who one is and that are relatively impervious to change. The discovery of such commitments, however, does not lessen the value of life history. To the contrary, it helps to define more clearly the nature of the educational project faced by the beginning teacher. It does this, in part, by forcing consideration of what contextual conditions are necessary for maintaining one's teaching commitments. Clearly, teachers ought to know what theories are driving their actions and be able to defend them. Teaching is a relationship with students, and definitions— theories—about the nature of students and learning bring with them definitions of self-as-teacher, and even of the good society, and the nature of knowledge and what is most worth knowing. The converse is also true. Teacher and student roles interact, sustain, and maintain one another.

Writing an educational autobiography brings with it the realization that there is no single authoritative story line—that the text evolves over time and in response to changing conditions and understandings. One's history, one's conceptions of self-as-teacher, can and do change. Carla, whose story will shortly be presented, nicely captured the point when she wrote: "If you ask me again tomorrow to tell you my life story, I might tell you a whole bunch of other things." After rereading his autobiography and looking backward over the year he spent in our certification program, another of our students observed in an interview that his history, his perception of himself, had changed. He had a new history, and he was different as a result: "[Writing] the educational autobiography was really interesting. How my perceptions have changed!" He admitted that his motivation to teach had been essentially negative, a desire to correct evils done to him. Seeing teaching through a teacher's eyes, he said, softened and changed his negative views of his teachers and of his school experience, and a different vision of his role as teacher emerged as a result.

We author our own stories, but these stories are written within social, political, and economic contexts that define what is seen as desirable, proper, and more importantly, possible. Constant scrutiny of one's values and beliefs is called for in relationship to the influence of context, and changes in context, on self and others, including students. Accordingly, the writing of autobiographies does not free teachers from their histories but rather enables them to take charge of those histories, to assert ownership, and to recognize their place as actors who can shape contexts and as authors who have before them choices that matter, that make a difference in the quality of schooling offered young people and in their own development as teachers.

Writing

The following is the life-history assignment we present to our students.

> Write an "education-related" life history. In the life history describe how you came to your current decision to become a teacher. Especially identify important people or "critical incidents" that significantly influenced your decision and your thinking about the aims of education, about the proper role of teachers, and about yourself as teacher. Consider your "experience of school," how school felt, and how you best learned and when you felt most valued,

connected, and at peace—or least valued, most disconnected, and most at war with yourself and with school.

A "critical incident" is an event that signals an important change in course, a shift in one's thinking (Measor, 1985). The term "education-related" is meant to be taken very broadly. Do not read "*school*-related," but "*education*-related." Perhaps most of our education takes place outside of schools; and a good many, perhaps most, of the people encountered and the events experienced that are educationally important have little to do with schooling. So think broadly and deeply.

Be patient with yourself. Recapturing the past may take some time. Getting started is often difficult, just as it is often a problem to know when to quit. Quit when you have nothing more you want to say and share. To get started, you might find it useful to make a listing of persons who have influenced you for good or ill, or of critical incidents. Some beginning teachers find it useful to start with the present and go backward, marching through names, dates, places, and seeking to recapture memories, feelings, impressions. Once you begin writing, memories will pop into your head and you will find that the storyline you are seeking to create will shift and sometimes dramatically change. A single recalled event may put an entirely different interpretation on your history than the one with which you began. You may discover some painful memories—Mrs. Prince, the cruel, abusive, boy-hating teacher who terrorized one of the authors during first grade—which have such an impact that everything else you write seems an addendum. It is likely you will find that although sometimes painful, writing is also a means to come to terms with hurt and to learn from it.

When writing of self, there are no right answers. Validity is replaced by authenticity. Does the story feel right? Does it capture you and your thinking? But if you leave writing feeling uneasy, do not be dismayed. Writing does not end the use of your autobiography. The methodologies presented will give you ample additional opportunities to think carefully about yourself as a teacher, and perhaps these will assist you to name your uneasiness. After all, your story is ongoing.

Three education-related autobiographies—two edited (to reduce their length) and one complete—taken from a recent cohort group follow.

Carla: "My Life Story . . . for Today"

I am the oldest child of immigrant parents. As such, I always felt different, a little odd. My parents spoke with an accent and did things differently from most people. Sometimes I remember being embarrassed by that fact, other times I enjoyed the uniqueness of my roots. Either way, my roots shaped many of my perceptions as I grew up, but I am only now beginning to see how.

Although I was born in Chicago, we lived in Canada for the first five years of my life. Much of that time was spent with foreign relatives visiting. I loved to listen to them tell me stories of what it was like where they lived. I also delighted in my ability to speak and understand several languages. I realized at a very young age that not everyone spoke a different language in their home or had foreign relatives with whom to speak different languages.

My parents wanted very much to have their children educated in "Amereeca," so they worked extremely hard to gain a visa to move back to the U.S. Much of the Latin-European approach to life that I had been accustomed to was gone. Kindergarten was not just the beginning of my education, it was the beginning of my "Americanness."

By the time I was nine years old, my parents were not too sure about the customs and habits of American school children (girls wore shorts under their dresses so the boys wouldn't see their underwear when they climbed on the monkey bars—but why are girls climbing on the monkey bars at school in the first place?).

. . . My father became a practicing psychiatrist and moved the family to a rich suburb of Chicago. Unfortunately for my parents, these people had even stranger customs than the ones we left [behind].

As time went on, my mother, brother, sisters and I became quite Americanized, but my father did everything he could to maintain his traditional ways. This was not a source of conflict in our home. It did, however, serve to illustrate to me how different cultures are and how much culture is part of every aspect of life.

By the time I entered high school two things were very apparent to my parents: their eldest daughter was very independent, and perhaps the money they had saved for her college education would be better spent on an island in the Pacific so she could be Queen. I did not get the island. I did, however, move myself, three days after graduation, to the Florida Keys.... [I did this] to assert my independence. It was . . . a wonderful experience. I worked and I paid for everything out of my own pocket (an amazing thing for a rich kid). I loved my independence. I became intoxicated by it, and knew from that experience that I never wanted to give it up. Moreover, I wanted everyone to enjoy the thrill of independence.

I became an activist. If there was a cause, I would be [involved]. I [was] a rebel. Actually, I didn't need a cause, I was just a rebel, outspoken and direct. The causes were all good ones, and they helped me to further shape my view of the world. Most importantly, they showed me that I must make a conscious choice to make [this world] better. If I don't, I consequently make a passive choice to make it worse.

My activism was a little out of place in the conservative [community within which I lived]. But [this] was for me all the more reason to speak out. Somehow, in the midst of all the protesting I went to college. Even more amazingly, I convinced my professors that I was a promising student despite being somewhat of a flake. At the University I worked haphazardly towards a television production degree. My work through the department was well respected and brought me both accolades and job offers (with much needed good pay). I was going a million miles an hour without a destination. Then I met [Rich], my husband. Things like destination began to be important to me.

. . . I had two children, a girl . . . (just turned six), and a boy . . . (just turned five). Right before they were born [my husband and I] decided to move his business to our home so we could both spend as much time as possible with our future kids.

Oh, yeah, the college thing. That's pretty much how I felt about it at the time. When my husband and I got married, I was working for a [motion picture company] and making independent documentaries. I was very successful . . . but was burning out [and felt unhappy]. College was definitely getting the shortest end of the stick. It all seemed to be a waste of time. I wasn't sure what I wanted, but I knew I was not finding it in school or with the work I was doing. So, I left. . . .

While raising the kids and working on our out-of-the-home business, I became more and more involved with my church. It is important to know that my church is very large, about 1,300 members, and I think about 1,200 of them are kids (okay, a slight exaggeration). Lots of kids and lots of things for kids to do made it easy for me to get involved with the youth ministry. Before I knew it I was running the Nursery, and a year later, I was teaching the seventh-grade confirmation class and running [other education programs]. Then it hit me: "Oh, yeah, this is what I have always wanted to do."

Then all the old tapes began to replay in my mind's ear: Mom: "Honey, you're too smart to be a teacher." Dad: "You can be anything you want, a doctor or a lawyer; don't settle for teaching." Carla: "But I have always wanted to be a teacher." Then my husband, a little fed up with my indecisiveness, said it. The words still echo in my head: "So, do it. Since when do you let other people tell you who or what to be?"

Off to college I went. I was going to be a teacher. "Damn the torpedoes, full steam ahead."

So, here I am, one year to go. I am still independent, but I don't need to be Queen. I am still an activist, but I have softened in my approach. And I am very active in my church. Now I am responsible for [even more of my church's educational programs]. . . .

When I become a teacher, the story will not be completed, though. I am and will always be a work in progress: changing, evolving, learning, and growing. . . .

I'm not sure if there are any central themes to my life story. Maybe that's because I was a little flaky for so long. I do recognize, however, that I am a product of the experiences, thoughts and emotions of my past, and I am glad of that.

I also know that this life story would be written differently on another day. Different things come to mind at different times. By no means can four or five or one-hundred or even one-million pages of information cover a life—even one of only thirty years. So, for this instance in time, the above is my life story (the *Reader's Digest* version at best). But if you ask me again tomorrow to tell you my life story, I might tell you a whole bunch of other things and skip what I told you here. Maybe that tells you the most about me and my life story.

"A Teacher's Worst Nightmare": David's Story

I was a teacher's worst nightmare for as far back as I can remember. Even as early as the first grade there were frequent visits to the principal's office due to fighting and other disruptive behavior, which only continued and increased in intensity as I grew older. Around the fifth grade, I added smoking to my already extensive list of undesirable behaviors and my classroom antics had escalated to such a degree that the school principal threatened to expel me. However, my father then came to the school and challenged that idea in a manner more verbally aggressive than he had ever before used in his weak attempts to discipline me. Apparently he didn't want me at home even more than the principal didn't want me in school, because I returned to class, much to the dismay of my poor teacher.

From that point on I went from bad to worse in a system that meant nothing to me. . . . Teachers—though not due to a lack of effort—simply could not reach me. By the eighth grade time spent with my pot-smoking, hormonally deranged buddies meant more to me than attending my classes, which I'm sure was more of a delight than a concern to some of my more frustrated teachers. I was on the path leading to juvenile delinquency, and it seemed that nobody was going to be able to reverse my direction.

Then, one of my teachers did something that I'm positive she was never taught [to do] in college, nor . . . ever imagined in a million years that she would do in the classroom: She lost it. The surprising thing is that she was usually the most tolerant teacher I had and I wasn't being any worse than I normally was in her class when it happened. Talk about the straw that broke the camel's back. She virtually exploded into a rage and attacked me. Had there been a weapon or sharp object within her reach, I am almost certain I would not be here today to tell this story. She approached me from behind with a scream that told me right away that I was in big trouble. When she finally reached me, this 120-pound woman grabbed me by the shirt and shook me like a rag doll. Then, as I dropped to my knees in an effort to recover my balance from the jackhammer effect, she dragged me out toward the hallway to do more damage, shaking me every so often just for good measure. After what seemed like an eternity of being dragged in front of the class on my knees, we were finally in the hallway, out of the sight of all but a few of the more daring students, who had recovered from their initial shock to storm the doorway and witness the completion of the murder. There she continued to shake me until the material of my shirt gave way and I fell to the floor. As I put my arms out to brace my fall and get ready to complain about my ripped shirt, she delivered a swift kick to my abdomen, knocking the wind out of me and leaving me unable to speak. As I lay there in my torn clothing, gasping for air, more embarrassed than I had ever been in my life, she leaned forward with a look of hate and disgust unequaled since the beginning of time and said, "You will *never* amount to *anything* in life!"

After that experience I hated this particular teacher so much that I simply decided that I was going to prove her wrong and make her eat those words no matter what it required of me to do so. Motivated by intense hatred, I began to reverse directions.

Although I would classify this experience as a critical incident in my educational life, I am still reluctant to give much credit to this teacher in regard to influencing my desire to pursue a career in education. At about this same time in my life, there were two other critical events that [need mention]. . . . That isolated experience reversed my direction or got me turned around, but the other two incidents are the ones that actually got me moving forward in the new direction I was facing.

The first event was the breakup of my family and the partitioning [dispersal] of the remaining three children into foster homes. It sounds tragic, but I was actually very fortunate to be placed with a wonderful family that was very education-minded, supportive, and disciplinary, three things that I had never been exposed to in my previous [family] situation. They were exactly what I needed at that time in my life.

The other event was the formation of a friendship with my high school basketball coach. Through my participation in a sport that I loved and my desire to become a great basketball player, he was able to teach me principles necessary for success in athletics that transformed this nasty, obnoxious, ungrateful student with a bad attitude into a hard-working, dedicated, committed, and disciplined athlete *and* student. To this day, whenever I think back on the influence of other individuals in my life and examples that I still try to follow, he is right up there at the top of my list.

. . . I discovered a hidden ability in math and science. Math equations that were hard for other students to do on paper I could do in my head, and chemistry assignments that were extremely difficult for others were relatively easy for me. Teachers and others saw these abilities and labeled me "engineer." But due to the example of my coach and a couple of other excellent teachers, I had already developed some feelings about teaching. However, when I discovered the monetary difference between the two careers, I quickly accepted the label of engineer. I felt that if I was intelligent enough to earn $50,000 a year, then it would be . . . an insult to that intelligence to settle for anything less.

Having thus been effectively brainwashed by society and the almighty dollar, I entered college as an engineering major. After the first two years I began to see my engineering classes as drudgery and found it more and more difficult to motivate myself to participate and get involved in the course work like I used to. My grades were slipping, and I went from tutoring to being tutored. I wasn't happy imagining myself [as an engineer]

. . . even with all the money. Whenever I thought about what I would really enjoy doing, it always involved sports.

So, I decided to go visit my old friend and basketball coach and discuss the issue. He simply told me that when choosing a career I should consider the other factors besides personal ability and income, things like personal enjoyment and satisfaction. He told me that these things would in turn influence important psychological, physical, and emotional factors in life such as what kind of attitude I will take to and from work, how it will affect the way I treat my wife and family, and even the way I feel physically.

Making serious considerations but still not totally convinced about changing majors, I happened to bounce the idea off my father during a phone conversation I was having with him shortly after my discussion with my old coach. He virtually told me the same thing, minus the tact and eloquence of the coach. He said, "Well, hell, if you do something you don't want to do just for the money, then you are no better than a prostitute." I changed my major the next day.

Needing a Job: Mary's Story

I wish I had an interesting story to tell, but there were no dramatic incidents in my life that brought me to my decision to become a teacher.

As is expected in my family, I went to college right after high school. I had no idea what I wanted to major in, so I just aimlessly took classes. Because I had no goal, I began to feel like I was wasting my time. I decided to take a year off to work full-time. A year turned into two years, three years, and then four years. Sometime during the last year I realized that I really didn't like my job and I definitely didn't want to do it for the rest of my life. At this point I began to take the steps necessary to get back into school. I told myself that this time I would come up with a plan to follow.

Upon returning to the university, I decided to start fulfilling a B.A. language requirement. I registered for a Spanish class. It turns out that this was a wise decision. That class was one of the best I have ever taken. The teacher succeeded in creating a friendly, comfortable atmosphere. I was amazed at how she could turn even a mundane grammar exercise into an enjoyable learning experience.

Because of that class, I decided that Spanish was the field I would like to pursue. I have been told that a language degree without teacher certification isn't very useful, so here I am, trying to get certified. Although I worry every day that I might not have what it takes to be a successful teacher, I know that I do have something to offer. I hope to discover what it is and develop it. In my future classroom, I want to try to create the kind of atmosphere that my favorite teacher created.

Commentary

To better understand the influence of biography on becoming a teacher and of how we use life history, we will consider how the themes found their way into student teaching. In order to do so, however, it will be necessary to provide additional information particularly about Mary.

In contrast to Carla and David's stories, Mary's entire education-related life history was one page long. It says very little about her, especially about her past. Yet silence sometimes speaks eloquently. Mary was a single mother. She worked nights as a cashier in a convenience store; this was the job to which she referred. Her overriding concern was to find a secure and predictable source of income that would allow her to take care of her child, a talkative and energetic six-year-old daughter. Mary was nearly overwhelmed by the demands of school, work, and child care. She came to class tired, kept to herself, said very little, and cut corners on her schoolwork, apparently to save precious time. Thus, the reduction of the life history to "why I became a teacher." She seemed more like a visitor to the classroom than a student. She resisted examining who she was until there appeared to be no alternative. Perhaps the turn inward was simply too painful or too enervating. Maybe she saw little purpose to the exercise. She wrote little, and we did little to encourage her to do otherwise, sensing that something more was going on than we were aware of. In truth, and quite in contrast to Mary's opening line, hers was a fascinating story of quiet desperation and remarkable courage, but one she felt unable to reveal. Carried by events, rather than controlling them, Mary seemed to live from day to day apparently trying merely to keep body and soul together until graduation.

During student teaching, the theme of being carried by events and unable to control them expressed itself in a variety of ways. Mary's central dilemma during student teaching was her difficulty with coming to terms with being an authority figure and in control of a classroom filled with lively youngsters. To survive student teaching, she would have to take control.

For David and Carla, and for Mary as we later discovered, two general themes emerged from their life stories: They felt they were outsiders, and that their histories were unusual if not abnormal. Both themes, as is discussed in the "Note to Teacher Educators and Students" section below, were made explicit and considered in class. For a time, as a young person, David felt like, and was, a victim; but in his rage at his teacher and through the helpful guidance of his new family, coach, and teachers, he began to discover previously hidden talents and to recognize alternative ways of relating to authority figures. Like Carla, he speaks authentically and powerfully about himself. Both he and Carla felt they were outsiders: the nearly "murdered" potential juvenile delinquent and the wealthy, immigrant-child "Queen." Mary also felt like an outsider, but for different reasons.

For David, feeling the outsider made him initially fearful to share his life history with others in the class as he wrote near the end of fall quarter: "I thought my personal life history was so abnormal that I would stand out like a sore thumb in class, isolated and unable to relate to the others." Through sharing his story, however, and to his great relief, he discovered connections: "[After sharing life histories], I realized that a lot of students shared experiences, emotions, and reasons for teaching that were similar to mine, and that these reasons were unique and [diverged] from the [expected reasons] for choosing a [teaching] career. I found that [discovery] comforting."

In addition to these two general themes, there were particular themes, peculiar to each person, that significantly influenced the kind and quality of their experience in our program and in student teaching. We begin with Carla.

Carla had no difficulty sharing her life history. "Damn the torpedoes, full steam ahead" nicely captured her approach to the cohort, to teaching, and to life. She took charge. She challenged and sometimes offended, but also reached out and sought to assist others in the cohort group, just as she sought during practice teaching to connect with students who were struggling. Carla's passion and independence lead to some minor conflicts with her cooperating teacher, a mild-mannered and skilled teacher, over how best to work with a student or approach a topic. With a good many students she had difficulty establishing open and productive relationships. Realizing that in good measure the quality of student learning was dependent on the kind and quality of her relationships with them, she began to reflect on those relationships: "I tend to be very outgoing and verbal. But this kind of behavior is not welcomed by all students." Carla confronted the contradiction between her much cherished "thrill of independence" that she sought for the students and her need to dominate interaction with them.

Carla, the "Queen," had difficulty accepting criticism of her work, which influenced our relationship with her as supervisors during student teaching. A few weeks into student teaching, we observed a math lesson on interest and change taught to ninth graders. Our observation notes included the following comments, which give a good sense of Carla's teaching practice early in the term: "Carla put rules on the board for [figuring] interest that confused the students because the assignment she wanted them to do required different operations. [She] made errors on the board that the students wrote down without protest as examples to be put in their notes—she didn't catch these until later when I pointed them out to her. She keeps on top of the kid's behavior—students rarely misbehave but a large percentage are not engaged." The feeling in the classroom was oppressive—no "thrill of independence" there. The students did not question her errors (although many recognized them) or ask questions about what they were to do, apparently because they did not dare.

The situation changed, dramatically, as Carla became increasingly unhappy with the quality of her relationship with the students and as we sought to help her address the contradiction evident in her thinking about teaching and how she worked in the classroom. A few weeks and much work later, (from observation notes) a very different classroom ethos had emerged: "[Students] are attentive, on task, and involved in the learning process. Your management program is effective and relatively nonconfrontational. Good work! . . . From the last time I visited your class—a couple of weeks ago—you've made enormous progress. You seem much more relaxed, without losing any control; your skills dealing with the kids are more [diversified] and comfortable."

Mary, in contrast, took few risks and kept to herself. The passivity evident in her life history, the feeling of being adrift and being dominated by forces larger than herself, proved to be the central personal theme of Mary's experience in the cohort. As noted, she encountered difficulty coming to terms with her authority within the classroom as a student teacher. The students controlled the class until she was forced to confront her passivity. She recognized the problem prior to practice teaching and fretted about it, but not until near the end of the term did she squarely face the issue, eventually recognizing it as central to her development as a teacher: "[My] overwhelming concern [is] my [lack of] presence in the classroom. I hate this 'control' thing, which is something I need to work on. . . . I am not scared anymore [by teaching], just a bit uneasy about being in charge."

Like his foster family, David wanted to provide students with a high degree of structure and support in order to help them find direction and meaning in their lives. He had a soft spot for pupils who, like himself as a young person, were alienated from school. Empathizing with these students, but fearing his actions would increase their alienation, David found it difficult to consistently enforce classroom rules and to provide the structure that he knew they needed to succeed. He was patient and caring toward the students and felt confirmed as a person when he was able to give advice, as his coach had earlier done for him, and thrilled when a student's performance seemed to improve as a result. Conversely, he was crushed when student performance slipped, and deeply hurt when students chose to "blow off" a class period or an assignment that he *knew* would help them. Moreover, and perhaps a bit like the teacher who sought his death, he found himself at a loss about how to respond to consistent acting-out. The kind of motivation that some athletes possess and that facilitates discipline was not available to him as a student teacher. Other sources of discipline had to be tapped, and this proved difficult. He had not resolved the dilemma at year's end.

Carla and David's life histories speak authentically. Both identified specific themes that later became crucially important in their quest to become teachers, to forge teaching identities. They uncovered sets of attitudes, values, and beliefs that proved to be sources both of strength and of difficulty in the classroom. In its own way, Mary's life history speaks authentically as well, although we only learned this later in the year. Mary said little because she had little she felt she could say. What she did say retrospectively spoke volumes.

A Note to Teacher Educators and Students

For a variety of reasons, not least among them the training orientation of teacher education, teacher educators frequently ignore what they tacitly understand: As with other teachers, what they teach will be filtered through and made more or less meaningful based upon a set of biographically embedded assumptions or preunderstandings held by their students. Some of what is taught will be ignored and discarded as meaningless because it does not fit current understanding; and recognized as self-confirming, other content, perhaps even less significant content, will be embraced eagerly. Ignoring the past does not make it go away. It lingers, ever present and quietly insistent.

Recognizing that all learners pick and choose what they will learn, all teachers, us included, use a variety of means— grades, tests, rewards, and punishments—to increase the likelihood that the content presented will be learned in the manner desired. Learning to teach, however, is not merely a matter of engaging or being forced to engage content—to know, for example, what is involved in putting together a comprehensive unit or even what are the most common reading errors of children. It is also a matter of learning how to direct one's professional development intelligently and to express self in a way that builds desirable and educationally defensible relationships with students and increases the enjoyment of teaching.

Who the teacher is as a person—the kinds of experiences had inside and outside of school, values, beliefs, and aspirations—has a profound influence on what the beginning teacher will or will not learn, but perhaps even more importantly, it shapes what he or she will become as a teacher. In teaching, the medium is the message, and the message is who the beginning teacher is: To teach is to express self.

Many beginning teachers come to teaching with relatively clear, but likely not fully articulated, conceptions of teaching and of themselves as teachers. Perhaps their parents or grandparents were teachers, and their conceptions of teaching are overlaid with the feelings of admiration felt for them. Perhaps an especially inspiring teacher challenged them in ways they would like to share with others. Perhaps, a bit like David, they hated school and desire to "fix things" so others won't suffer as much. Or, maybe they played school as little children and feel "called" to teaching like Carla. In addition to these experiences, each beginning teacher has spent literally thousands of hours sitting in classes as students, engaged in what Daniel Lortie (1975) called an "apprenticeship of observation." They are familiar with schools and feel more or less knowledgeable about teaching. Taken together, these kinds of experiences and the understanding and attitudes that come from them are the bedrock of professional development, of who the beginning teacher thinks he or she is and wants to become as a teacher (a professional vision or "dream") and—swapping images—the seeds of socialization to teaching.

For beginning teachers, switching to the other side of the desk may bring some surprises, however. It certainly did for Carla, David, and Mary. Teaching looks quite different to a student about to become a student teacher from how it looks to an experienced teacher. Teachers and students see different things and, to a degree, have different concerns. Preunderstandings about teaching and about self as teacher born of student experience and brought to teacher education are inevitably naive, perhaps misleading, and sometimes blatantly false. Prejudices blind. Prejudices cripple. Prejudgments—judgments lacking explicit justification—blind by cutting off other, perhaps more fruitful, sensitive and responsible ways of understanding and framing a problem or building a relationship; they cripple by unnecessarily constraining opportunities to learn and by truncating one's professional growth.

To confront preunderstandings, we have argued that a turn inward toward self is required. But turning inward can be a risky business, and sharing the results of the turn even frightening. Fearing retribution or a bad grade, the beginning teacher may not wish to uncover, let alone reveal, some views or beliefs. This is a difficult problem. Ethically, teacher educators must not and cannot compel students to disclose more about themselves than they wish. We are not, after all, in the "molding" business. Teacher educators can only invite, not compel, the "good." More about this issue follows. At this point, we need to underscore the importance of trust and of an honest and sincere effort to explore self, of which writing an "educational autobiography" or "life history" is a part. Without trust, risk is unwise, yet risk is essential to maximizing the educational value of each of the methodologies presented in *Becoming a Student of Teaching*.

Related Research

The need to mine the past for insight into the present finds a good deal of support in recent research on teacher development (see Ball & Goodson, 1985; Goodson & Walker, 1991; Hargreaves & Fullan, 1992). How best to do this remains a lively question. There are several different approaches to writing and using life histories or autobiographies, which represent differences in purpose. Perhaps the earliest work related to teacher education was done by the students of Ross Mooney, a pioneer in the field. Mooney's students wrote autobiographies and explored their own development as a lens through which to think about teaching and learning (see Riordan, 1973). In his early work Pinar (1980; 1981) drew upon psychoanalysis and developed a method, "currere," that begins with regression and seeks a healing synthesis. Raymond, Butt, and Townsend (1992) encourage practicing teachers to engage in "collaborative autobiography." Teachers write and share their stories as a means for helping them to understand one another's experience, identify "collective concerns," and eventually engage in school-based projects that aim at creating institutional conditions more conducive to teacher development. Our focus on preservice teacher education in this part of the book distinguishes our approach from these and others (Goodson, 1981, 1991); and as a result, our aims are both more modest and, at the same time, when seen in relationship to the other methodologies we will present, perhaps a bit more ambitious.

Conceptions of Self

For us, as for most of these writers, a great deal hinges on how we conceive of the self. A distinction made a number of years ago by Berger and Luckmann (1966) between primary and secondary socialization is a useful point of departure. They suggested that secondary socialization—the process involved in taking on an identity as a teacher, for instance—takes place against the background of one's primary socialization in the family, which produces a relatively stable conception of self. Secondary socialization, they observe, "must deal with an already formed self and an already internalized world. It cannot construct subjective reality *ex nihilo*" (p. 140). Jennifer Nias' (1989) distinction between "core" and "situational" selves represents a similar distinction.

Often when one first enters a new situation, demands are made contrary to the core self which, as noted, is relatively resistant to change. In such contexts we must in some degree be other than self in order to function in institutionally valued ways; and to be not self is to be miserable. This other self, a "situational" self, using Nias' term, may also be relatively consistent with the core self, and one feels more or less at peace as a result. In either case, knowing oneself enables role negotiation from a position of power; one acts, rather than reacts, to contextual demands.

At a time when it is increasingly difficult to achieve a core self (Gergen, 1991), a stable "I," that feeling of continuity in an ongoing story that is "my life," turning toward and recapturing the past takes on additional significance. It is a means for discovering self.

Specific Questions and Issues

We turn now to a set of specific questions and issues related to using life histories or autobiographies in teacher education.

Sharing

Once the life histories have been written, we ask our students (either in small groups or in a large group) to share briefly the "high points" of their stories. What they do not wish to share with their peers they need not share. We are careful to remind them of this, just as we are careful to remind them of the importance of being respectful to presenters.

Themes—shared concerns or issues—are identified. Typically, themes are of two kinds: particular and general/common. Particular themes, of the kind discussed earlier such as Carla's tendency to dominate others, relate to patterns of belief and action embedded in an individual's story that have a bearing on their work as teachers. General themes, ones that cut across stories, also impact classroom performance but represent commonalities among stories and, therefore, tend to reflect wider, contextual issues. General themes are of interest here.

A decision will need to be made about how best to pursue commonalities. One approach we have used is to identity general themes or problems, to group the beginning teachers according to commonalities, and have them explore one or more of these in depth and in relationship to teaching, school contexts, and the conditions of teachers' work. This approach requires that students be helped to turn their shared concern into a researchable problem statement, be connected with appropriate literature, and then be assisted in ways that will enhance and broaden their understanding. The results of these inquiries should be shared with the entire group. Although time-consuming, this has been a useful and powerful way of assisting students to confront aspects of their past (in particular, constraining influences on their development), to identify alternatives, and to build a sense of community within the group.

A second approach, used because of time constraints with the group from which the quoted life histories come, is to treat the general themes and problems less directly. Instead of becoming the basis for a specific inquiry, they become ongoing threads to which we periodically return. Some assignments, for example, may include one or another aspect of the concerns raised. We have found the student teaching seminar to be a particularly fruitful arena for this activity. One of the common themes that emerged in discussion from this group, and these three and additional life histories, centered on the problem of being an outsider, of not fitting in. Instructionally, this was a particularly powerful theme because it related closely to the study of student culture, which included reading the book *Jocks and Burnouts* (Eckert, 1989), which was about to begin. The feelings associated with being an outsider provided a means for connecting emotionally and intellectually to both types of students, jocks and burnouts, and for exploring the ways in which school structure and teacher behavior relate to, and in some ways sustain, student categories and, through categories, affect. A second theme that emerged focused on the victimization of young people. This also proved to be a powerful theme, especially given the political context of late twentieth-century America. Other themes may also emerge.

A third approach is to avoid commonalities altogether, and to treat the autobiographies as simply personal statements that will be returned to from time to time. In this instance, the focus is on particularistic rather than general themes.

Ethics

As noted previously, students should not be compelled to reveal more about themselves than they wish to reveal. It is extremely important that the classroom be characterized by a climate of trust, where risk taking is not only accepted but honored. This is especially important when values associated with the "core" self are at stake; these are values and beliefs that represent a significant personal investment. To accomplish this aim, we have found it necessary to downplay evaluation. If sorting of students is institutionally required, and often it is, the burden should be placed on quizzes or other assignments unrelated to revealing self. Written comments on the life histories should encourage and honor student effort and honesty, not bear judgement. Moreover, students need to be assured that what they have written will be held in confidence. Thus, the three education-related autobiographies we have included were published with written permission and with the understanding that only fictitious names would be used.

By not formally evaluating the student education-related autobiographies, some students have mistakenly understood that the work is unimportant. A few are pleased to discover that a page or two of superficial writing will receive full credit. This has been an ongoing dilemma, as Mary's writing suggests. A good many students, however, will produce rich and interesting documents *provided* they fully understand that they are writing *for themselves* and that a good piece of work, an authentic expression of self, will prove most valuable over the course of their certification program and perhaps into the first years of teaching. This claim is based upon data gathered from beginning teachers who were asked to evaluate the quality of the certification program and of their experience within it.

The education-related life history becomes the first entry in the *Personal Teaching Text*. It serves as the backdrop against which the beginning teachers will assess much of their development over the course of the year we are together because it is the source of one's ideals. Periodically, as part of reviewing their development, they are asked to reread the history and, in a review of the personal teaching text, assess their development in writing. Thus, a poorly written, inauthentic, and superficial life history haunts them. This, too, we carefully explain.

Roles

We have found that reading our students' life histories affects how we view them. In some instances, where our experiences blend with theirs or where a story represents a particularly touching or compelling tale of self-discovery, empathy develops and bonds build. Knowing our students in this way has forced us to review perhaps with greater care than otherwise the possible implications of our actions on our students as, for instance, with Mary when we accepted work that might otherwise have been rejected. Moreover, knowing our students in this way has compelled us to reveal more about ourselves and our backgrounds to students than perhaps might otherwise have been the case (see Bullough, 1994). Knowing them encourages intimacy as does working with them over the course of an entire year. Finally, knowing something about the background of our students has enabled us to make our programs more responsive, and especially allowed us to function in more sensitive and, we believe, more effective ways as supervisors during practice teaching.

CHAPTER THREE

Analyzing Personal Teaching Metaphors

Introduction

One of the most daunting challenges faced by beginning teachers involves negotiating a role within new and unfamiliar contexts. As a student teacher this process is especially complicated because you are, in a sense, just passing through your cooperating teacher's classroom and school. Feeling like a visitor, and vulnerable, some student teachers are sorely tempted—and, in some ways, pressured by established patterns of interaction and expectation—to become imitations of their cooperating teachers. Because they are not their cooperating teachers, however, the best that can be hoped for is to become a comparatively poor imitation of the real thing.

Role negotiation is at the center of professional development. To think of this process as one of passively adapting—even for strategic reasons such as fearing a poor evaluation—to what is believed to be necessary in order to fit into the new context with minimal disruption or distress is to accept artificial limits on that development.

Negotiation is never simply one way. Despite contextual pressures to conform, when negotiating a role the communities one seeks to join are changed in subtle ways, just as the person in some ways changes. Even as a student teacher, your presence in the classroom alters the context, and will alter the nature of the relations your cooperating teacher has with pupils.

The challenge of negotiating a role is multifaceted. On one hand, as a beginning teacher, you want to realize your ideals in practice. On the other, you want to fit in. Here's the rub: "fitting in" may require that ideals be set aside or compromised. Inevitably conflict of varying degrees exists between ideals and what appear to be contextual imperatives to behave in institutionally expected ways. Facing such conflicts some beginning and experienced teachers engage in one or another coping strategy like "strategic compliance" (Lacey, 1977) where there is the appearance of conformity without a change in beliefs. Sometimes ideals are set aside, perhaps painfully, and accommodation takes place; one becomes what the context demands. And sometimes teachers resist pressures to conform and work, instead, to alter the context to make it more hospitable to one's ideals.

Whatever the outcome, beginning teachers need to be acutely aware of the process of negotiation itself if they are to be able to direct it. Beginning teachers must be not only students of teaching but also students of their own development. To be such a student requires knowledge of self and of context *and* knowledge gathered in systematic and ongoing ways about the *interaction of self and context*.

Contexts and the communities that sustain them can be characterized in many ways. One distinguishing feature is found in the metaphors that bind a community and which "mark off boundaries and define conditions of membership" (Taylor, 1984:17). For example, in secondary schools "teacher is expert" is an especially powerful and institutionally accepted role. Along with it comes a view of teaching as "telling," and a student role: "empty receptacle in need of filling." To fit into many secondary faculties, to be a "teacher" in these contexts, means buying into these metaphors.

Representing embodied experience, metaphors also play a significant part in the formation of beginning teacher ideals. This is so because of the fundamental place metaphors hold in human thinking as a means of producing coherence and of making sense of life (Lakoff & Johnson, 1980).

The identification and exploration of metaphors is a means for gaining a window into the taken-for-granted assumptions that characterize a context and that drive action (Bullough, 1991). By their nature metaphors represent a simplification of experience (Dickmeyer, 1989), and their analysis provides a parsimonious means for getting a handle on the interaction of self and context, which is the complex and contradictory process of role negotiation. Through analysis light is shed not only on self but also on context, which enables identification of the ways in which context constrains one's realization of ideals, as well as ways in which ideals are immature or in other ways limited. In this way, alternative visions of teaching, ways of being with young people, can be identified and explored. For beginning teachers who are uncertain of who they want to be as teacher, the identification and analysis of teaching metaphors is a means for beginning to find oneself, to achieve the coherence of thought and perhaps action that is central to negotiating a role, a "situational self," that resonates with one's inner or "core" self (Nias, 1989). Moreover, because changes in one's teaching metaphors signal changes in conceptions of self as teacher, the focus on metaphors provides a point of reference against which to critically consider the socialization process.

Writing

The analysis of metaphors may take one of two different and complementary directions. One direction focuses on the analysis of beginning teacher language, seeking to identify ways in which sense is made. For example, beginning teachers might be encouraged to explore their use of language to describe and define students. In this way assumptions embedded in thinking are uncovered. One of our former students, a beginning teacher in a working-class junior high school, for instance, found himself speaking about students as "beasts." When he was asked about the use of this metaphor, he immediately recognized that the term had slipped into his language unnoticed and accurately represented his growing frustration about his relationship with students. He realized his use of the term signaled a serious problem that demanded attention, and began to consider ways of making changes. A second direction, the one suggested here, emphasizes the identification of personal teaching metaphors as ideals for practice, ones that invite conformity. With beginning teacher education students, this approach focuses first on self and later on context.

After an introduction to the place of metaphors in thinking, and some of the related research (a portion of which will be shared in the section entitled "A Note to Teacher Educators and Students"), the students are invited to imagine themselves in the classroom and to think about what it is they are doing, what the students are doing, and how the classroom feels. They then write: "Drawing on your life history, identify a metaphor (or metaphors) that captures the essence of yourself as teacher."

Throughout our year together we periodically invite our students to reconsider their metaphors in the light of their increasing experience as teachers and as students of teaching which includes considerable time spent observing and analyzing teaching both in classes and through videotape as well as planning and conducting the "short course," a unit taught prior to student teaching. A few weeks after the initial writing, they are again asked to think and write about their metaphors in class. A November "update," for example, included the following questions:

1. What is your personal teaching metaphor?

2. Has your metaphor changed? If so, into what? Has it been confirmed?

3. What factors/experiences have led to the change or resulted in the confirmation of your metaphor? Do you have a new metaphor?

4. Do you have any concerns about your metaphor?

The results of the updates are shared through discussion. In response to these questions, a lively discussion ensued this term, as in the past. Those who said their views were changing were encouraged to describe the changes and then to talk about what experiences prompted the change. Thus, we focus on the interaction of self and context. They were in schools at the time and had just finished writing classroom ethnographies (see chapter six). Based upon their increasing involvement in schools, many concluded their views of students and of the work of teaching were inaccurate and naive. A few expressed discouragement; they asserted that the students would not allow them to be the kind of teachers they imagined themselves to be. These students began to see the ways in which self definitions bring with them definitions of other. In response to this view one of the optimists in the group remarked, "You have to hold on to the belief that you can make a difference." Clearly, a number of students' conceptions of self as teacher had been jolted by increasing experience with students and in schools. How they chose to respond to the challenge was of crucial significance in their development.

Subsequent updates followed about every three or four weeks. One in March asked these questions, and again the students wrote:

1. Has your metaphor changed or been confirmed?
2. What factors/experiences have led to the change or resulted in confirmation?
3. After the short course [during which time they taught a two- to three-week unit prior to student teaching] and looking ahead to practice teaching, how confident are you about your conception of yourself as teacher? Do you have any concerns or worries? If so, what are they?

Once again, a lively discussion followed, which concluded with the question, "Do you feel as though you are increasing the knowledge and gaining the power necessary to direct your development as a teacher and achieve your metaphor?"

Three examples of personal teaching metaphors follow. Each example is drawn from student writing (including metaphor updates and reviews of personal teaching texts) gathered over the course of the year. Once again, these materials are presented with student permission. The first example comes from Mary, who was introduced in chapter two. Prior to reading Mary's metaphors it may be helpful to briefly review her life history. You will note that initially, she was unable to generate a metaphor although she had a general image of what she wanted her class to be like. Later, a metaphor emerged. The second example comes from Terry, a beginning junior high school art teacher. Initially Terry thought of herself as a guide, but this view evolved and became increasingly complex as she reflected on her development and teaching ideals. The third example, Martha, presents aspects of the most common metaphor possessed by secondary teachers, "teacher is subject matter expert." This metaphor, and its variations ("coach," where the emphasis is on skills rather than content, and "master," among others), brings with it powerful images that grow out of one's love of a discipline and experience as a student, particularly as a college student.

Mary: Bridge Builder

October 8, first writing:

> I don't know how to state it succinctly. I just don't want any of my students to dread my class. I want it to be something they look forward to, a place where they feel comfortable enough to offer their own ideas and opinions . . . [Students] should be . . . responsible for one another's learning. All my years of schooling have shaped this view. I just sort of intuitively knew that teachers didn't have to embarrass students or put them on the spot to get their point across. I have been fortunate enough to have a couple of teachers who have been successful in creating environments in which the students felt comfortable enough to contribute and to take risks. These teachers de-emphasized incorrect answers and encouraged participation.

November 14, update:

> When we first wrote about teaching metaphors, I could not come up with one. All I knew was that I wanted to create a non-threatening environment where all students could participate and, hopefully, learn something. Although no single word or phrase can sum up what I want to be, the word "bridge" covers part of it. I want to be able to create a bridge between the content and the lives of the students. I want some aspect of the class to personally touch and engage each student. The idea of

teacher as bridge occurred to me after having personal contact with students. Some of them are just so needy, interaction with the teacher is crucial.

Writing, December 12, review of personal teaching text:

> I want my students to feel good while they are in my class. Therefore, I vow that I will never embarrass them or put them on the spot, as I have seen quite a few teachers do. An issue which has emerged for me is that of making connections. My teaching metaphor turned out to be the teacher as bridge. I want my class to mean something to each student. I have started thinking about, and have discussed with my cooperating teacher, how to engage different types of students. Some students seem to turn off when they are invited directly into the discussion. This distresses me. But at least now I know some different strategies I can use. The overwhelming concern for me is, of course, discipline. Directing the energy of the seventh graders that I will be teaching during my short course and student teaching will be a huge task. I will have to be on my toes at all times to keep control. And I don't want to come across as too serious or unfriendly (once again, I'm back to the affective aspect of teaching).

Mary taught the short course, a two-week unit in Spanish for junior high school students. Like other students she was asked to identify and analyze a problem that emerged during the short course. Here is part of what Mary wrote (March 3):

> I wasn't in control of the class. But . . . I have *never* been an authoritarian in any area of my life, and I don't want to be one in the classroom. Being an authoritarian goes against my concept of myself as a teacher and doesn't help create the kind of atmosphere that I want. I need to come up with some kind of strategy to bring the class to order that is compatible with my personality.

This said, Mary was not discouraged. She found much that was encouraging about the short course: "I left feeling good. I can do this because I care about the students. I can connect with this age group. Most of the students want to make a connection; they wanted to know me and to know things about me." This experience prompted her to write in an update:

> My metaphor . . . has been confirmed. I originally meant it
> as a bridge between the students and content. But it has
> been confirmed in a more important way. . . . Yes, the
> bridge between content is there but the students seemed to
> be reaching out for a personal relationship with me. They
> wanted to make a connection, and so did I. . . . I am very
> confident with my conception of myself as teacher because
> I know that as long as I keep caring I will be just fine.

Shortly after this writing, Mary began practice teaching,
which she excitedly anticipated, fully expecting to "knock 'em
dead." She taught four Spanish classes, seventh through ninth
grade.

Writing, April 29, update:

> My metaphor has been crushed. I have been crushed.
> Some days I feel like I don't want to teach because
> everything is so negative. I have to be so negative to keep
> these kids in line. I never wanted it to be that way. I
> thought I could create an environment, full of mutual
> respect, where everyone could feel free to participate. My
> metaphor was "teacher is bridge." I wanted to help
> connect the students with the content and the social aspect
> of school. I wanted relationships (connections) with the
> kids, but it's impossible when they don't show me respect.
> So, I don't know what my metaphor is now. Maybe
> teacher as supervisor? I have to be so strict about talking
> in class that my idea of a comfortable atmosphere where
> everyone can contribute isn't coming about. There are
> bright spots, however, in this dreary picture. (I hate being
> a disciplinarian—it goes against my personality.) There
> are periods when things go well (never entire days) and
> those are what keep me going. When things are bad, they
> are really bad; when they are good, they are fantastic.

Following this writing, the cooperating teacher and the
two of us who worked with her from the university increased
our assistance efforts. We wanted Mary to succeed. Our help
took many forms, including ongoing and nearly constant
feedback on her teaching, help with planning and curriculum
design, and advice on classroom management and on how better
to structure the classroom to gain the respect she desired. Mary

worked hard to implement those suggestions that made sense to her, and with some good results.

Writing, May 27, analysis of personal teaching text:

> I can't believe the end is finally here. I didn't think I would ever make it to this point. . . . I survived. I am finally starting to feel more like a teacher than a student. However, I still feel like I am the baby sitter, not the parent. . . . Through the course of my student teaching, I discovered my strengths and worked on my weaknesses. I found that I can be authoritative when I have to. I found that I am very patient with the students, and flexible when it comes to methods and lesson presentation in order to reach [kids]. The only disappointment I had this quarter was that I wasn't able to create the type of atmosphere that I would have liked in my classroom. The students wouldn't let me.

At year's end, and in interview, Mary spoke of the changes she went through in her thinking about herself as a teacher. She regretted being forced to give up her initial metaphor, although it endured as an ideal, and wondered if another context would allow her to realize her dream. She doubted it, however:

> I feel like I have to be watching the students, all of them, every second. You have to be able to watch 30 people at once. You have to be doing one thing and out of the corner of your eye be able to tell quickly that somebody is not doing what they are supposed to be doing and tell them so. So, right now, I just feel like a supervisor and disciplinarian. I'm hoping that when it is my own classroom and I have the whole year with the students, I can get that out of the way at the start and they will get routinized, and then I can worry about the bridge part. Maybe that will come later. . . . Right now, [for me], teacher is disciplinarian or authoritarian or supervisor or something like that.

Terry: Teacher Is Guide and . . .

Initially, Terry, a beginning visual arts teacher, thought of herself as a guide, a "person with some experience and knowledge in an area, yet willing to try new things, unsure of all the answers—one who is still learning and gaining knowledge." She also thought of herself as an "explorer," a guide into uncharted territories. She held this view, she said, because of the "ever changing face of the art world. There is so much happening in the world in the visual media that no one can ever know everything. So, I will never see myself as 'the expert,' because there is an unlimited supply of new information, the rules are always changing, developing, growing. My hope is that I can change along with the world and give new experiences to my students."

Writing, November 11, update:

> I'm beginning to realize that junior high students need set boundaries. They are pushing limits at every chance. They are trying on new and different identities; somehow I must establish the regulations of my classroom. I need to add something to my view of myself [as teacher] that will address this problem. I really hate the image of "policewoman" in the classroom. Yet I'm not sure what other image could establish the rules [that are needed]. Maybe I need to incorporate some parenting. Parenting—teacher as sometimes parent. An adult that sets goals and limits, rewards a job well done or a valiant effort . . .

Writing, December 12, review of personal teaching text:

> I am struggling with my teaching metaphor. The first set of images has proven to be idealistic and somewhat naive. To be a guide and explorer, you must have someone following you. The reality of the junior high classroom is that the students are testing roles and rules; in this kind of atmosphere it may be hard to expand their worlds if you are fighting for the right to lead. Yet the second image has faults also. I am not at all sure that I want to parent 200 students a day. . . . I haven't found a metaphor that can describe the kind of teacher I want to be.

After the short course, Terry's images of herself as a teacher gelled into "teacher is artisan" (March 3, metaphor update):

> At some point during my short course I reflected on my experience and struggled to find a word or image that combined all the parts of my new experience. My first metaphor now seems ideal and naive, and the second addressed the part of a teacher that must deal with management and discipline problems. Now, I see teaching as a developed set of skills that are used to express knowledge to students. I see myself as an artisan.

April 29, update, halfway through practice teaching:

> Teacher as artisan seems to still fit, yet it's changed! I find my skills as an artist are not as strong or important as my skills as a teacher most days. There are times when the student as apprentice is overwhelmingly strong. The students need a mentor/parent so much. I am fighting to be a strong influence without dreaming about these kids. I want to see them be successful. Yet I want to be able to turn it off at the end of the day. Some days, that is easier than [in] other days. I still feel that [teaching] is the most right thing I have ever done!

May 27, review of personal teaching text done at the conclusion of student teaching:

> I have been struggling with changing my metaphor. As an artisan you must have apprentices that are interested in your skills. I find some of my students really do not care about the skills I have to teach; this makes teaching a more difficult process. Yet, as an artisan you sometimes parent, guide, and pressure your apprentices into completing their work. That part of the metaphor fits very well with who I am in the classroom. I use everything, anything, to get students involved. I am developing a sense of who the students in my classes are both as individuals and as a group. This has helped in my planning and helped me set [reasonable] expectations for finished projects.

Martha: Teacher Is Subject Matter Expert

Martha—a quiet, very private, and (as she described herself) a "very competitive" beginning high school chemistry teacher and honors student—initially thought of herself as a "helpmate," one who helps young people achieve their own goals. It was, however, her love of chemistry and her desire to share it that was most central to her understanding of herself as teacher. Update, March 3, following the short course:

> The times I feel the most successful and good about myself is when I explain a concept and I see a light go on or when I see a student do a problem that they couldn't do before. It makes me feel good about expending the energy to learn my subject that I know it well enough to teach someone else. The short course was good for me because I taught a subject that troubled me for a long time, and it still is my shakiest area. I feel that if I can teach that, I will do fine in other areas.

Martha summarized the changes in her thinking after practice teaching in her last review of personal teaching text when she wrote:

> At the beginning of the year I was the most concerned about the teaching aspect of being a teacher. I worried that I wouldn't be able to get a concept across to my students. I have found out that this is almost second nature to me. This is the easy part. Towards the middle of the year I was concerned about classroom management. I had problems, but not any that weren't solvable to some extent. My most pressing concern before I began student teaching was being able to think of myself as the authority in the classroom. I knew that if I was insecure the kids would pick up on that and make my life difficult. I did have some problems with this at the beginning [of practice teaching], but I quickly adjusted, and so did the kids.

It was during the period when she was most concerned with authority that her reliance on the "expert" metaphor was most evident. Writing in the review of personal teaching text, March 12, following the short course:

The short course helped me realize that during my three years at the University, I have learned a lot. I know something that I can teach my students. . . . I believe I know my subject well enough to explain a concept many ways, and I can field questions without much stress at all. This was an extremely important discovery for me to make. . . . I want to be respected in my classroom as an authority on my subject, and an intelligent, organized individual who cares about the students. . . . I am nervous that at first my [youth] will be a problem in obtaining respect as the authority figure in the classroom, so I think that I will have to have very clear goals and rules for the class, and I will have to strictly enforce those rules. But I also think that after I have established myself as the person in charge, my youth will help me establish the kind of relationship I want with the students.

Commentary

Like perhaps most beginning secondary teachers, Mary thought most about getting content into students' heads when she thought of teaching and of herself as teacher. She wanted to be a "bridge" across which content and student could meet. There was, however, an emotional dimension to her ideal, one evident in her life history, that over time emerged clearly and became increasingly important to her self-conception: She wanted to be friendly with students, to avoid embarrassing them, to create a "nonthreatening environment," and to have a "personal relationship" with them. Clearly, this is what she wanted from her own teachers for herself and what she hoped to give to students. She feared being singled out for attention by teachers, and she wanted to be cared for. Making emotional "connections" is how she expressed these values; and her metaphor expanded as a result and became increasingly complex.

Practice teaching shocked Mary and shattered her dream, at least for a time. Teaching, she discovered, was more than a matter of making content lively in order to assist students to connect with it, and of caring. Like perhaps most beginning teachers, she found the demands of managing large groups of students distressing and struggled with being in charge. Mary had never been in a position of authority before, and it frightened her. The context of teaching seemed hostile.

What Mary discovered was that teachers' concepts of themselves as teachers bring with them definitions of "other," of the students and parent roles in education, that may or may not be reasonable or fitting. She noted that the students wanted to make emotional connections with her, to "know things about me"; but she discovered that too few wanted to cross the bridge and embrace Spanish, and she did not want nor know how to compel the crossing. To her dismay, caring about the students did not produce respect or engagement, as she had assumed and hoped. In response, she fell back on familiar and unpleasant ways of interacting with students, and she was "strict," an "authoritarian." She did so because this is what she believed the situation demanded, and what the students expected.

Young people are a powerful force in the classroom, and the most significant source of change in thinking about self as teacher. This is so because it is generally to them that beginning teachers look for self-confirmation. Just as teachers seek to influence pupil behavior, pupils influence and shape a teacher's behavior as roles and relationships are negotiated. As noted in the introduction, the student teacher's position in this negotiation is complicated and, in some respects, weakened because the classroom into which they enter is not their own. For Mary, as for the other beginning teachers, the classroom environment was ordered by the cooperating teacher to reflect her self-definition; roles had already been negotiated and patterns of interaction set. Thus, Mary was not necessarily engaging in a foolish flight of fantasy when she longed for her own classroom unencumbered by the presence of her cooperating teacher. Perhaps she was right: a change in contexts might enable her to better realize her metaphor. Experienced teachers sometimes comment on how important a change in context has been to their own development. Some contexts are more hospitable to some metaphors than are others.

Terry gives us a glimpse into a common problem faced by beginning teachers as they negotiate a role. As Terry worked with the students, the importance of content dropped, while she placed increasing value on establishing caring relationships with the students. For some beginning teachers, particularly those who think of themselves as more like students than like teachers or those who embrace one or another nurturing metaphor (like "parent" or "mother"), the relationship often takes on unexpected dimensions. Teacher and pupil become too close. Terry encountered this problem as she found herself trying on a parent role with the students. To be a parent places students in the role of children; and children rightfully demand and usually get a great deal from parents. Children-students expect intimacy, and teachers who set up this expectation and respond to it are likely, just as Terry feared, to dream and worry about their students and their problems. Terry recognized some of the limitations (some arising because of large class size) of this way of relating to students and yet still found some elements of it compelling.

Other aspects of Terry's struggle to find a metaphor are enlightening. It is with respect to establishing the desired relationship with young people that she thinks about teaching skills. Implicitly she knows that teaching *is* a relationship. Knowing this, however, only frames the problem in a useful way, it does not solve it. In fact, as she reflects on her relationship, the role of teacher becomes increasingly complex, which we take to be a healthy and positive development. Naivete vanishes. As an artisan or master, she knows that some students will not accept the role of apprentice that she seeks to impose upon them. Comfortable with this self-understanding, and believing that the student role it brings is a desirable one, near the end of practice teaching she is actively engaged in developing skills and identifying resources that will enable her to establish the relationship she desires with the students. Her aim is to adjust the situation to make it more fitting to her conception of teaching, and not to comply as Mary did.

Like Mary, Martha struggled to be an authority in the classroom. To address her fears, she appealed to the authority of the expert. Martha was a chemist, and she played the part very well. Her lessons were carefully planned and executed. Student performance went up, somewhat. But ironically, the longer

Martha taught the less she enjoyed the role, yet she felt unable to change it. What bothered her was that she did not feel, using Mary's language, "connected" to the students. She felt they did not care about her, although she cared about them. In interview she remarked, "I want the kids to like me, most of them don't. . . . They are kind of resentful and resent how much they have to work." To the question "How does it make you feel to have the kids not like you?" she replied, "At first it was hard. Now it doesn't bother me so much. I'm a little more used to it. It is not so much that they dislike me, they have no opinion of me as a person, I'm just a teacher."

Each of the three teachers discovered limitations of various kinds in their teaching ideals and in the contexts within which they student taught. They addressed these limitations differently. Mary set aside her metaphor, believing there was no alternative and looked forward to the time when she would have her own classroom and feel ownership. She "strategically complied" with the demands of the context. Terry engaged in an ongoing exploration of herself in the classroom, and was sufficiently skilled as a teacher and forceful as a person to make changes in the context along the way. Martha settled on a role early and stuck to it even when it became increasingly unpleasant to do so. For Martha, being a chemist was fundamental not only to her conception of herself as teacher but as a person; it represented a "root" metaphor, connected closely to a cluster of values and beliefs central to her core sense of self and not merely an institutionally valued role. It is little wonder this self-understanding proved resistant to change; she valued it and the context supported it. The identification and analysis of metaphors is not likely to result in the change of such foundational conceptions, but revealing them may assist beginning teachers in their quest to form more hospitable contexts within which to work.

For each of the beginning teachers increased experience with students and reflection on their metaphors made the role of teacher increasingly complex. They became more sophisticated in their thinking about themselves as teachers and about their professional development.

A Note to Teacher Educators and Students

Two lines of research are of particular importance to our use of metaphor analysis (see Bullough with Stokes, 1994). The first centers on the place of images in learning and problem solving and the second on narratives. Calderhead and Robson (1991) nicely capture the general view underpinning much of the work on images.

> Images have been found to fulfil an important role in chess playing, medical diagnosis, and certain types of problem solving. In order to solve certain problems, it is suggested one has to develop a mental model or image. . . . Generalizing to a teaching situation, one might expect teachers in various problem-solving aspects of their work . . . to draw upon images of lessons, incidents or children to help them interpret and solve teaching problems. In fact, being able to recall images, and to adapt and manipulate these images in reflecting about action in a particular context is possibly an important aspect of the task of teaching. . . . Images, whether representations or reconstructions, provide us with an indicator of teachers' knowledge and enable us to examine the knowledge growth attributable to different training experiences and the relationship between knowledge and observed practice. (p. 3)

These images—rich or poor, elaborated or sparse, vivid or vague—operate as "implicit theories" (Clark, 1988) that guide the practice of teachers; they represent the "subconscious assumptions on which practice is based" (Johnston, 1992:125). Moreover, they "are not usually consciously articulated without some assistance" (Johnston, 1991:125). They need to be made explicit.

The concept of image is, as Calderhead and Robson (1991:3) note, a rather "crude" one. We hold images of many things, abstract to concrete: good and bad government, good and bad families, good and bad classes and students, good and bad lessons, and so on. No set of images is more slippery or perhaps more abstract, yet of greater importance educationally, than that associated with conceptions of self. In part the difficulty is a result of the impact of the vast cultural and social changes brought by the shift from a modern to a post-modern age, which makes achieving a coherent self difficult. Nevertheless, all situations demand a degree of coherence, a story line born of experience that allows a measure of predictability and stability in interaction and relationships. The need for coherence is a practical matter of having to cope with reality (see Witherell, 1991)—and six periods of thirty hormonal teenagers is reality!— and of needing to interact with others (see McCarthy, 1991).

Practically, images need articulating, and to articulate images is to tell a story, a self-narrative. To tell a story is to create a coherence of meanings, perhaps to impose a pattern (Olney, 1972:326), that allows consistency of interpretation and action. Besides creating coherence the story has another important value captured by Suzanne Rhodenbaugh (1992:398) in her discussion of why some poems grip her, producing a "heart's canon": "It may be the poems become important because they contribute to a *myth of self* I'm making, a self I long toward, one that understands more, is more generous, is kinder and wiser than I am." The story, a "myth of self", serves as an ideal type, something we long for. Elbaz (1983) noted in her study that this is just how images operate for teachers; they invite, rather than compel, conformity.

The recent work on the role of narrative in teacher socialization represents a second line of supportive research (Connelly & Clandinin, 1988). By moving to narrative, we have shifted from vision to voice. At first blush this would seem to be a problem until it is realized that we "see" through language; and language creates the world in its own image. Put differently, we see through our metaphors; images are metaphorically embedded (Collins & Green, 1990) and embodied experientially (Lakoff & Johnson, 1980).

Metaphors often form a story's theme or line (Bruner, 1990); they stand between story and image. As such, they provide a promising means for clustering images for exploration and analysis of teacher thinking and provide an avenue for self-exploration.

Implicitly, teacher educators have long recognized the intimate relationship between metaphors and teacher identity.

Some years ago Earl Pullias and James Young (1968), for example, created a list of teaching roles that took the form of: "A teacher is . . ." A teacher is a "guide," they said, "an example," and so on. Surprisingly, "one's relation to the world can often be reduced to a few words describing how one thinks and feels" (Norton, 1989:1). Perhaps the most powerful teacher role is embedded in the metaphor that a teacher is "one who knows," a master or expert. It is this metaphor that seems to come to mind most readily as representing the essence of "teacher" and is, as noted, institutionally most supported particularly in secondary schools where it is taken as being commonsensical. Martha certainly knew this, as did Terry. The institutional strength of this understanding is remarkable, as evident not only in how school is organized structurally but also in student, teacher, and parent expectations. Moreover, other metaphors are discouraged.

For a teacher to be master or subject matter expert, it is necessary that students, as "other," become disciples, imitators, or mimics of those in the know. And here's the problem: As Terry noted, a good many students do not want to be cast as disciples, yet disciples they must be if teachers are to be masters. But this is not all. For the master, teaching is telling, or shifting images, a matter of filling a "dry-well" (Sternberg & Martin, 1988:557); and filling a dry well, as Martha discovered, is often no fun at all. As each teacher discovered, metaphors reach out, interact, and define one another and simultaneously define the other.

Thoughts associated with metaphors may conflict not only when personal and institutional metaphors clash, but also when they do not fit our "myth of self." The result is what St. James would recognize as the condition of "double-mindedness," the inability to will one thing (Kierkegaard, 1956). Double-mindedness—wanting to be a chemist and expert but wanting to be liked and needing to feel close emotional bonds with students—impedes consistency of action within the classroom, because there is no coherent story line. And the teacher seems adrift. Moreover, metaphors may not only conflict; some may be educationally limiting, if not harmful. Think, for instance, of the educational significance of the metaphor "teacher is policeman." For policemen-teachers students become criminals!

Thus, there is more at stake to exploring self through metaphors than just the inner workings of self. For beginning teachers, coming to terms with who they are as teachers and the assumptions that underpin their thinking about teaching requires coming to terms with that which is not self: most importantly, students. Exploring teaching metaphors is not, then, only important because it is a means for assisting beginning teachers to articulate and consider who they think they are as teachers and what they want to be but also because it simultaneously enables exploration of coevolving conceptions of other: students, the disciplines, and so on. It is particularly important to note that the metaphors held by teachers both enable and limit student opportunities to learn. Their consideration, then, necessitates that the ethical and moral implications of different conceptions of self as teacher, as well as different relations with the other, be confronted and criticized. Finally, exploring metaphors is a means for considering the ways in which different contexts enable some meanings while they inhibit others. In secondary schools, it's easier to think of teaching as telling than as the exchange of cultural capital or as mothering, for example. As such, the identification and analysis of teaching metaphors is a means for gaining perspective on one's own socialization. We turn now to a set of issues and a few problems related to metaphor analysis.

Getting Started

As noted, we stress to our students that they should reread their life histories when seeking a metaphor or metaphors that capture their views of themselves as teachers. Also, we introduce the topic by discussing the centrality of metaphors in thinking, in particular drawing on the work of Lakoff and Johnson:

> Just as in mutual understanding we constantly search out commonalities of experience when we speak with other people, so in self-understanding we are always searching for what unifies our own diverse experiences in order to give coherence to our lives. Just as we seek out metaphors

to highlight and make coherent what we have in common with someone else, so we seek out personal metaphors to highlight and make coherent our own pasts, our present activities, and our dreams, hopes, and goals as well. A large part of self-understanding is the search for appropriate personal metaphors that make sense of our lives. (1980:232–233)

In teaching, as in life generally, metaphors are central to the process of sense making.

We ask, for example, what the discovery of the pump did for our understanding of the human heart? We share our own metaphors for teaching, one of which is "teaching is conversation" (Bullough, 1994), and explore by way of example the implications of these metaphors for practice as guiding theories. We have also discovered that for some students visualization is helpful; we encourage them to close their eyes and imagine their ideal classroom. We ask them to focus on how that classroom feels, what they are doing, and what their students are doing while in the room. Then, they write.

Generating Metaphors

Some students, like Mary, have difficulty identifying metaphors. We have found that for the vast majority of our students, authentic metaphors do eventually emerge and a little patience is all that is necessary. For a few, however, metaphors never come. A very few students never quite understand what a metaphor is. And, some do not want to reflect on their conceptions of themselves as teachers because they either think they "have it" and they see no purpose to the exercise or they are generally unreflective. Additionally, for a variety of reasons a small group of students have difficulty because they assume there is a right answer, a single metaphor that is them and that will endure.

To address these problems we encourage a few students, after the first writing, to rethink what they have written or to expand on it. We urge them to turn inward, be patient, and focus on naming their images of themselves as teachers. For those who do not understand what a metaphor is we talk individually, and this seems to help. Often they "know" but are unfamiliar with

the label. With those (and there are a very few) who produce
silly metaphors that indicate an unwillingness to turn inward,
we prod gently and seek to better explain the purpose of the
methodology. And finally, we stress over and over again that
there is no universal, single, best teaching metaphor. We remind
them that all metaphors have limitations and break down as
comparisons are made. Moreover, we suggest that as their
thinking becomes more complicated, other metaphors may
become more compelling than those initially generated, and that
this is the way it is supposed to be; it is a sign of development as
a teacher.

Student Reactions

We have sought through interview and questionnaire to gather
data that would help us better understand the strengths and
weaknesses of the methodology. Some students do not find the
methodology helpful, but clearly most do, particularly during
the early stages of teacher education. A few of our students find
that by the end of teacher education the value has lessened
because they have settled on a comfortable role and self-
understanding. This is to be expected, and celebrated, provided
the role generated is ethically and educationally defensible. Our
questionnaire included the following question: "Was the focus
on the identification and exploration of personal teaching
metaphors helpful?" Typical comments included: "Yes. Because
of the written metaphor updates I was able to see where I was
(mentally, developmentally) at certain times during the year. The
updates forced me to think about, and put into words, my ideas
and assumptions." Another wrote: "I thought the metaphors
were very helpful. When I started the cohort in the fall, I was
very nervous about what it meant to be a teacher. I certainly
couldn't imagine it then. The metaphors worked for me because
they made me examine my feelings about myself as a teacher,
which helped when I began teaching." A third student wrote:
"Yes, very much so. It allowed me to re-evaluate myself
periodically and be self-critical. . . . Through the metaphors I was
able to look back on my progress and realize I was beginning to
think like a teacher. . . . I was able to look at what I was

becoming as a teacher and decide whether I was headed in the direction that I wanted to go." And a negative comment, which illustrates some of the difficulties noted above: "Not really. I hate to compare myself in a metaphor. Each of us is different in terms of our personalities. Each of us is unique and will teach in a different manner. I think the metaphor is actually restrictive in describing ourselves. Maybe a multiple metaphor?"

Methodologies for Exploring School Context

CHAPTER FOUR

School Histories

Introduction

The school context influences what curriculum is implemented, what relations are established between and among teachers and students, and even the role teachers play in local decision making. Take tracking, for example. It makes a great deal of difference to your role and relationships with students if you join a faculty that is committed to ability grouping or one committed to discovering ways of working effectively with heterogeneous groups. And yet, despite the importance of context in shaping the quality of classroom life, teacher preparation, especially training approaches, tends to ignore a variety of contextual issues and instead focuses almost exclusively on classroom practice. Further, because you have spent a number of years in schools as a student, these contexts have become familiar, taken for granted. Inquiry into school history is a way to make these familiar contexts "strange." By doing so, a number of critical issues about context can be posed, including the influence of mandated curriculum on teachers' work and student learning, how the teacher culture shapes educational experience, and even how common school structures such as ability grouping help shape student and teacher expectations.

The purpose of raising such issues is not to prepare teachers to fit easily into schools; this would still reflect training assumptions. Rather, the aim is to identify questions and a point of departure for inquiry that will enable you to shape the structures, values, and policies that help form the teacher role and teaching practice. Undoubtedly, you will work in a school context that differs from your current student teaching placement, but the questions posed through the study of school history can help you keep contextual issues in mind as you make the transition to your first year of teaching.

It is important to note at this point that while context influences how you approach teaching, it does not determine it. Teachers and others act on and shape the school context, just as the context influences those who work within it. Thus, a study of school context is a matter of considering not only organizational structures, such as the formal curriculum or the administrative hierarchy, but also the way individuals and groups have reshaped the context. To understand schooling requires that events and structures be situated historically in relationship to past policies and practices and to wider cultural developments.

It should not be assumed, however, that school histories are only about context. As is true of all the methodologies described in *Becoming a Student of Teaching*, the histories involve both issues of context *and* self. While context is emphasized here, it is inevitable that part of the history will involve placing yourself within the context studied—to consider from your standpoint the nature of the organization and culture.

Writing

There are three stages in writing school histories as we use them. Stage 1 involves problem formation and data gathering, stage 2, school description, and stage 3 involves making interpretations and identifying themes. A description of these stages follows.

1. *Problem formation and data gathering.* In the first stage of writing a school history, you will be asked to conduct informal observations and interviews and review school policies in a general way to see how this information might shape a problem or issue of interest to you. Once a problem is identified, you should begin collecting data that address the identified problem. You may work in teams. Those of you teaching in the same school can

divide up the work. For example, some of you could do observations while others interview school faculty.

Regardless of how the team decides to collect data, you will need to determine the types of interview questions that will shed light on the issue or problem identified. When interviewing, care must be taken not to ask leading questions. In addition, confidentiality is essential as is gaining permission from those involved in the study to conduct interviews and visit classrooms.

2. *School description*. This stage involves using the data collected to describe the school. If, for example, your observations focus on the types of interactions found in a remedial class as compared to an honors class, observation notes could be used to make comparisons of teacher roles, student expectations, and teacher-student relationships in the two settings. The purpose of the descriptive stage is to put into words what you see in the classroom. In doing so, avoid trying to account for all aspects of the school.

Once a draft of the description is written, it should be shared with other beginning teachers. Sharing will help you identify areas that are unclear or perhaps overly judgmental and help you identify themes underlying your description.

3. *Identifying themes and making interpretations*. The transition from description to a thematic organization signals the third, or interpretive, stage. Themes are reoccurring patterns in the data. For example, if the data indicate that teachers interact more with boys or with girls, then the issue of gender and teaching may become a theme around which the data are organized. Once identified, the themes are used to locate readings that speak to the issues you have raised. An example may be helpful at this point. If you find that a key theme in the school studied is the influence of tracking on student relationships and learning, then you need to search out readings that focus on this issue. The readings are intended to help you develop an argument, and to see

how your interpretations compare with others'. Put simply, the readings make it possible to start a dialogue between yourself and others who have produced knowledge about teaching. Be cautious: keep in mind that the knowledge you produce comes from a case study and does not provide a foundation for generalizations about schooling. Also, the readings should not be used to turn your school history into a typical academic research paper complete with footnotes and bibliography. Instead, they should allow you to contextualize the themes presented by connecting your insights to those of others. The readings should not overwhelm your voice; a balance should be sought between your private theories and the more public ones presented in the readings.

Once insights gained from the readings are integrated into your themes, the next step is to make sure that the interpretation considers why the particular structures, commitments, or patterns found at the school came into existence. Interpretations of this kind may require that you look beyond the school context and consider the wider influence of educational policy. For example, if your focus is tracking, you may want to explore why tracking came into being and how it changed over time.

After attempts are made to relate the school histories to policies and practices outside the school, you will be asked again to share your histories. The intent of the sharing, in this instance, is to locate gaps that make the story difficult to follow, clarify themes, and further articulate the perspective you bring to the school history. Your perspective should be apparent; there is no need to pretend to be neutral, because that is not possible. It is better to be up front with your views than to pretend yours is an "objective" account of the school. After receiving feedback, a final draft is written and shared with other preservice candidates, teacher educators, and practicing teachers.

Three abbreviated and edited school histories taken from a recent cohort group follow.

Central Heights High: A Clash of Cultures

The "baby boom" [following] World War II . . . [produced] a growth-spurt that forced the [Salt Lake City School] District to reconsider its educational structure. Home to the three "central city" high schools—East, West and South—Salt Lake School District was forced to open yet another high school to accommodate the record 42,000-plus students flooding the system. Central Heights High School was built as a direct result of this population spurt.

The area surrounding Central Heights is . . . fairly [prosperous]. . . . Central Heights has a reputation for being a predominately Caucasian, higher socioeconomic [level] school. It has remained the most highly populated of the district high schools, and has enjoyed the affluence from which it draws its main population. However, this changed in 1988. As Salt Lake City began to change and the city population began to diminish, the need for South High School was called into question. Because the housing in this [area] is much older and oftentimes more run-down than housing elsewhere, it is often inhabited by young, childless couples, the elderly, and the poor. Young families tend to move to the suburbs . . . to buy "starter homes" in what are often considered safer, more appealing areas. [In contrast,] a larger number of [poor] minorities moved into the South High area as the property value and rent decreased. . . . [These changes threw] . . . the entire city into a controversy concerning the question of closing one of the oldest and most beloved schools in the state. Parents, teachers and students alike were concerned that [closing South] would "negatively impact" their [own] school and the education it was providing. On the other hand, the population surrounding South continued to decline.

There was also the concern that leaving [South] open would lend itself to segregation of sorts and that the public perception would be that the district could not stand up to the parents and faculty of the [two more affluent] schools [who were against the integration of South High students]. Leaving South open because the more prestigious schools did not want the minorities in their schools was a dangerous pre–*Brown v. Board of*

Education view, and district [leadership] was wary of getting caught in such a legal and social trap. Thus, the district felt it had no option but to close South High despite the protests and controversy that followed. South's population was dispersed throughout the remaining three high schools, and Central Heights High received a little over one-third of the students and became the ESL (English as a second language) magnet school, which draws students from throughout the district. Thus, [the] Central Heights minority population was drastically increased (the effects of this increase will be discussed later).

Central Heights High School currently houses approximately 2,100 students in grades 9–12. Of these students 76 percent are Caucasian, 12.5 percent are Hispanic, 1.7 percent are Pacific Islanders, 6.9 percent are Asian, .85 percent are African American, and .33 percent are considered "others." Given the diversity of the population at Central Heights, I was shocked by what seemed to be a nearly all-white student body in honors and "regular" English classes. In four class periods I counted only ten minority students, and when I asked the instructor where the minorities were he told me that "you will rarely find minorities in classes like these." I was afraid to ask why.

From what I had seen and observed in the classrooms and halls, I assumed that Central Heights had no more than 10–12 percent minority students. I was surprised when I discovered the actual figure was 24 percent, and I couldn't help but ask myself just where Central Heights "was keeping" its minorities. The "mystery" was solved, however, when I began observing remedial and basic skills courses, which were literally filled with minority students. It was almost as if Central Heights was attempting to somehow hide its minority students by keeping them in such courses, and the image that came to mind was that of the "bastard child" hidden in the attic of the Victorian mind-set. Whether intentional or not, most of Central Heights minority students are in one way or another involved in the remedial, basic skills or ESL programs, and are being tracked into programs that may not necessarily suit their needs and best interests.

According to Jeannie Oakes in her book, *How Schools Structure Inequality*, the decisions that are made concerning a student's placement are often reached "on the basis of counselors' assessment of their language, dress and behavior as well as their (perceived) academic potential" (12). Thus, given the history of Central Heights as being a predominately white, middle-class school, it is natural to assume that the teachers, counselors and administrators make judgements about students and their potential according to what they perceive to be the norm: white, Anglo-Saxon, middle-American students. This also applies to the results of standardized tests, which are often gender and race biased and fail to account for individual differences. Last year at Central Heights an incident occurred that rocked the foundations of this kind of thinking and forced the school to reexamine its policies and attitudes toward minority students. A Hispanic student approached his counselor for a scholarship application and was rejected because he did not, according to the counselor, "look like someone who could win a scholarship." The boy was one of the school's top students and ended up winning over $20,000 in scholarships! The counselor never did give the student the application he requested. When questioned about her actions by outraged parents and their attorney, the counselor repeated her justification, unaware of its prejudicial overtones and the impact of such generalizations. The counselor was eventually forced to resign.

[I observed] very little interaction between minority and majority students, and the various groups tend to stick together. . . . When asked about race relations at Central Heights High School, students, both minority and majority, came to the same conclusions: students tend to form "cliques" or groups which exclude others who do not fit the criteria for the group. For example, one student that I interviewed told me that he wasn't very sure about the rest of the student body because he "mostly stayed around the jocks—the guys who play sports." This was not unusual, and after I had interviewed several different students I got the impression that the student body at Central Heights is very fragmented and divided. It is almost as if there are several small schools within one, each possessing its own culture, values and goals. You can observe this phenomena in the halls between classes and at lunch—cheerleaders gathered with cheerleaders; "jocks" wrestling on the lawn; "brainers," or academic students, studying in the halls; and minority students gathered together in the parking lot. The district itself has noted this division among students and has attempted to involve students living outside the Central Heights community (mostly minority students transferred from the former boundaries of South High) by chartering "activity buses" to pick students up and take them to school activities such as games, dances and pep rallies. Sadly, the idea failed. Buses returned empty, and it became necessary to discontinue the program for lack of interest.

Whether it was lack of interest that killed the program or a feeling of disassociation, or not "belonging," on the part of the minority students, it is evident that Central Heights has a problem. My interviews revealed that minority students feel separated and distanced from the rest of the school, despite the efforts of the district, the school and the faculty. I can't help but blame the tracking that is going on in the "attic" of Central Heights as the cause. It is impossible for students to gain respect and understanding for one another when they are being inadvertently separated and segregated. In order to truly mend race relations at Central Heights, administration and faculty must reexamine their curriculum, methods and attitudes to ensure that all of their students are getting the education they deserve. More emphasis should be placed upon integrated, multicultural education rather than upon tracking and structuring the inequalities that exist within the system. Jeannie Oakes contends that tracking systems more than often fail and, in the process, backfire on those who subscribe to them. Perhaps this is what has happened at Central Heights despite good intentions.

Some of the teachers at Central Heights think that there is nothing wrong with "the way things are currently done," [others] feel that there is much to be done at Central Heights. When asked what approaches to teaching style, curriculum and management need to be altered to suit the needs of all students [one teacher] agreed that there needs to be more cooperative learning approaches taken with students and that assessment needs to be more flexible and reflective of the different ways that students learn. Citing portfolios as an example [this teacher] explained that her Asian students hated this method, but her Hispanic students loved the approach and were very successful.

In general, the faculty at Central Heights feels that the integration of South High is an advantage rather than a disadvantage. Most view it as a source of "new blood" and liveliness of new ideas and attitudes that has made them more aware of how and what they teach. Most are optimistic about the future of Central Heights and are concerned with the issues plaguing the school. Increased training, community input, less tracking—all of these are ideas which were mentioned to me as suggestions for improving race relations and the overall situation at Central Heights.

It is now time for all to work together to bring Central Heights up to par by detracking the remedial and basic skills programs through more innovative, creative methods of teaching and assessment—methods that apply to everyone and ensure individual success and, in the process, ensure the success of their school. Also, all students need to feel that they belong at Central Heights, and in an attempt to remedy race-related problems, the school has formed a Diversity Committee this year composed of students and faculty who work together to address issues and concerns throughout the school. Together they decided on a school theme of "Strength Through Diversity," and administrators and faculty alike have taken it very seriously. The students, however, are a different matter. According to the results of my interviews and observations, even more needs to be done to incorporate the entire student body and insure individual recognition and success.

What Is a Middle School?: The Story of Northeast

Physical changes are the most noticeable change for students in these ages. . . . Sexual maturation is another element that is changing at this time. . . . These changes cause anxiety for many students. Appearance becomes very important, and students worry when their changing bodies do not meet the cultural norm depicted in advertising and other forms of media. [Rapid] mental changes are also taking place during early adolescence. . . . Students also undergo tremendous social and emotional changes during the early adolescent period. Children in this period are breaking away from parents and family and moving toward the peer group.

This is also the time when a child's self concept is at its lowest. Young teens crave attention and do not discriminate in how they get it. They also become very egocentric. They have a tendency to monopolize telephones, bathrooms, and television. "They think the whole world is watching them and that pimple on their chin" (What Is a Middle School—Really, p. 3).

The Middle School Model

A general definition of a middle school is [that it is] an "institution that truly seeks to meet the needs of youth in transition between childhood and adolescence" (This We Believe, p. 14). These children no longer belong in an elementary school, but are not yet ready for high school. . . .

A model of a true middle school has been developed by the National Middle School Association. While this is only a model, it is important to understand the ideal concept of a middle school in order to [assess] Northeast's progress in implementing the concept. Using the publication by the National Middle School Association and information in a pamphlet on middle schools by Paul S. George, I have synthesized the information to explain the elements of a true middle school that is based on student needs rather than a notion of what students should know.

1. *Educators should be knowledgeable about and committed to the unique characteristics of this age-group.* For a middle school to succeed, it is imperative that teachers and administrators are committed to helping and understanding students in this age-group.

2. *Skills through exploration.* Exploratory curriculum is the key for success with middle school students. Because of

the many personal changes facing the students [they] learn best through brief, intense interest-based activities.

3. *Balanced curriculum based on student needs.* Balanced instruction recognizes that middle school students are no longer children but are not adults. Instruction will balance academic goals with the special developmental needs of students.

4. *A range of organizational arrangements.* A variety of organizational arrangements, including block scheduling, multi-age grouping, developmental age grouping, and alternate schedules, . . . [help] middle schools meet students' needs.

5. *Varied instructional strategies.* Students in middle school have a broad range of skills and abilities but they do not achieve in a uniform manner. Therefore, methods of instruction should vary.

6. *Evaluation procedures compatible with young adolescents.* Evaluation procedures should minimize comparisons between students, because of the self-conscious nature of middle school students. Progress reports highlighting the individual accomplishments of students should include comments by both the teacher and student.

Northeast Middle School: The Context

Northeast Middle School opened in 1958, and currently has about 790 students in seventh and eighth grade. The school population is generally from a lower socio-economic level. This is evidenced by the 40% of students who receive free or reduced lunches. Many students also live in single-parent families, many are on welfare, and quite a few live in foster homes. The school population also consists of about 28 percent minority students, including Latinos, African Americans, Asians (including Pacific Islanders), and Native Americans. These groups bring a unique cultural diversity to the school, and also bring special needs.

Northeast Middle School has worked hard to become a middle school. Seven years ago (1985) the principal, Dr. McCoy, saw the need to adopt a different format for Northeast. At the time Northeast was operating as a junior high school, in essence, a small high school. As an administrator, he saw that the junior high format was not meeting the students' needs, and determined that Northeast would become a middle school. Ms. Baron was chosen to assist him at this time.

The concept was not well accepted in the beginning. The faculty did not see the need for change and neither did the community. The administration decided that rather than make drastic changes, they would move slowly and take one step at a time. The school is still working on adopting a full middle school model.

Ms. Baron, [currently the] principal, has the charge of hiring teachers. She looks for teachers who are interested in middle schools and who understand middle-school-age students. Many teachers were already teaching at Northeast when the school became a middle school. Many of these teachers have adapted and become an integral part in adopting the middle school model, but some are not enthusiastic about the change. They continue to teach in styles more suited to high-school-age students. During interviews, students mentioned teachers who used a more active, hands-on approach as being better teachers than more traditional teachers.

This active, hands-on approach is stressed in teaching at Northeast. The school mission statement developed by the school community council states: "The mission of Northeast Middle School is to provide a safe positive learning environment which encourages and recognizes active learning. . . ." Terri King, a social studies teacher, was mentioned by six students as being their favorite teacher. When asked why she was their favorite teacher, they noted that she taught with activities and a hands-on approach. During one observation, she used political cartoons from the newspaper as a way to help students understand the current presidential election and allowed students to come to their own conclusions as to the meaning of a chosen cartoon.

Kathryn Tucker, an English teacher, used small groups to enhance students' writing skills. Each group of students came up with a topic to write on. The students were to use one of six styles of writing being discussed. The teacher and students then evaluated whether each group had accomplished the intended goal. The teacher and students actively worked together to learn the intended concepts.

A teacher who was not well liked by the students spent a great deal of time lecturing to the students and dealing with discipline problems. Students felt they misbehaved in the class because it was boring and the teacher treated them like "babies."

[On an organizational level] the school is also trying to do away with tracking. Resource, learning disabled, intellectually handicapped, and behaviorally disabled students [are placed] in the regular classroom as much as possible. Because students are not grouped by their special needs, their self concept is thought to be improved. Although this is the goal, the school still has special classes for most of these students. Northeast has the largest number of special education students in the district (130 students), [which] presents a special challenge to the school. Math students are also tracked so those with better math skills can move forward to higher-level math.

This is the first year at Northeast the teachers have worked in teams. The teachers are in groups of four and include a teacher from math, science, social studies, and English. . . . Wherever possible the classrooms of team members are in the same area. Teachers meet together one hour each week during class time and one hour after school to discuss their students and the progress they are making. During the class-time meeting aides take the place of the regular classroom teacher. At this [point], teachers are not [yet] integrating their curriculum. This is a [future] goal.

Students at Northeast receive a regular report card, but at the present time Northeast considers itself a "failure-free school." If a student receives below a D-, the student is given an incomplete. The students and the teacher work together for three weeks to make up the grade. If the student has still not done sufficient work to pass the class, he/she is enrolled in a Saturday class where work is continued on the project. Students who fail to complete the work in the Saturday class must take summer school. Every effort is made to help the student. Students who are at risk of failing in school and dropping out are referred to a special program called the "Strong" program. These students are not in regular classrooms, but spend the day with a teacher assigned to meet their special needs. Some of these students are trained for jobs, since it is supposed they will not complete high school. . . . Not every student remains in school, but at least the school is attempting to help students at risk remain in school.

Interpretation

The middle school concept is beginning to be successful at Northeast. Not all teachers, parents, or students are enthusiastic about the concept, but overall the middle school format seems to be making school more palatable for early adolescent students. In many ways the school is following the middle school model, but the school has also incorporated its own personal style. . . . Some parts of the model will be incorporated at Northeast in the future.

The administration is working to hire educators who are committed to young adolescents, but it is not easy to remove teachers who do not enjoy students in this age bracket. Some newly hired teachers find they do not enjoy the students as much as they originally thought they would. One teacher, for example, has struggled all year to work with her students. She has had difficulty controlling classroom behavior, and as a result, she dislikes her students, and they dislike her. Ideally, all faculty members would work well with young adolescents, but this is [idealistic] and difficult to find in real situations.

Middle schools require changes in the teacher [role]. To facilitate these changes the school is holding seminars to help teachers [understand] the middle school model. . . . At Northeast, some teachers have done a good job of [changing their approach to] curriculum, while others have not done so. This will continue to be a challenge at Northeast. The middle school's focus on varied instructional strategies is another point in conflict. Some teachers successfully incorporate a variety of teaching methods in their classroom such as cooperative learning groups, simulations, and independent exploration of topics by students. Other teachers still spend a great deal of time lecturing students in a traditional manner. Time will tell if teacher seminars will [change] those teachers who are less committed to the middle school concept.

There are still some aspects of the model that need to be incorporated into the school. The school is still working on a balanced and integrated curriculum for all students. The first step was forming teachers into teams. It is hoped that next year, teams of teachers will work together to integrate the curriculum. Sometimes at Northeast content takes precedence over student needs. The blame for this cannot solely be placed on Northeast's faculty. Outside influences, such as the board of education and the state legislature, also determine what and how certain subjects will be taught in the classroom. These expectations limit teachers.

Northeast Middle School is successfully incorporating the ideals of a middle school. It is hoped at Northeast that further integration of middle school concepts will make the school even stronger in the future. Overall, I think Northeast is making a positive impact on students and the community. Hopefully, students will continue to make sufficient academic progress so that the middle school model will continue to receive support from the school district and the community.

The Complexities of Gifted Education: Lakeside High

In January of 1993 I face the responsibility of student teaching at Lakeside High school where I have been assigned to teach tenth-grade honors English. In researching the circumstances I will teach under, I found that a proportion of the students in my class are ninth graders who participate in an extended learning program (ELP) and have, therefore, skipped ninth-grade English and advanced directly to tenth-grade English. [Knowing that I will be] teaching gifted students, I have researched the history of gifted education in America and observed, in depth, the gifted program at Lakeside High School. Thus, this paper presents a brief history of gifted education and details the program I will be working with at Lakeside High School.

History of the Gifted in American Education

In the developmental stages of the American education system Thomas Jefferson recognized the importance of identifying and training intellectually gifted children. Influenced by Plato's *Republic*, Jefferson put forth a bill . . . which proposed that in order to eventually fill key positions of leadership in the new country, promising youths should be educated in universities at public expense.

Jefferson's goal was that "the best geniuses will be raked from the rubbish annually, and sent to William and Mary College. By this means we hope to avail the State of those talents which nature has sown as liberally among the poor as the rich, but which perish without use, if not sought for and cultivated."

One of the first special programs in the education of the gifted was initiated in the schools of St. Louis, Missouri, and ran from 1868 to the end of the nineteenth century. This program allowed for the gifted to skip grades in what was called "flexible promotion" and allowed high-achieving students to complete six years of grammar school in four years. Between 1900 and 1926 many school districts recognized the needs of gifted students and set up special programs to accommodate them, including flexible promotion, special classes, and select schools for high academic achievers. The object of these programs was usually to accelerate the education of gifted learners because, as it was argued, children of high intelligence should be educated separately from slower learners so that they could excel to be the nation's leaders.

During the 1930's and 1940's [interest in] gifted education continued. During this time the idea of progressive education was in favor, and special isolated classes gave way to enrichment programs that were taught in the regular classroom. Instead of going faster, the gifted were taught at the same pace as other students. However, they were encouraged to study current material in greater detail and depth.

[In] 1957 a dramatic change in gifted education occurred. Following the Russian launch of Sputnik, Americans realized that other countries were doing more to train their best minds. As a result U.S. educators began to dramatically improve and expand educational programs [for] the gifted, and the federal government encouraged states to put a strong emphasis on the development of special programs.

In 1972 Congress created the Office of the Gifted and Talented within the Office of Education, and two years later they funded Section 404 of Public Law 93-380, known as the Special Projects Act. This act provided $2.5 million every year to state and local agencies for a variety of gifted education projects. Six years later, President Jimmy Carter signed Public Law 95–561, which is known as the Educational Amendments of 1978, and authorized five years of funding to elementary and secondary programs. Title IX-A of this bill is the Gifted and Talented Act [which] promises increasing amounts of money to state education agencies to help them plan, develop, and improve programs designed to help gifted and talented children. Fortunately, the bill also provided grants for training [teachers] who work with gifted and talented students.

Although this bill was passed nearly fifteen years ago, it initiated growth in the study of gifted and talented education and promotes the belief that every human being is a unique individual with an equal right to the full development of his or her potential.

The history of gifted education shows an increasing recognition of the rights, the needs, and the value of the gifted and talented person in society.

Change

In 1986, when the Salt Lake School District decided to close South High School, the Extended Learning Program, which was housed at the school, became homeless. Amongst the confusion of school boundary changes and student transfers, the future of the ELP program became a debated issue. Fortunately, parents, school administrators, and students at Lakeside High saw an opportunity to improve the image, priorities, and academic standards at their school. With change in mind, they adamantly fought to have the ELP secondary magnet program located at Lakeside High.

Currently no ELP teacher at Lakeside High instructs only ELP classes. The additional training through workshops and seminars is beneficial to a much broader base of students and is available to all teachers who choose to participate.

Although the majority of teachers welcomed the ELP students, some were hesitant to have twelve-year-old students in their classrooms. Fortunately, smooth communication between the counseling center and faculty has served to avoid [some] conflicts with those who wish to teach only regular students.

In addition to counseling services, parents of the ELP students have effected change in the PTSA and Community Council. As members of these volunteer programs, the parents of gifted students see that the needs of their child are addressed and met.

Further, the younger ELP students have transformed the image of a typical high school student. Freshmen are no longer the youngest class, and some seventeen-year-old seniors compete with twelve-year-old, seventh-grade gifted students. As a result, the emphasis on gifted education has [changed] the expectations of students, as well as [some] teachers. Teachers, counselors, parents, and students seem to expect excellence and high achievement. This year Lakeside accepted applications from 693 potential ELP students, and only 70 could be accepted. Obviously, the program has encouraged the elementary feeder schools to change their expectations and students' goals as well.

The elementary magnet program is housed in two locations. Valley Elementary school has classes for grades kindergarten through six, and Mountain Central Elementary School has classes for grades four, five, and six, with intentions of expanding to lower grades. Both schools offer a complete elementary curriculum which is "extended" in specified ways, with ability grouping taking place across the level boundaries. For instance, at Valley all teachers teach math at the same time, and the students move to the classroom where their level is taught. Further, as part of the regular school day experience, minicourses, such as music appreciation, art appreciation, foreign languages, literature studies, and computer literacy are offered at each grade level.

[As a consequence] full-time elementary students are better prepared for the transition into a similar secondary setting, where full-time extended learning is available and expected.

Emotional and Social Needs

The academic transition into ELP is difficult for some students who are not accustomed to a high school setting. . . . Recognizing [the problem], the entrance requirements to the program have slowly evolved into a more comprehensive matrix of instruments that measure the academic and emotional maturity of the prospective students. In fact, over the last two years the dropout rate of dissatisfied or unhappy students has dropped to one-tenth of where it used to be. Further, the teachers, administrators, and students that I interviewed agreed that although not all ELP students are equally motivated, most are prepared emotionally and socially to meet the demands of the program.

It is the aim of the Extended Learning Program to meet the needs of each student. Thus, the ELP class consists of only seventy students. . . . Although the administrators claim that ELP students are not favored or treated differently from other students, the administration also boasts of treating each student according to his or her individual situation. In the 1991 annual ELP report Director Connie Jean Larsen reported that in Lakeside High's program "the whole student is our concern." . . .

Moreover, the ELP at Lakeside High is the result of years of changes throughout the history of gifted education, and in the Salt Lake City School District. . . . Feeder schools, parents, teachers, administrators, counselors, and students have changed [somewhat] and, in doing so, have [altered] the academic priorities and goals at Lakeside High. The vast array of students and their individual achievements speak best for the entire program. In fact, Justin Culley, a Lakeside High alumnus who entered in the first class of ELP students, summarizes the effect of the program: "The ELP program at Lakeside is good. It works.

It prepares students for college in a way that, in my opinion, cannot be obtained through mainstream high school. What it boils down to is that for those who feel up to the work, the benefits are valuable beyond measure, especially at this stage in life when they are preparing to enter the real world." Fortunately, "the real world" of education is beginning to recognize and meet the complex needs of gifted students.

Commentary

To better understand this methodology, and its strengths and limitations, we will consider the three examples in relation to some of the purposes set out earlier. In moving from a description of the school context to making interpretations about the context, we suggested that a starting point is the identification of themes. The Central Heights and Northeast studies are somewhat successful in this regard. The Central Heights study centers on the clash between minority culture and the more affluent white culture. The Northeast study also is successful in developing themes: a comparison between the theory and practice of middle school education, and the difficulty of school change. This said, we should note that while themes are present, the histories are organized chronologically rather than thematically. This is not surprising. Few people think of history as anything other than a chronological accounting of events.

In contrast to these two studies, the Lakeside history of gifted education remains at a descriptive level. It is a favorable accounting of the structures and policies in place that eased the transition to high school. Themes are not developed, nor are questions posed. More than anything, it is an endorsement of the program. While the purpose of school histories is not to criticize all that is occurring within a school setting, a critical eye is necessary if questions are to be raised about the influence of the context on teachers and their work.

Even if one moves beyond description and develops themes, interpretations need to be compared with "outside" authors who address related topics. The Central Heights study is most successful here. Although including only one reading on tracking, the reference strengthens the anecdotal evidence that minority students bused to Central Heights were missing from the honors classes. The author of the school history and the outsider, Oakes, came together to illuminate the clash of cultures at Central Heights.

The Northeast and Lakeside histories include more readings, but they are used differently. The middle school study begins with a cursory but helpful review of the literature on middle schools and the account of gifted education draws on a number of interesting historical sources. Unfortunately, these readings are used more to provide background information than to further the analyses. In the study of the school with the "gifted" program, for example, the readings are used to support the values of the program, but do little to raise questions about it. In the middle school study the readings have a more important role; they are used to set up a contrast between middle school policy, what authors suggest the middle school should be like, and how schooling is practiced at Northeast. But the author does not use the readings to consider if the gap between policy and practice is a problem or a benefit. As a consequence, the assumptions of the author and the practices put into place as part of the move to a middle school go unexplored.

In our introductory remarks we stated that school histories should include a policy analysis that reaches beyond the specific school context studied. The difficulty of making a broader analysis is evident in all three studies. None do more than suggest the wider forces affecting the practices and structures found in the school. For example, we might ask, how have government policies affected the clustering of minorities in cities? Or, how has the vanishing national support for middle schools affected practices within these schools? These are important questions that would lead to a more in-depth understanding of the complex factors influencing the school studied. However, this said, we also understand that not only is the lack of time a problem in addressing such complex studies, but teachers need to start their interpretations of context close to home and only after much work can they address the relation between wider policy issues and context. Our sense is that as preservice teacher education becomes more closely linked to in-service activities, the possibilities for viewing the relation between the school studied and the wider context become more likely. It is the training organization of our programs, more than anything, that limits inquiry into wider concerns. Such concerns need to be introduced over longer periods of time and when developmentally appropriate.

Writing a school history is useful for conceptualizing one's work as a teacher and for beginning to uncover how that work is shaped by events outside of self. In particular, the writing process should help raise a set of questions about context which later can be asked when you enter your first year of teaching. The accounts of Central Heights and Northeast middle suggest a number of provocative questions about context. The Central Heights study raises questions about tracking and its influence on students representing different cultures. We suspect that the author of this text would carefully examine situations where students were homogeneously grouped and, specifically, where this type of grouping reinforced cultural and social class divisions. It would be too speculative to suggest what this beginning teacher might do if she found herself in a similar situation, but it is likely that she would be able to speak knowledgeably about some of the limitations of tracking. In contrast, the Lakeside study should have also led to a consideration of tracking, but did not. The study accepted the ELP program uncritically. The middle school study conducted at Northeast raises two questions which could easily be taken into the first year of teaching. One question is the relation between public theory, or school policy, and its practice. Examining this relation enables teachers to see gaps between what faculty and administrators are trying to do and what is actually happening, and points to some "spaces" where teachers have the freedom to experiment with alternative pedagogies. The other question concerns the issue of school change. In particular, this query points to the importance of hiring and retention practices in thinking through the effectiveness of reform efforts.

Unfortunately, the ELP study does not seem to raise any questions to be taken forward by the author as she enters the first year of teaching. There is a set of questions begging to be asked about gifted education and the relationship between "gifted" students and others in the school, but these questions have not been posed. As a consequence, implicit values are not examined.

A Note to Teacher Educators and Students

One difficulty in doing successful school histories is that they require a number of skills that need to be developed and supported before the process begins. The three stages of the school history process will serve as a guide for discussing how these skills can be cultivated.

Stage One: Problem Formation and Data Gathering

The primary challenge in stage one is data collection. While our intent is not to produce sophisticated methodologists, it is important to become familiar with a few ways to conduct observations and interviews and develop questionnaires. The way we support these activities parallels many of the assumptions that underlie the methodologies discussed in *Becoming a Student of Teaching*. In particular, we start by having the students do a very short pilot study. To begin such a study, the students literally wander around the school and talk to teachers, students, and administrators. These informal observations and chats, which can be accomplished in a few short visits, help establish a tentative focus for the school histories. Once an issue or problem is set by the members of the study team, observations, interviews, and questionnaires are planned to gather data systematically. The questions that will structure the questionnaires or interviews are shared with us to get feedback, as are issues concerning the observation of classroom practice. Outside readings such as Agar's *Professional Stranger* may prove helpful as a resource. Once feedback is given, team members might try one interview or observation session. The purpose of these trials is not so much to collect data, but rather to identify problems associated with conducting observations and interviews and using questionnaires. Again, problems are shared with us and with other beginning teachers to generate possible solutions. Part of the feedback that needs to be given involves advice about situations that might put the beginning teacher at risk. For example, if a beginning teacher asks questions of teachers on the staff in the school within which they will student teach, and asks these questions in ways that alienate these faculty members, the school histories can create problems for the novice without producing much insight. Teacher educators must steer novices away from confrontational questions that will put the school staff on the defensive. Feedback should also be solicited from faculty working with student teachers to make certain they understand and support the process.

Stage Two: School Description

Transforming data into description, a story, is difficult. We find that students often summarize the data in a short list, such as how respondents answered interview questions, and then write the description without any supporting evidence. Links between data collection and the story told are not clear. Others will use so much data that the story or description never comes through. The challenge is to find a balance between the data provided and the story told. The middle school study seems to capture this balance.

> "The mission of Northeast Middle School is to provide a safe positive learning environment which encourages and recognizes active learning. . . ." Terri King, a social studies teacher, was mentioned by six students as being their favorite teacher. When asked why she was their favorite teacher, they noted that she taught with activities and a hands-on approach. During one observation, she used political cartoons from the newspaper as a way to help students understand the current presidential election and allowed students to come to their own conclusions as to the meaning of a chosen cartoon.

One way we have found that helps encourage balance is to have students go through their observations and interviews several times and then, without the data in front of them, simply describe the event or perspective expressed. Once a tentative description is written, the student is encouraged to go back to the data and insert quotes or excerpts from field notes that support the story told.

Stage Three: Interpretations and Themes

The interpretive stage is the most difficult. The first challenge is to identify themes. Having students look at the types of themes developed in well-organized published qualitative studies can be helpful. We have also spent time looking at the author's point of view and how his or her arguments are constructed. Discussion of these issues provides some insight into the difficult but important activity of making sense of data.

Another vital part of this stage is the integration of outside readings into the study. Some students are not sophisticated in doing library searches. It is helpful, as a consequence, to begin any consideration of "outside" readings with a trip to the library and a discussion of the types of resources that can be obtained. We then have a follow-up session which helps beginning teachers make choices about which scholarly work to focus on and how to quickly summarize the arguments found in a particular article, research paper, or text. While this is time-consuming, if an aim of teacher education is to foster students of teaching, knowing how to locate and summarize literature is important.

A final point about this aspect of the school history needs further elaboration. As noted, sharing insights is important. It is important as a way for students to help one another produce an understanding of context, and for developing an emergent form of community. While classroom practices can often be changed to some degree to fit a teacher's vision of what is good education, school structures which shape the boundaries within which decisions are made are more difficult to change. Changing context often requires group discussion and action. Generally speaking, neither teacher education programs nor the school context supports such discussion. Instead, there seems to be a trend of continuing isolation among teachers. One way to challenge this trend, particularly within preservice education, is to use school history texts for discussion. Through them, common concerns and interests can be identified and built upon. For example, after school histories were finished, a discussion that followed focused on several common concerns, including tracking and its influence on culture, and the issue of teachers who are resistant to change. Even the author of the "gifted" study could see how tracking had negative effects on minority cultures. Another way to further an emergent form of community is to talk about the difficulties and possibilities of doing a team project. School history teams work differently, and understanding their effectiveness, or lack of it, can be an important part of developing more collegial relations during the first year of teaching.

Given that emergent communities are never formed overnight, and that school histories are complex projects that require a considerable amount of time, these studies are likely to be most effective if they are conducted in stages over a quarter or semester, or seen as an integrating methodology that summarizes and focuses what has been learned about self and context. If the methodology is used over a quarter or semester, beginning teachers could be working on this long-term project as they are utilizing other methodologies. For example, the Shadow Study (see chapter five) or the Textbook Analysis (see chapter seven) could easily be part of the school history. The only change required would be to make certain these methodologies, in part, speak to the question or questions central to the school history. On the other hand, if school history is seen as an integrating methodology, it could occur at the end of the preservice program and be used as a way to pull together insights gleaned from other methodologies. In either case, what is most important is that beginning teachers be given the time to take on the difficult work of understanding the school context.

The History of School Histories

Understanding the history of this methodology is an important part of developing a rationale for the study of school context. The use of the local context as a focus for research has a long tradition in both sociology and anthropology. In sociology, the notion of "nearby history" became popular in the mid-twentieth century. Nearby histories were thought to be the most natural and logical way for sociologists to understand the relation between context and the broader historical currents of society. Studying local contexts, according to proponents, made the process of reaching decisions more reflective and intelligent (Kyvig & Marty, 1986, p. 103). Anthropology added to this research orientation by pointing out that nearby histories should focus on not only individuals and structures but also culture. Anthropologists traditionally did not study their own contexts. They did, however, focus on the way patterns of interaction, institutional structures, and artifacts influenced the traditions and rituals of a particular culture. In the 1970's educational researchers combined the sociological approach of nearby history with the cultural approach found in anthropology and began to study aspects of the local school culture (see, e.g., Willis, 1977).

School histories build on both traditions. They encourage beginning teachers to examine their own school context and utilize these studies to produce knowledge about the influence of school practices, policies, and structures on the teacher role, teacher-student relationships, and the type of curriculum offered to students. Further, they show not only how school culture is made and remade over time but how culture influences the type of education offered to students. In this way school histories owe much to sociological and anthropological traditions.

CHAPTER FIVE

Ethnography: The Shadow Study

Introduction

Walking into a classroom for the first time may feel a bit like walking onto an empty stage, but this stage is never empty. In subtle and sometimes not so subtle ways, teacher and student relationships are already defined by the context of schooling, and the habitual and accepted ways of interacting and of working that characterize institutional life and culture. Life in the classroom is bounded by institutional priorities and the structures that sustain and maintain them.

Boundaries produce cultural continuities, patterns of understanding and interaction that function as norms governing practice. Yet, as beginning teachers quickly discover, even within the same school context classrooms differ. How is this possible?

The norms that govern schooling help define school culture and shape teacher and student relationships, but they are not monolithic. They do not form a tightly woven cloth. Each generation of beginning teachers must be inducted into the culture, but induction is never fully successful; the fit is never perfect. There is always some tension—sometimes a great deal of tension—within established norms and ways of interacting and between these norms and the beliefs and values of individual participants within the culture. Tension produces what might be termed, for lack of a better phrase, "wiggle room" within the patterns of schooling. Wiggle room enables each generation of teachers to negotiate and, in some ways, recreate the teaching role. Wiggle room makes alternatives possible. Thus, norms powerfully shape but ultimately do not determine teacher or student practice, for that matter.

As constructed patterns of meaning and action—historical creations—norms require identification and scrutiny. Understanding them enables beginning teachers to see why teaching and schooling are as they are and to begin to consider the ways in which norms both enable and constrain meaning and action. When norms are accepted as right and proper, such understanding enables the negotiation of a desirable teaching role. Similarly, when they are found wanting, such knowledge is crucial to identifying wiggle room, the space within which alternative ways of thinking and acting can be tested in relative security. Without knowledge of wiggle room, and of how students and teachers operate within it to soften and redirect otherwise oppressive institutionalized role expectations, the pressure of norms and the structures that maintain them likely leads to teacher disengagement and passivity. Exploring wiggle room, in contrast, plays to teachers' sense of agency and strengthens the belief that people can and do make a difference.

There are many ways of gaining knowledge of the norms that shape school and classroom life and of locating wiggle room. One way is through a simplified version of ethnographic research. Ethnographers, those who conduct ethnographic research, study culture. Culture is commonly thought of as the customs, practices, and traditions that characterize, distinguish, and give stability to a group. More generally, it is "the knowledge people use to generate and interpret behavior" (Spradley & McCurdy, 1972:8); it is knowledge of shared norms or rules. Typically, ethnographers study "cultural groups" (such as Native Americans) as outsiders. Our focus, in contrast, is the culture of the school and of the classroom studied by one who seeks to become a participant. Being an "insider"—or more accurately, one who seeks to become an insider—presents some difficulty. Sometimes it is difficult to be critical, and sometimes criticism comes too easily, as when seeking confirmation of a viewpoint. Both dangers can be tempered if data is gathered systematically, and if it is attended to carefully and allowed to "speak."

When preservice teachers study the culture of the school and classroom within which they will engage in practice teaching, they begin to see how context shapes and constrains practice and how students and teachers deflect, redirect, and resist pressures to conform. In this way, they are encouraged to consider ways in which they too can adjust the context to better realize their aims. Reflection on context can lead to action. Moreover, by studying culture through interviews and observations, they develop a set of methods which are useful for examining new settings when they formally enter the profession as first-year teachers.

Shadow Study

The Shadow Study is intended to help you begin to understand how students construe classroom and school life, how they have internalized, reshaped, or rejected institutional norms or, put differently, what they do with their wiggle room. The degree to which students have internalized, or failed to internalize, institutional norms and what they do with their wiggle room have a profound influence on what teachers are able to do with their own wiggle room. Without question, students are powerful socializing agents, whose expectations of teachers and classroom behavior constrain and shape teacher thought and action (see Bullough, Knowles & Crow, 1992). As teachers struggle to find a place within the classroom and school, they do so in relationship to their pupils and the roles they have forged. Knowledge, then, of how students make sense of their experience in school is crucially important to successful teacher role negotiation, particularly since the quality of the relationship with students and student performance form the backdrops against which teachers, especially beginning teachers, judge their performance in the classroom.

The tendency among beginning teachers is to generalize from one's own experience as a student to others' experience and to act accordingly. While it is inevitable that when making sense of the behavior of young people you will draw on past experience as a student and perhaps as a parent, this experience needs to be recognized for what it is: partial and limited. The study of child and adolescent psychology and of diverse cultures helps broaden one's perspective, but clearly there is no substitute for spending time and talking with young people, particularly when their backgrounds differ significantly from your own, as they likely will.

Writing

The following are the guidelines we give to our students on how to conduct a Shadow Study.

> The purpose of the Shadow Study is to begin to understand how students experience and make sense of their life in schools. With the help of your cooperating teacher, identify a student and obtain permission to follow him/her for an entire school day. Pick a student to "shadow" whom you find interesting, and who comes from a background different from your own. Make certain he/she understands what you are doing and why. Take notes that will help you recall significant events or comments. Do your best to get to know the student and to understand his or her feelings about school and about teachers. There is much that you might attend to: How does the student spend his/her time? What seems most important to the student during the day? What topics and issues demand attention? What events are found upsetting or irritating? What kind and quality of relationship does he/she have with other students and with teachers? How important are teachers to students? Does the student have any power? Whatever focus you take, conclude your paper by describing what, in your view, school is like for the student—what kind of experience is school?—and what part teachers play in shaping that experience.

The Shadow Studies are discussed in class. It is during this discussion, and drawing on the life histories, that comparisons are made between experiences—beginning teacher and shadowed pupil—and attention given to the diversity of ways of making a life in schools. At this point a problem should be noted:

A good many of our students have difficulty identifying a pupil to shadow. They feel uncomfortable and awkward; they are outsiders. One beginning teacher wrote: "I approached the study with mixed emotions. [One side of me] couldn't wait to get into the world of a high school student. [But] . . . knowing I would be [with] high school kids and seeing an intimate part of their world caused me [to feel] uncomfortable. . . . I felt out of place." The temptation is to shadow a little brother or sister or the child of a friend. Neither is acceptable. Being uncomfortable is to be expected, even hoped for. Nevertheless, it is not always possible to gain the permission of a student who is most challenging and interesting, and sometimes compromises must be made, as we will shortly see.

Three abbreviated and edited Shadow Studies follow. Veronica's study is the first. Veronica did not get to choose her student. Despite this, Veronica's study proved to be a source of rich insights into school life and how a young woman made that life tolerable. Tangi's is the second study. Jamal is an outgoing minority student who showed Tangi a side of life within South High School that was enjoyable and quite different from her own experience in high school. Mick's is the third study. Mick chose a friend's son to "shadow" thinking the day would be comfortably spent. He was wrong.

Veronica's Study

The student I shadowed is Janie C. Janie is a sophomore at South High. I met Janie through her seventh-period English teacher, who offered her seventh-period class extra credit points for participating in the Shadow Study. Two people from the class volunteered. I chose Janie mainly because [my cooperating teacher] indicated that she needed the extra credit to make up for some absences. [My cooperating teacher] characterized Janie as a "good kid" who seems to be enthusiastic about school and life in general; except when she is absent, she generally completes her assignments on time and doesn't cause problems in class. I first contacted Janie by phone and found her to be very personable and outgoing. She seemed to be at ease with me immediately. I explained the nature of my assignment, and we arranged to meet before school on the day of the Shadow Study. After several conversations with Janie and my observations at school the day of the Shadow Study, I decided that I would like the first part of this write-up to focus as much as possible on the student's perspective of school. Consequently, in an effort to achieve accuracy and authenticity, Janie and I have collaborated on this portion of the write-up, and it is written from the point of view of the student.

A Day at South High (Student's Perspective)

Well, I'm here a little early because I have to meet this lady who's going to follow me around at school all day today. She goes to the university or something, and this is some kind of an assignment she has to do, kind of to get an idea of what life is like for a high school student, I guess. I don't really mind doing this with her; it might be kind of fun, and besides, I really need the extra credit in English. I'm supposed to meet her over by the [school mascot]. There she is. "Hi, I'm Janie. You must be Mrs. H. Well, my first class is drama. It's right here in the auditorium. Let's go in."

"Look at that. There's coke spilled all over the floor. . . . I wonder if they're going to turn the house lights on in here or if we're going to have class in the dark. Our regular teacher is pregnant and won't be back for at least at month or two, so we have a sub in this class. Yeah, the stage crew is always in here when we are. You get used to the noise after a while. Besides, everybody in this class just talks most of the time, anyway, especially since we have had this substitute teacher." She's reading something from a paper about a story or something we're supposed to do on Monday. That's the next time we have this class. How come she didn't say anything about this [assignment] before? I don't really understand [it]. I guess she wants us to retell a story. She's reading to us from some children' storybook, but I really can't hear her too well (the stage crew does seem especially loud today); and with the lights off in here I definitely can't see the pictures. Oh well, she said that was an example of the kind of story not to use, so I guess it doesn't matter if I couldn't hear it. I wonder what kind of story I can get. Okay, I get it: we're not supposed to read the story; we're supposed to retell it *in our own words*. I understand that part. But what are these criteria and activity sheets she keeps talking about? I wonder if I could transfer to stage crew? They seem to be having a lot more fun. Why does she keep reading these stories? They are really boring! Okay, we have the rest of the period—that's about 50 minutes—to work on our stories for the next time. The only problem is, I don't have a story to work on. "What, Ms. T. [the teacher]?" "No, we don't have a story yet. I guess I'll go to the library later and try to find one." Oh, everybody seems to be leaving. I didn't hear the bell ring. It's not supposed to ring for about five more minutes. I guess we can leave if we want to, but I better not, since I have this lady following me around today. We'll leave when the bell rings.

The next class is upstairs—third period—Life Skills (school days are divided into odd and even, with periods running 80 minutes each). We're going to meet in the classroom to watch Channel One and then go to the computer room. "Yeah, I [Mrs. H. (Veronica)] already know how to use the computer. I took word processing in the ninth grade." "What? Yeah, this should be pretty easy for me." Channel One is pretty boring today, as usual—more stuff on the presidential election. "Yeah, the class next door always comes in here for Channel One. They don't have a TV in there. There aren't enough seats for everyone, so we usually just stand around while it's on. Sure, it's hard to hear, but we don't really have to listen to it anyway, so it's no big deal." Now it's time for the announcements; oops—as usual, we can't hear them. Well, Mrs. J. says we can just go on down to the computer room then. Oh, I forgot my assignment. Oh good, she says we can finish it today in computer. "Let's go to the computer room—it's this way." The computer teacher isn't there, and Mrs. J. doesn't know anything about WordPerfect. That's okay. I know how to work this. She said we should help each other. What are we supposed to be doing again? Oh, okay. Write something about technology and how it affects our lives. "How do you spell technology? Never mind, I'll use the Spell Checker." Oh, that lady who's with me, Mrs. H., knows WordPerfect. Mrs.

J. asked her if she can help some of the other kids until the computer teacher gets here. Okay, I'm done. "Do you have a copy of the assignment that's due today?" Okay, this is pretty easy. I'll just fill this out and turn it in, and I can talk with Sharon and Tess until the bell rings.

"Okay, let's go. Next class is history—it's just down this hall and around the corner. I have to stop at my locker, but it's right on the way." Oh, here's Mr. P. He always yells "Quiet!" when he comes into the room, then he calls the roll and passes back our homework. He seems to be acting nice today—probably because Mrs. H. is here. Those girls better be careful passing those notes, because if they get caught, he'll probably explode. Oh, I thought we were just going to watch the last part of the movie today, but I guess he's going to talk for a while first. Boy, I hate these notes he puts up on the overhead. His writing is hard to read, and he never leaves it up there long enough to copy it all down. "What? No—I mean I don't know. I wasn't really listening. I was trying to copy down all the notes." Now he's saying something about page 55 in the book: "If you want to look at page 55 in the book." I don't want to look at page 55; I just want to finish copying these notes and then watch the movie. This is actually a pretty good movie we've been watching—*The Last Emperor*. It's about some guy from Japan or China or something. Oh, there's the bell. I guess we'll see the last part of it next time. I have to hand in my extra credit notes before we leave.

"Okay, we only get 30 minutes for lunch. No, I never go to the cafeteria. I usually just run over to the [convenience store] and buy something to eat. Want to come? Okay, let's go." Well, we better be heading back—the bell's going to ring in about three minutes. "Yeah, lunch goes by pretty fast; we don't have too much time to eat or anything."

"This class is a pretty good one. English isn't my favorite subject, but Mrs. B. usually makes it pretty interesting. We have been reading *I Heard the Owl Call My Name*. Have you read it? Yeah, it's pretty good." Looks like we're going to start with free writing today. I'm glad we're going to talk about some ideas we can write on. I can never think of anything to write. Oh, yeah, that's a good idea. I can write about the two characters in

Chapter One and why they have a hard time understanding each other. Okay, time's up. That wasn't so bad. I actually had enough things to write about for the whole ten minutes. We're going to have a test on the first seven chapters on Monday. Now we're working with a partner to make up some questions for the test, only the questions can only start with the words on the board. This is kind of hard. "Mrs. B., what about 'Who is Jim?'" "No, 'who is' isn't on the board." "Well, I guess I can reword it to start with 'who did.'" Let's see, who did Mark first meet when he arrived? "Is this okay, Mrs. B.?" "We're done. Now we can work on this crossword puzzle for the rest of the period. If I can get this all done now, I won't have to do it at home. There—almost done. Oh, there's the bell. "What? Oh, sure. No problem. Anytime. It was fun hanging around with you today. Nice meeting you, too. Bye."

A Day at South (My View)

Janie corroborated that the "stream of consciousness" presentation above was fairly typical of most of her days in school. . . . I have to admit to some disappointment at what seemed to me to be the tedious and lackluster nature of Janie's day. . . .

The experience Janie had in her first-period drama class was appalling to me. Drama is an elective, so presumably most of these kids are in this class because they are interested in the subject. However, the outrageous conditions under which the class was expected to be conducted (stage crew shouting, banging things around, turning the lights on and off) and the substitute teacher's apparent lack of preparation and engagement with the kids seemed to produce an overwhelming sense of apathy among the students. Most of them barely paid attention to her during the entire class period; those who did, like Janie, found a way to use the time somewhat productively but not to fulfill the assignment that was given them. It seems completely ridiculous to me that a teacher would give students 50 minutes of class time to complete an assignment when none of them had any advance notice to bring materials with them to do so. The assignment was to retell a story, but not one of the students had a story with them to work on. Several students asked if they could go to the library to find a story, but they were not allowed to leave. The teacher read three children's books to the class as examples of stories that would not be good candidates for retelling—there was no modeling of what a good retelling looks like. It is not surprising to me that none of the students worked on the assignment during the class period. I feel the time could have and probably should have been used for teacher-guided and structured practice; as it was, 50 minutes of potential instructional time was virtually wasted. One student was reading a book; Janie's group was practicing for an afterschool musical production; most of the students were just talking. The group nearest to me were discussing their favorite types of alcohol and mixers. *No one appeared to be working on the assignment,* although the teacher did eventually walk around the room and ask the students, "Do you have a story to do?" Each group apparently put her off with some vague remarks about working on it later, which she appeared to accept before moving on to the next group.

The next class was a little better. This class, "Life Skills," is a new class designed to teach students personal skills, thinking skills, technology literacy, career exploration, and communication skills. Today was apparently technology literacy day. Although the Channel One time was essentially [a waste], time in the computer room did seem to give some students who were heretofore "computer illiterate" at least a nodding acquaintance with WordPerfect. As mentioned above, however, the computer teacher's absence when the class arrived posed a problem for the regular teacher, who knew nothing about the WordPerfect program. Since I am fairly knowledgeable with WordPerfect, I was immediately drafted to help the students get started. If I had not been there, I assume those students not familiar with the program would simply have waited the 15 or 20 minutes it took for the computer teacher to arrive, or tried to figure it out on their own with help from one of their fellow students. At least these students were engaged in doing something, not just sitting, although most of them finished well before the end of the period and spent the rest of the time talking with one another.

Janie's next class, fifth-period history, was also an eye-opener for me. I guess I really have been out of high school too long, because I was somewhat stunned by the teacher's manner with students. He began the class by shouting at them and continued to treat them in a rude and condescending manner. I was even more surprised when Janie confided that she felt he was "being nice" today because I was there. My immediate thought was, "If this is nice, I'd hate to see him when he's being rude." After roll call, the teacher launched into a lecture on the history of civilization in China. During his lecture, he turned out the lights and posted some handwritten notes on the overhead projector. He moved up and down the aisles in the classroom while he lectured, but the attention of nearly every student seemed to be directed toward copying down the notes on the overhead. This behavior was reinforced by the teacher, who would pause at intermittent points in the lecture and demand, "Haven't you guys finished writing this stuff down yet? I'm ready to move on; you're going to have to learn to move faster." The content information being presented was really quite interesting, but the manner of presentation had me "zoning out." Following the lecture, the class watched a part of the film *The Last Emperor* until the end of the period. Perhaps some background information on the film had been given in a previous class period, although if it was, Janie couldn't remember much of it. None was given the day I was there.

After history, we had our frenetic lunch period. We barely had enough time to run across the street [to] buy a sandwich and drink, wolf it down, and run back to Janie's locker and then to her last class. It was, however, the most active part of our day. It seems a shame that some portion of the time that was wasted in this morning's classes couldn't somehow be added onto the lunch period to enable the students to take ten deep breaths before returning to class.

Janie's last class was the highlight of the day for me. I admit I am biased because English is my area of expertise, but I also sincerely felt that Mrs. B. made a genuine attempt to employ various activities to help students with different learning styles to find a way to relate to the novel they were reading. She took the time to brainstorm with the class to make sure everyone had an idea before requiring them to complete a ten-minute free writing exercise. The students came up with some great ideas dealing with their reading, and I was shocked to realize that this was the first class all day in which I had observed any kind of meaningful class discussion. Most of the kids were writing during the free-write time. The partner activity composing test questions also seemed to engage most of the students, and the teacher moved around the room a lot monitoring the groups, helping them with their questions, and trying very hard to engage reluctant participants. Since this was the last class period of the day, I think it would have been very easy for many of these students to give in to fatigue and eschew the class activities, but it appeared to me that most of the students were involved and interested. . . .

Based on my experiences during this day, I have come to the conclusion that the teacher's role is crucial in shaping the student's experience. It seems to me a "bad" teacher can cause a student to have a bad day at school; it also seems to me that too many bad days in a row could kill any desire the student may have had to succeed in school. If I had to give the four teachers I observed a grade for the day, I would have to rank them as follows: first period—F, third period—C, fifth period—D, seventh period—A. I realize that allowances ought to be made for the fact that first period was taught by a substitute. It is entirely possible, and perhaps even probable, that the regular drama teacher is much more effective and dynamic. It is also possible that the four classes I attended on this day were not a representative sample of the teaching being done in the school; in fact, I sincerely hope that they were not. However, the mere fact that one student had to spend one day in a place supposedly dedicated to learning and growth with relatively little in the way of intellectual stimulation until the last class of the day seems to me to border on the tragic.

If my observations of Janie's day at school can be considered in any way typical, educators have a long way to go to fulfill the public trust and to provide students with the kind of nurturing and enriching environment to which I believe they are entitled.

Tangi's Study

For Jamal, school is, among other things, a large gathering of available and cute women. As we walked through the crowded halls at South High School, Jamal was waving, admiring, talking, and sighing at numerous girls. He explained to me after his first class (English) that we needed to make a run to his car for some Advil for M'Lisa, his old girlfriend—not to be confused with his new girlfriend, Meg. "See," he explained to me as we walked to his car, "I dated M'Lisa for about 10 months and then she made me mad and so I broke up with her, but now we might . . . you know?" "Get back together?," I said. "Yeah." Then I asked him, "Well, what is that?", pointing to the ring hanging from the necklace he was wearing. "Well, this chain my dad gave me and this is Meg's ring, but don't tell M'Lisa that because she thinks it's my sister's ring." "Oh," I said. He smiles, proud of his carefully executed plan.

Jamal took me on a tour of the school during second class; it was a slow day. During the tour, he would stop at the door of a classroom, "Wait, she's cute" and make a gesture with his head: "Come here." A girl would appear at the door, and as he walked away he would say, "You've been mean to me this year." She would say, "No, I haven't," and he would say, "Yes, you don't even talk to me anymore." She would follow until the false accusations were revoked. Another line he used was, "I've got a secret for you." Again, he successfully captured the girl's attention.

[Despite all of this sex play], it's not that school isn't important to Jamal; [it is]. At one time he expressed concern because he forgot to hand in chapters 7 and 8 for his business math class. But he doesn't know where his book is. In fact, he doesn't know where any of his books are because he has forgotten his locker number and his books and various assignments are scattered between several different girl's lockers—and he can't remember who has what.

He also expressed concern about failing his biology class, but talked as though it was an inevitable fact. He can't find his book and just missed another class. He saw his biology teacher in the hall and said, "I need to talk to you. Are you in your classroom after school 'cause I came to see you and you weren't there." "Jamal, I'm always in my classroom after school. Where are you?"

He also told me about his anxiety to take the ACT test. He said, "I need to get at least a 26 so I can go to the University and play football." But he said that he doesn't want a football scholarship because he doesn't want football as a career. He doesn't know what he wants to do, exactly, which is why he says that he doesn't want to leave high school.

"All I know," he said, "is I want to make lots of money." Right now he works at a drive-in theater sometimes until three o'clock in the morning. On Saturdays he sometimes works 14 hours. He needs the money to make his car payments and repairs. . . . And (I'm assuming) he needs the extra cash to entertain his many female friends. He and his buddies [have] already picked out the tuxedo they're wearing to the Prom— black with pink satin collar and pink cummerbund.

Jamal is an enjoyable kid; he is witty, smart, and considerate. The teachers I spoke to about him said he's a good student *"when* he comes to class." He made everyone laugh in first period with his quick wit as he defended himself and his friends as they were being tried as witches and warlocks. However, his love of socializing is what interferes with him getting to class. I asked him what he does when he sluffs: "Hang out, go to breakfast, usually." He cuts class after lunch because, he said, "I just get caught up and then it's just too late to go [to class]."

Jamal has great relationships with adults. We spoke to many of his teachers and adult friends while walking around the school. He says the principal is quiet, but he really likes his counselor, whom he introduced to me. About the counselor, he said: "He's cool and he's going to help me get my time down for football." He says he likes all of his teachers; he couldn't pick a favorite. It was obvious to me that for teachers, Jamal is a hard student to get upset with [in part] because he is so honest. Most of his teachers joked with him about not coming to class, but in the end they praised him as a "good kid" and a "pretty good student."

As you can see from my study, Jamal is definitely the shaper of his own world in and out of the classroom. He doesn't hide the fact that he sluffs to his teachers (though he might say, "Mr. S., it wasn't my fault"), and he is perfectly honest about missing his books and assignments. All during the day he was very up-front with me about his life inside and outside of school. He said that he was in one fight at the beginning of the year because someone told him this guy was going to "flatten him" at a party. Jamal said, "I just went up to discuss it with him and he said a few things I didn't appreciate and I punched him." He hasn't had any problems since then. I respected his honesty with me.

Jamal [has lots of confidence], especially with the ladies and adults in the school. He is friendly to everyone; he doesn't seem to limit his friendships to one group of students. He was especially considerate about introducing me to everyone, including his buddies. When he said to me, "I'm going to take you to breakfast," a girl behind him said, "She's here to watch you in school." He said, "Hey, she's following *me* around" (pointing to his chest), "and I'll show her what I do."

As it turns out, he just took me on a visit of the neighborhood in his car—where his grandma lives, where he went to junior high school, to the gas station—and finally he dropped off his mom's Visa bill. If Jamal feels like going to class, he does. And if he doesn't, he can tour the classrooms to visit the ladies, maybe go to breakfast with [his buddies], Kent and Jason; and if he gets caught [sluffing], most likely he can smooth-talk his way out of a sticky situation. That's the way he likes it.

Mick's Study

This may be the most unique Shadow Study you receive. It turned out to be a jolting experience. I knew from the start who I was going to shadow. . . . Ed's the son of a family I have known well for several years. That is the central reason I asked him, because I believed it would be a comfortable situation for both of us.

Since I'd been working in Hood Junior High School as a volleyball coach, and Ed is on the team, I see him on a daily basis. I have constant interaction with him and his father. . . . So we set up the time last week for the two of us to get together before school and spend the day doing this assignment.

I should have realized that something had happened in Ed's life. He lives [in a lower socioeconomic area of the city] but attends Hood, [which is in a better-off neighborhood], because of poor performance and citizenship in his old school. He is an excellent athlete, and his grades have improved dramatically since [transferring]. I am still unaware of his problems in his "old community," but as for the new situation, my eyes were opened. . . .

On Thursday, when we had originally agreed to meet, I was ditched by Ed. He neither showed up nor called the school. When I saw him that afternoon at volleyball practice, I asked him where he was. He told me he had forgotten, and was just running late that morning. I set up a time [to meet] the next day. I got a list of . . . his classes. . . . [The next morning] I went to the principal's office to double check the room numbers Ed had given me. To my surprise, [the principal] said he was in with the vice principal and I "could do the shadow study on him right out the door." I was informed that he and a friend had been caught smoking marijuana at the bus stop that morning, and since he was already on a waiver to attend school, he was immediately expelled. . . . I felt like *my* world was out of skew. Here was a boy that I have known for several years. A young man I saw everyday as an athlete . . . being kicked out of school for using drugs. Dozens of thoughts and emotions struck me simultaneously. What would his parents say? What would I say to Ed? How was I going to explain to the team that their captain was caught doing this?

The principal told me I could join the meeting with the boy and vice principal. I declined. I felt I had no business going in there. [I waited outside. The door opened.] Ed looked horrible. He saw me, then our eyes met. His glance went directly to the floor. He stumbled over a couple of chairs as he made his way to the door of the office, and I caught his attention and simply asked him if he was alright. He only shrugged his shoulders and solemnly [walked] to his locker to collect his things.

I went into the vice principal's office and asked to speak to her. She knew who I was and was in no way reluctant to speak with me concerning the matter. She handed me the report that had been filled out [on Ed]. [She told me that] Ed was so stoned that he could not even remember his address or phone number. He had scratched it out two or three times, and eventually had to look it up in the phone book. She said he had freely admitted his guilt and would never be accepted back into that school again.

I was devastated. Why didn't I know more about what was going on in his life? How could I have not noticed [that something wasn't right]? Then I began to think back over many practices when Ed didn't seem like himself, or times when he moved as if in slow motion. Were these other occasions when he was using? I also remembered him on these occasions using foul language and doing other things that seemed out of character. . . . I wept that night. If I . . . only have students for a few months, how can I make a difference in their lives? . . . I felt like a failure. . . . How does a student who is . . . popular, successful, and [apparently] happy deceive us so that we [teachers] can't help. . . . I thought I knew this young man. I felt as though I had some power. Now . . . I believe he had all the power. . . .

Commentary

The form of Veronica's study immediately stands out. She does not think of Janie as an "object" to be studied, but as a co-participant within a culture whose insights were valuable and deserving of respect. They share the context and, in varying ways and degrees, the struggle to make sense of it meaningfully. Although Veronica is a beginning teacher and Janie one of her future students, Veronica does not yet think of herself as a teacher. They are both students, and this proves to be an important bond.

Veronica seeks to preserve Janie's voice within a setting that appears little interested in what Janie has to say. To

Veronica the day was almost unbearably tedious, but to Janie it is simply the way school is. She does not expect anything to be different: School is supposed to be deadly, and teachers boring and disinterested in students. Within this context Janie has learned how to take advantage of the opportunities that come along during and between classes to engage her friends, which, despite it all, makes school life relatively enjoyable. Janie expands what turns out to be a considerable degree of wiggle room given to her by her teachers. Unfortunately, the origin of this wiggle room, at least as Veronica sees it, is that Janie's teachers—except her English teacher—do not care about pupil learning. Janie really doesn't complain, however. For Janie, school seems to mean enduring long periods of relative boredom in order to interact with friends whenever possible.

Veronica was appalled by the condescending manner of Janie's history teacher and wondered, openly, why so little learning took place during the day. This is not the way it is supposed to be, and she begins to think critically about the teacher's role and responsibilities: "It seems to me a 'bad' teacher can cause a student to have a bad day at school; it also seems to me that too many bad days in a row could kill any desire the student may have had to succeed in school." Things were better, Veronica thinks, when she was in high school. Janie's teachers, Veronica concludes, betrayed a public trust: "Educators have a long way to go to fulfill the public trust and to provide students with the kind of nurturing and enriching environment to which I believe they are entitled."

The picture Veronica presents of Janie is of a young person who drifts through school, doing only what she needs to do to get by. There is no passion for learning, little engagement, but lots of brief and enjoyable encounters with friends. Like most of her teachers, Janie is little interested in learning. She is interested in avoiding trouble, however; she knows where the boundaries are to her passive student role. In most ways she is a good student, one who does what she is told and causes no trouble; she deserves better from her teachers. The teachers, Veronica thinks, have failed Janie.

Jamal skillfully manipulates the school context; likely he would be labeled a "resister" (Willis, 1977). He understands the institution and its norms and uses this understanding to resist unpleasant aspects of institutional life and make his life as enjoyable as possible. He maximizes his interaction with friends, and minimizes institutional control through his disarming honesty and winning smile. Teachers enjoy Jamal's personality and give him a large degree of slack; school rules soften in the light of Jamal's grin. But there is a dark side to this playful relationship: The norms of schooling are not challenged, and most importantly, Jamal is not encouraged to study. Unlike Janie, Jamal makes no pretenses. For him the value of school is strictly social, and yet he worries about his future. Although Jamal fails to see a connection between attending class and test performance, the upcoming test for admission to the university looms large and there is no manipulating the norms that govern college admission. Apparently, no one has taught him that there is a connection. He wants to play football but claims to not "want a football scholarship because he doesn't want to make football as a career." One gets the feeling that Jamal is a confused boy who wants to put off making some very important but inevitable decisions as long as he can. In the meantime, he plays, and plays hard, and teachers seem unconcerned.

Unintentionally, Ed breaks Mick's heart. Mick thought he had a close and open relationship with Ed, the volleyball captain. What he discovered was that Ed had a private life that excluded adults, a closet life lived outside the norms of school. Shocked, Mick wonders what he could have done to help Ed and, perhaps feeling a little guilty, recounts missed signs that something was wrong. In despair, Mick wonders what a teacher can do to help young people when they spend so little time together, an hour or so a day for a few months. Yet, he feels he failed.

To Mick, Ed was a successful "jock," a good and popular student. While true, this conclusion blinded him to times when Ed behaved in uncharacteristic ways, like during practice when he swore and moved slowly. Mick lost sight of the person under the label. But it was too late. Ed was expelled from school for going outside what was deemed acceptable behavior even for a jock.

Each study illustrates aspects of how young people find a niche in school and build a life. They also underscore how important relationships with friends and teachers are to the quality of that life, and how important wiggle room is to those relationships, but also how school norms shape interaction. For a good many young people, like Janie and Jamal, the value of schooling is intimately tied to the quality of their social lives. Veronica, Tangi, and Mick thought it should be otherwise. Perhaps it was different when they were in school, but it is more likely that they have simply forgotten. We do not know. This said, Jamal and probably Janie see school in some ways connected to their future and do what is necessary, but in their own way generally stay within the institutionally acceptable bounds of the student role even though Jamal pushes those boundaries outward. Recall, Jamal is a good student *"when* he comes to class."

Teachers are centrally responsible for providing an engaging academic climate, but too few do. Some schools are characterized by a culture and norms that allow little education to take place. Publicly, of course, this would be denied, but privately norms operate that actually discourage learning and encourage minimal performance from both teachers and students. Facing such a culture, where learning is of little value, students find other ways to be occupied as they put in their time—and they must put in their time! Janie's English teacher resists these pressures, and students learn as a result. But not all teachers share this teacher's vision, and the students suffer. Some teachers—and these views would emerge in interviews with them—have given up on their pupils, believing they either cannot or will not learn.

From Janie's portion of Veronica's study, one gets a glimpse of how the day is organized for some students. Between classes and at lunch life roars by, and bells bind every activity. By "hanging out" and going "to breakfast," Jamal openly takes time from the school day for his social life, while Janie, perhaps like most young people, secretly steals it and attempts to cover the theft: In public places they live private lives. This is what wiggle room is for.

A Note to Teacher Educators and Students

Unlike most of the other methodologies presented in *Becoming a Student of Teaching,* the value of the Shadow Study and of interviewing teachers is not directly supported by research, although their value is attested to in interviews and questionnaires given to our students as they exit the program. They may best be thought of as representing elements of ethnographic research which aim to uncover the meaning of a context to participants.

The theoretical support of the Shadow Study, however, is considerable. As Riseborough notes, students are "critical reality definers" (1985:262) for teachers, and as we have said, beginning teachers, in particular, look to students for confirmation of their self definitions. It is crucially important that beginning teachers know something about how pupils make the context they share with teachers meaningful because together they must make their way within the institution. Moreover, such knowledge is a means for ameliorating the "narrow, pessimistic perspective on pupils" that beginning teachers frequently develop (Diamond, 1991:35). Rather than being seen as enemies, students come to be seen as persons who share a context with teachers and who, like teachers, are trying to forge a meaningful life within a set of sometimes rather tight-fitting institutional norms.

This said, as Veronica reminds us, teachers enjoy a superordinate position and have a surprising amount of power by which norms within and without the classroom can be reconstituted. Teachers have a moral obligation to exercise this power with, and on behalf of, their pupils' learning and for the purpose of improving their own work environment.

Preparing to Conduct the Study

Prior to conducting the Shadow Study, our students are given selected readings that address student cultures (Eckert, 1989) and address particular ways in which the institution shapes and responds to those cultures. Because of its power within schools to shape interaction and understanding, special attention is given to labeling and tracking (Bullough, 1988; Oakes, 1985). It has been our experience that many of our students are too comfortable with schooling labels and the norms associated with them, and use them too easily as means for accounting for how pupils and teachers make sense of school life. It is important to note that young people have different relationships with school and with teachers and respond to norms and make and use their wiggle room differently. Young people may be "cowboys" or "burnouts," for example, which signify an unfriendly institutional relationship (see Bullough, Knowles & Crow, 1992, chapter nine). Other students have labels (like "gifted") placed on them by the context of schooling, which signal institutional acceptance and the promise of a high degree of conformity to established norms. We stress the importance of attempting to look beyond and under labels—the institutional and cultural shorthand that so seductively defines reality by prejudging it—and that beginning teachers need to become wary of them as a means for relating to young people and for understanding their behavior.

Sharing the Studies

The three Shadow Studies presented are based upon spending only one day shadowing a student. Lengthening the time spent will produce richer data, but not necessarily more useful interpretations. Aside from getting to know students better, the value of the Shadow Studies is centrally tied to the discussions about them and, later, the classroom ethnography. We have organized these discussions around a cluster of questions which we will share, along with a few reactions to them, noting that they are more suggestive than definitive. You may well find other questions more helpful than these.

First, what was the day like for the student? How much was your shadowed student's experience of schooling like your own as a student? What was different? Where differences are noted, they are explored. For example, Veronica notes that she did not recall school being so boring. Others shared her recollection, while many disagreed. Teachers were identified as the critical variable, underscoring their power and educational responsibility. But differences in school contexts, and especially in tracks, were also mentioned as important. Different tracks reflect different norms. Social class and culture often surface as well as reasons for differences in experience.

Second, what was most important to the student? What were the sources of his/her greatest pleasure and disappointment during the day? How was the student treated by teachers and other students? Answers to these questions also present occasions to compare and contrast experiences. A common perception is that academics are less important to the shadowed students than they were to the beginning teachers. This is not surprising, since most of the beginning teachers were very able students and a large percentage of those shadowed are from lower tracks, as one would hope, given the assignment. Inevitably, a discussion follows of how important social interaction is to young people, how hard teachers and the institution of schooling work to constrain rather than build on the gregariousness of youth, and how school cuts off and opens up opportunities to different types of young people based upon criteria that seldom have anything to do with ability: school norms favor some young people over others. Exploring why this is so and how students respond is crucially important.

Third, who holds power within the school? How powerful are students to shape their educational experience? What are the sources of their power? How powerful are teachers? What are the sources of their power? How do students come to terms with teacher power? These questions direct the students to consider teacher-student relationships and the teacher's role and responsibilities. In his ability to play one set of school norms off against another and to explore his wiggle room, Jamal illustrates some of the covert and overt aspects of student power. In principle, young people always have the power to refuse, to resist institutional demands, but in practice refusal to conform either leads to withdrawal from the institution, and perhaps expulsion as in Ed's case, or finds expression in institutionally nonthreatening ways: students sluff class, do only portions of their work, and talk when they are supposed to be working. Power may also come from collaborating with teachers: Jamal cuts a deal, and teachers "wink" at his "misbehavior." Sharing norms with teachers and invested in serving institutional interests, student body officers are allies who are granted privileges. In all cases, student power must be understood in relationship to teacher power and to the costs and benefits of compliance or resistance.

It is the abuse of teacher power by failing to exercise it for the sake of student learning that prompts Veronica to conclude that lunch period ought to be extended. But Veronica hints at a more radical relationship of teacher and student power when seeking to preserve Janie's voice. She seems to want teachers to share power, to hold it *with* rather than *over* students. Perhaps this is a reflection of still thinking of herself as a student primarily and not yet as a teacher, but we think not. If young people are to become active participants in their own education, then there is no alternative but for teachers to share power, and for this to happen different institutional norms may need to be created. As an aside, the same argument is now being made for teacher-administrator relationships: power ought to be shared.

Inevitably, discussion leads to the exploration of the role and responsibilities of teachers, and in relationship to the institutional, social, and political context of teaching. A beginning teacher asked, after Mick shared his study, whether it was reasonable for him to expect that he, or any teacher, should have known what was going on in Ed's life that led to drug usage? This type of question is crucially important to beginning teachers who are thinking seriously about who they are as teachers and the kind of relationship they want to have with pupils, and are beginning to discover the limits of teacher power.

As mentioned, you may find other questions more useful than these for guiding discussion. And you may wish to include some of these or other questions as part of the written assignment. This decision is related to what work comes before and after the Shadow Study, how much time is available, and whether greater emphasis is placed on written interpretation and evaluation than on description. We have emphasized description. We see the Shadow Study as a continuing foray into a set of issues to which we will often return throughout the program.

CHAPTER SIX

Ethnography: Classroom Study

Introduction

The introduction to chapter five also serves as an orientation to this chapter. We need add only a few words. Through spending time in your cooperating teacher's classes, you will know that classes differ in subtle and not so subtle ways. Caution is in order, however: It is easy, given these differences, to neglect the patterns of interaction that define normative behavior. It is these patterns that concern us in this chapter.

Having spent many years in school as students, school and classroom norms may be invisible to beginning teachers or, when recognized, are assumed to be natural rather than constructed. When norms are assumed to be natural, simply part of life within classrooms, wiggle room goes unnoticed and the ways in which norms constrain and shape interaction and understanding are ignored. Socialization is assumed to be passive, a matter of fitting in rather than of negotiating a place within the context. The implications of such views of socialization are far-reaching; one catches a glimpse of the shadow of training. When fitting in is the driving ambition of beginning teachers and when teacher educators think of their job as assuring a quick and tight fit, the wider professional community is impoverished, albeit slightly. The accumulative effect, however, can be devastating. Communities and the causes they champion remain vital only when socialization is, and is understood as, a dynamic process of reform and renewal, where seeking membership involves testing boundaries and exploring and challenging accepted ways of thinking and acting. In this way the novice becomes part of the professional conversation and embraces the dual responsibilities of strengthening practices that are deemed life-enhancing while scrutinizing and perhaps helping alter those found wanting.

Teacher Interview

Both interviews and observations are essential tools for studying culture. Prior to conducting the classroom study, we require our students to formally interview their cooperating teacher. Just as the Shadow Study focused on how pupils construe classroom and school life and what they have done with their wiggle room, it is fundamentally important to carefully consider how teachers make sense of their experience as teachers. Knowledge of this kind is central to understanding how classroom norms are constructed and operate. Aside from providing essential knowledge about the teaching context and how it is made sensible, the interview has the added benefit of strengthening the beginning teacher/cooperating teacher relationship.

Arranged in advance, the interview begins with questions that seek background information about the teacher, which often proves to be knowledge essential for comprehending how meaning is made. How long has he/she taught? Where did he/she study? What factors influenced his/her decision to become a teacher? The aim is to begin to understand the teacher's actions in relationship to life history and values. Questions then follow that seek to reveal the teacher's understanding of his/her role, ideal and real. Questions like these are asked: What do you find most and least satisfying about teaching and why? How do you spend the majority of your time? Would you spend your time differently if you could? Why or why not? Describe your relationship with students, other teachers, administrators, and parents. What are the major institutional and personal factors that shape these relationships? How much influence do you have with these groups and how much power do they have to shape your life in school? The answers to these questions often prove very revealing. How teachers understand their responsibilities and what they think about students, for example, profoundly influence what they do in the classroom. Decisions about what and what not to teach and how to approach a lesson are grounded in just such understandings.

The interviews are written up and then shared in class. Commonalities inevitably emerge as a result of the similarity of teachers' work across settings where, for instance, teacher isolation remains a factor of life (see Bullough, 1987; Gitlin, 1987). But important differences are also identified that reveal differences in teachers' personalities and the work contexts that enable satisfying and interesting teaching roles to be negotiated. Sources of teacher power are also revealed, indicating in various ways that teachers take advantage of wiggle room. The discussion is informed by readings on the nature of teachers' work in schools, including studies of sources of teacher job satisfaction and dissatisfaction. The crucial point is that you start exploring how your cooperating makes teaching sensible, perhaps enjoyable. The classroom ethnography follows the teacher interview and builds on it.

Writing: The Classroom Study

The following is the classroom ethnography assignment we present to our students.

> Ethnography, simply stated, is the "work of describing a particular culture" (Spradley, 1980:3). The challenge is to grasp how those within the culture understand it, how they make sense of their experience. Identify a class that you will be student teaching and that you find interesting or challenging. Your task is to gather data—through observations, informal and formal interviews, and whatever other ingenious means you can come up with— that will enable you to describe how the classroom environment is understood and recreated by the teacher and students. What are the *formal* and *informal rules*, the *norms*, that give order to the classroom? In what ways are they enabling and limiting of meaning? What roles do the students and the teacher play and what is the relationship

of these roles to one another? How do the students and the teacher experience the classroom? What are the key words, metaphors, ideas, and concepts that they use to give meaning to the classroom and to structure their experience? Try to get *underneath* surface appearances by asking not only What do I see these people doing? but, *What do these people see themselves as doing*?

Begin your paper by describing the context and the players: the school, the classroom, the teacher, the students, the subject area and level. What kind of school is it? What kind of kids?

As you observe, look for *patterns* of behavior and of language. Look for events that disrupt the patterns, which often reveal otherwise hidden norms (for example, what happens when a student acts contrary to classroom routine?). Listen for comments—pay attention to the language used—that reveal the meaning of events. Again, the aim is to get on the *inside* of the culture of the classroom, to become knowledgeable about it, so that you may eventually become an effective agent within it.

The assignment is given and questions quickly follow. Inevitably a student will ask, "How much time should we spend observing?" A second question follows on the heels of the first: "Is it acceptable to spend one entire day in a classroom, instead of observing one or two classes over an extended period of time?" To the first question we respond with a question: "Having already spent quite a bit of time in the classroom observing, how much time do you think it will take to complete the assignment?" This question provides an occasion for further exploring the task. It is quickly realized that what is being required is extremely complicated, and a good deal of time will be needed if useful insights are to be produced. Generally speaking, our students, at least those who produce interesting studies, spend several consecutive days with a single class— sometimes two—observing and talking with the teacher and students. To assist them we typically have cancelled two or three of our classes with the understanding that the time will be spent in the schools. We explore the second question in light of the challenge before them. "Is it possible," we ask, "to get depth of understanding in one or two days of observation, even when several class periods are observed?" They realize it is not possible.

After the ethnographies are written, conclusions are shared in class and comparisons made. At this time it is not unusual to have a few students complain that the writing task was too vague, that we should have told them specifically what to look for. As an aside, some teacher educators intentionally keep the task vague (see Teitelbaum & Britzman, 1991). Other students counter that if we stated specifically what to look for, then what would be seen would be what we wanted them to see, and this also has drawbacks. Generally speaking, our experience has been that it is best to resist the temptation to be prescriptive. The feeling of being adrift for a time is a common one among ethnographers, and a feeling productive of many interesting and lively insights that might otherwise not emerge if one enters a cultural context expecting to identify examples illustrative of conclusions reached by others from studies of different contexts. Concerning the latter point, it is worth noting that some of our students have produced studies that challenge research conclusions—public theory—presented to them in one or another class reading. We celebrate such moments, seeing them as occasions to confirm a central value underlying the propositions presented in chapter one: Teachers are producers of legitimate knowledge.

A final point: A good many of our students need reminding that their first task is *descriptive*, while the second is *interpretative*. In their writing they need to not only describe the context and what is going on within it but also attempt to understand the meaning of events to students and teachers. Those who spend comparatively little time in the classroom looking, listening, and asking or jump from class to class find it very difficult to move beyond description, as we shall shortly see.

Three edited and abbreviated ethnographies follow. The first is representative of studies that present generally interesting descriptions that are of importance to the writer but fail to move beyond description in part because too little time was spent observing. The second (written by Mark Pendleton, whose name is used at his request) and third studies present efforts to understand the meaning of events, one through production of a single, unifying concept (the "social contract") and the other through a flood of insights of lesser generality that center on the students' power to shape classroom culture.

Lots Going On: Nikki's Study

Grant High School is an old school located [in a working-class neighborhood]. Most high schools in the city have the same curriculum, and similar extracurricular events and activities. However, national standardized test scores are generally lower for west side schools, [like Grant], than they are for schools on the more affluent east side. . . . To add to the seemingly lower [quality of] education available from Grant, a teacher informed me that an option was given to students which allowed them to choose to attend one of the four other schools. . . . Therefore, the students left at Grant are the bottom of the barrel and are not too involved in school.

Despite these circumstances, Grant High School's scores on national tests have risen dramatically in the past year. A large part of this is due to the school's participation in a [vocational education] program called Passport, which is an effort to restructure the educational system [by linking the schools with local business]. The principal is very enthusiastic . . . and supports many of the teachers' ideas which promise to improve . . . education.

The school is set up on a block system which means the students have eight classes. They go to four extremely long periods each day. They go to the even periods one day, and the odd periods the next. Although this gives the students an extra day to do their homework, they also have more time to forget what they have learned before they attend that class again.

The mathematics classrooms are located in a building behind the main school. This building does not seem to be territorially divided by the students, since no particular group of students hangs out in the halls or around the building. Therefore, all students may feel comfortable to use this building. . . .

The math department has its own faculty room in this building. This room unites the math teachers, as they are able to retire here during lunch and discuss students, lesson plans, or any problems they may have. However, each teacher has a unique teaching style. . . .

As you enter [my cooperating teacher's room], the students' desks are arranged in neat rows to your right. The students have assigned seats according to the alphabetical order of their last name. The teacher's desk is directly in front of you, facing the students' desks. Windows line the wall beyond the teacher's desk. Lists of the students' grades hang on the wall opposite the windows. There are few decorations in this classroom.

[My cooperating teacher] has been teaching for a long time and is looking forward to retirement in a few years. His teaching style is the traditional arrangement of lecturing and then letting the students work on homework in class. His years of experience allow him to know how to handle his students.

He knows what to realistically expect from the students. When discussing grades, he said that you cannot expect all the students to be an expert on the subject when they leave the class. The students who come most of the time and learn something deserve to pass; those students who learn more should get the better grades. . . . Each day a student accrues points for coming to class on time, bringing [his or her] book, taking a daily quiz, and turning in [his or her] homework. The daily points are then averaged and the grades are posted on the wall so the students can see where they stand.

The class period begins by going over the homework. Students are encouraged to ask the teacher to work problems from the homework which they have questions about. He calls on students to participate in working the problems. After the students cease to ask questions about the homework, he has them take a short quiz. Then new information is covered by doing the even-number problems from each section of the homework. And the students are allowed to work on their homework for the rest of the class period.

The students are shown how to do the homework before the test is given, so that they can work on their homework after they finish the test.

The relaxed atmosphere in the classroom comes from the informal rules which exist. Food and drinks are allowed in the classroom. Students are allowed to get up and sharpen pencils or throw garbage away at any time. The T.A. passes out homework while the teacher begins answering questions about homework. The students pass a stapler around the room to staple their homework pages together. And the students are allowed to talk while doing homework, and during quizzes and tests. The teacher emphasizes, however, that simply copying answers does not promote learning and is therefore considered to be cheating.

I observed an algebra 1–2 class twice. There were a few students from different student groups. There was a cowboy, a greaser, and a few minority students. About half of the class seemed to be quiet students who were doing what they had to do to get a good grade. And there were a few students who seemed not to care about what was going on.

One day was a big test day. It was amazing to me that there wasn't a lot of cheating going on because the teacher actually left the room during part of the test. A few students chatted about events, but in about five minutes most were busy working. One boy offered to pay another boy to do the test for him. The other boy replied, "I'll do it, but I can't guarantee the answers will be correct." That was the end of that discussion. Another boy, who had not been paying attention in class, obviously did not know how to do much of the test and was looking around to see if he could see someone else's answers. After seeing that the students around him were guarding their answers, he began doing what he could on his own.

During the test the teacher posted a new sheet of grades on the wall. Some students came up during the test to see how their grade was doing. Others waited until after the test. I thought it was interesting that some students, who had a lot of the answers during lecture time, did not come up to see their grades. They just began working on their homework after they completed the test. . . .

The next time I visited, the class seemed extremely subdued. It may have been the stormy weather, or the end of a term and beginning of a new term, which caused them to be so sleepy. But whatever it was, there was little interaction between the students. In fact, the teacher taught almost the whole 85 minutes because he felt the kids would get more out of the time that way. He said the kids were so sleepy that many of them would have just put the books away after he stopped talking.

I also observed a geometry class three times. The students in this class were generally more aware of the rules of good student behavior. They knew when it was appropriate to behave in different ways. It was definitely the harder class to observe. When it was test time, they settled right down to take the test. When it was homework time they either did homework or quietly talked among themselves.

There seemed to be a couple of groups of students who liked to talk in this class. The main group . . . surrounded a cheerleader. After the test this group did act up a little and began trying to throw a paper ball into the garbage can until the teacher put a stop to it.

Through talking to a few students, other people, and through my own retrospection [*sic*], I have come to sense that the major feeling of the students is that school is important. At least the diploma is important to get a better-paying job, but the students fail to see how math relates to their lives and their futures.

I feel I can fit into the teacher's classes. I hope I can continue the comfortable atmosphere of learning . . . without losing control. . . .

Making a Contract: Mark's Ethnography

Mrs. G.'s eighth-grade English class is located in a side hallway of . . . Orgill Junior High School. The walls of the classroom are painted white and there are windows on two sides; but they only provide views of other parts of the building. The building itself is old—they say around one-hundred years. The hallways look old and tired. . . .

Orgill Junior High School lies situated on the top of the . . . Valley and directly below the widening mouth of [Sandstone] Canyon. The abruptness of the mountains behind the school is startling. The . . . neighborhoods that feed Orgill are well-off, though there must be some exceptions. Mrs. G.'s English class is a calm, homogeneous collection of students. Mrs. G. is a calm woman of around forty who loves what she does. I think the students catch on to that.

The first time I talked to Mrs. G. she asked me if the English department at the University teaches classes on how to teach writing. I told her I had not taken one yet. When we arrived at her classroom, she showed me a few books written by teachers who had generated good reading and writing programs in their classrooms. *In the middle* (Nancie Atwell's book) is the only title I remember. She asked me again what I knew about the writing process, and I just answered around her question. I could tell that she was excited about writing—and excited about getting the students to write. I think Mrs. G. looks at teaching as a craft, or as a nurturing exercise. She involves the students in exercises that nurture the skills she wants to see. She uses interesting assignments—I was involved in them; I enjoyed doing them with the class and learning something in the process.

Mrs. G. begins every class with a ten-minutes reading time. The students bring their own books to class. She told me that if she did this at a different school, she would have to supply the books because the kids would not have any books at home to bring. Even at Orgill it took a while for the students to bring their own books. When I was there everyone had a book and everyone read quietly for ten minutes. They talk about their books. She introduces new books. They seem almost as excited about it as she is.

One of the days I sat in her class we came together in groups of four and read each other's books. In order to participate I picked *Lost Horizon* off her shelf and passed it on to the next person in our group. We had about five minutes to read from each of the four books. Two of the books were high school books about high school situations. Mine was a classic and the other one, brought by a boy, was a gruesome modern thriller. I did not read much of the modern thriller, and the other two were almost interesting. If I were Mrs. G. I would have a hard time being non-judgmental about the books being brought to class. Yet she accepts almost all the books her students bring. She just wants them to bring books.

For me the time passes quickly in Mrs. G.'s class. I smile often at the things she has the students do, and I smile at the things the students actually do. The students amaze me. They have a lot of energy; but I cannot remember seeing or hearing any one of them really speak out and react against something Mrs. G. was doing. This could be the way eighth-graders are, but I really did not see any disruptive behavior. They read and wrote and listened when they were supposed to. . . .

I think Mrs. G. sees herself as someone who is slowly and softly immersing her students in reading and writing. I also think she is aware of her success. She knows when the students are really enjoying what she is doing with them. I think the students see themselves as going along with what Mrs. G. wants. For them, enjoyment comes and goes. Talking and interacting with one another is what they naturally do. They do that in between and during exercises. Some other classes I have seen have a very thin border between the hallway and the classroom. Others have too much of a border, and the silence is tense. Mrs. G.'s class is neither tense nor wild. Of course the students try to get out of assignments; they lie and cheat—if that is what they normally do. But this is harder to do in her classroom because most of the assignments come in the form of reading logs, journals and book reports. A lot of people think of English as a lot of busy work. I did not see much busywork—work for the sake of being occupied—in Mrs. G.'s classroom. What I did see is the kind of quiet learning that comes from a gentle exposure to language and literature.

There are other things in Mrs. G.'s classroom that make it more [typical]. Clothing, physical appearance, names and name calling—society speaks everywhere. Orgill is a Channel One school, so they watch it every day. Mrs. G. does not like it, but she does not oppose it. There must be a million minute things that add life to Mrs. G.'s classes. I feel like I need to name all of them, while I only know a few of them. I do not feel baptized into the culture. [I was given] a name, and I think that is the first step to conversion. . . . In Mrs. G.'s class I was introduced as Mr. Pendleton—an observer from the University. My relationship [with the students] was instantly formalized. I realized that the "Mr." tag is necessary, but I was disappointed. [I wanted something less formal].

As I watched Mrs. G.'s class, and a few others, I realized that there was a social contract being carried out by two consenting sides. I feel that the first thing necessary to making a contract is the identification of the two sides: "I am this; you are that." After the two sides are identified and made distinct, then agreements can be made. Both sides make promises. Both sides forfeit certain rights so that both sides can gain other, more important, rights. Both sides acquire roles that are mutually beneficial. The substance of the acquired roles is a combination of the initial identifications and of the subsequent release and gain of rights or privileges. The day-by-day implementation of the social contract provides a basis for the continual process of [coming to know] one another. I have tried to get to the bottom of this "classroom ethnography" stuff, and this is what I have come up with. . . .

I think what Penelope Eckert said in *Jocks and Burnouts* and what [Bullough] said in *The Forgotten Dream* applies directly to the social contract, although in a general sense. All kinds of teachers and all the kinds of students, in all the behavior they exhibit, always and inevitably participate in the social contract of American public education. The questions in this situation are: What is at stake? What is being lost or gained? What is really going on—what are we agreeing to? . . . There does not seem to be any escape from the sides and the roles that the contract demands or encourages. Once someone enters the domain . . . they will fall into a slot—there is no other possibility. The only way to nullify the contract is to enter into another one. . . . Ironically, . . . the social contract is less structured yet more complex [than at first it appears]. Boundaries of the sides blur; the roles can blend into each other. . . . Maybe the blending occurs when everyday life overrules the institution for a while. All the people in the classroom slip out of their roles because for a moment they are knowing and being known [differently]. Yet still, in an instant, if either a teacher or a student jumps back into a rigid role—by either making a demand or by resisting one—then the spell can be broken. I wonder now which is the fulfilling of the social contract—being social by filling a role and exchanging rights, or being social by finally giving up the roles and the rights and seeing eye to eye. . . .

A social contract is the foundation of Mrs. G.'s eighth-grade English class. All the in-class reading, all the exercises in writing, and even Channel One—there is a contract behind them all (especially Channel One, which is naturally a lucrative one). Once I entered the classroom and I was called Mr. Pendleton, I knew I had joined a side. My "Mark" was given up to acquire a "Mr." I really did not have a choice—the contract [operating in this setting] demands that I be a mister. Seeing eye to eye is probably best left for the devout—university students and their professors. Knowing and being known takes a long time. . . . Mrs. G. has accomplished a lot in the space and time she has been given. She and her class understand one another. She wants them to love reading, and they bring their own books to school.

Student Power: Laura's Study

The classroom I observed is at Taft Junior High School, a relatively new school. I would not consider this school to be a "big bucks" junior high, but it is clean and has some technical devices such as a small computer lab (about 20 terminals) and a TV in every classroom. The houses around the school look clean and small to medium in size. This makes me think that the school is in a working- or middle-class neighborhood. . . . According to the teacher, the student body consists mainly of Caucasian students; several Tongan, African American, and Hispanic students; and some Asian and Native American students.

The classroom I observed is located on the outskirts of the school building. There is only one other classroom in the hallway, and the hallway is far from the main office, cafeteria, and library. Because the classroom is far from these heavily trafficked areas of the school, I did not see a lot of students or other teachers walking past the door. The hall was quiet so the students (about 20–25 in each period) and teacher could focus their energy on what happened inside the classroom rather than be tempted to find out what was happening out in the hall. All of the students I observed are ninth graders who represent a range of academic skills and possess varying degrees of desire to be in school. . . . The English class I observed emphasized literature because the English department is organized so that writing and literature are taught separately and the students take a semester of each every year.

The teacher, Mr. H., has been teaching junior high English for the past seven years. Through observing his classroom and talking with him, I [learned quite a bit not only about how he teaches but also what he values as a teacher]. One of his main concerns is good discipline. In his disclosure statement (written at the start of the year to inform parents of teacher expectations) given to each student when they entered his class, he defines good discipline: "Good discipline is the pleasant atmosphere where a teacher's relationship with a class has encouraged every student's self-control and participation." From what I saw, good discipline is that which produces [student passivity]. The students show self-control when they sit in their seats, do the assignments, and respond when the teacher asks them a question. I came to this conclusion because I heard a lot of comments such as "Open your book and read the story" and "Answer this question in your journal," which were directed at individual students who were staring at the wall or playing with their pens. . . . The few students who did not do their assignments were quiet and did not attract the teacher's attention.

The teacher's desire for control is also reflected in the seating arrangements. Rather than a traditional setup with the students' desks facing the teacher's desk at the front of the room, the desks are on each side of the room facing each other with a large aisle down the middle. When I asked him why he had chosen this arrangement, he replied that with this arrangement he can be close to the students and see what they are doing because no one is in the back of the room. Instead of the rows being five to six desks long, the rows are only three to four seats long. If he is close to the students, then he can monitor their activities. This seating arrangement also gives him the opportunity to approach each desk quickly. . . .

Another one of Mr. H.'s main [concerns is to see] that each student participates and receives individual attention. He told me that when the students are participating in class discussions, he feels they are receiving individual attention. So, when he would lecture or have student discussions he would randomly call on students to respond to questions. He mentioned that when he calls on students, he is particularly concerned about getting the silent student to participate. He is aware that some students hate this procedure, but he feels all students should be comfortably saying the answers as well as writing the answers.

Although Mr. H.'s formal intention is to give all students individual attention, the informal rule is that boys receive more attention than girls. When he would call on students randomly, he called on a boy about 75 percent of the time. . . . I was surprised to see Mr. H. point out that the term "heroes" can be either boys or girls, since most definitions and textbooks leave out the term "heroine." It seems to me that the formal rule is to give equal attention to both boys and girls, but his actions [conveyed something else]: boys receive more attention and opportunities to talk in class than girls.

Mr. H.'s philosophy that students receive individual attention when they are called on to participate in class created a different learning environment in each of the three periods I observed. This is because different kinds of students influenced the atmosphere in each class. . . . In first period the students did not participate in class very often. At first I thought that the lack of participation was due to the early hour and that the students were simply tired. But this hypothesis was refuted when I came to first period one day and found sixth period. The change was due to a schedule rearrangement for an assembly. Even though it was the same time of day, these students answered the questions and half of the students showed the desire to participate by raising their hands. In first period, some students discovered that they could beat Mr. H.'s system by responding to questions with a shoulder shrug or by saying "I dunno." They found out that eventually Mr. H. would tell them the answer. One day in particular it seemed as if the students had all made an agreement to remain silent. The teacher sensed their attitude and said, "Sometimes I get the feeling that you just don't want to answer me." Even though the students say they do not know the answer, Mr. H. told me that there are about four students who know all the answers on assignments and tests. When these students are called on in class, they will say they don't know because that is the expectation in that period. . . . Even though the teacher feels participation is essential, the students in first period have decided not to respond to the teacher. The contradiction of teacher and student expectations has created a dead feeling in the classroom because there is no connection made between the teacher and students.

However, this is not the case in second and third period. The majority of the students in these two periods respond when they are called on. In first period I could not determine which students in particular had established the attitude of the class, but in second period I felt the class atmosphere was determined by a group of three or four girls. These girls appeared to feel comfortable talking with Mr. H. and discussing literature in front of the class, and they did their assignments when asked. Because of their willingness to participate other students followed along. . . .

Although third period also participated in class discussion and answered questions, this class was not controlled by one small group of students. Instead, three or four groups of students created the atmosphere in the class while those students who did not belong to a group sat quietly, listened to the groups talk, and participated when Mr. H. called on them. I sensed a little competition between the different groups to dominate the conversation and control the classroom. Because of this competition, third period was noisier than the other two periods. . . .

Through listening and observing . . . I was able to discover some of the key concepts and attitudes which [shaped] the learning atmosphere in each classroom. . . . I was able to [gain insight into] some [aspects] of the roles the teacher and students played by listening to repeated phrases. One phrase Mr. H. used often when talking both to students and with me is "with me."

He told a couple of students to "stick with me and you'll get better grades." Sometimes when a student was not paying attention, he would look at him/her and question, "Are you with me?" These types of phrases imply that the teacher is the source of important information in the classroom. When the students are with the teacher, then they are learning because the teacher has the knowledge. They need the teacher's guidance to discover knowledge. If the teacher plays the role of the source of information, then the students can tap into that information only when they recognize the teacher is the source.

One of the most common phrases used by students in all of the classes is "What are we supposed to do?" The phrase indicated that the students see their role as one in which they are people who must meet requirements and conform to expectations. Since the teacher records grades and gives assignments, then the students' role is to fulfill the teacher's requirements. It is important to note that the students say "we" rather than "I" even though the speaker really wants to know what he/she is supposed to do. This illustrates that the students see their role collectively. A student is not a single person, but one who is part of a student body.

To me Mr. H. frequently made remarks such as "You must always be the teacher or they'll take you to the cleaners" and "Keep the teacher-student distance or else they'll take you to the cleaners." This metaphor, "they'll take you to the cleaners," suggests that both the students and the teacher have the ability and power to control the classroom, but the teacher's power is superior to the students', since the students gain control only when the teacher relinquishes power. This metaphor also suggests that once the teacher's superiority has been cleaned away, then it is too late; the teacher cannot regain authority from students. . . .

I also discovered some informal rules of the classroom when Mr. H. relaxed slightly on control. . . . This happened every day at the end of second period when the TV turned on so the students could watch Channel One, a nationally produced news show anchored by teenagers. The students generally got out of their seats and walked around or sat on their desks and talked with each other. Since this type of activity is just the opposite of that which he expected while lecturing, I concluded that the informal rule states that if Mr. H. is not the main source of information, then good discipline is not essential. . . .

Another time that his discipline stance relaxed was when he was dealing with certain types of individuals. One of the girls who is influential in shaping the attitude in second period was often out of her seat to look out the window or talk with a student across the room. In the same class there is a boy who is out of his seat just as often and for the same reasons. However, when the teacher gave out grades and citizenship marks, the boy, who received the lower grade of the two, was scolded for being out of his seat constantly. The teacher only made comments about a missed quiz to the girl student. . . . Students with good grades are given . . . privileges because they are "good students." The fact that Mr. H. relaxes somewhat on his good discipline stance when dealing with "good students" illustrates [an] informal rule.

Throughout my observations it seemed to me that Mr. H. continued to organize his classroom in a similar manner for each period, but the students in each class reacted to his rules and expectations in different ways and, thus, created different learning environments. . . .

Commentary

Nikki's study includes some interesting descriptions of the context within which she will eventually practice teach, but little interpretation. There are moments when she raises a question or uncovers an issue, but she does not push herself to get to the meaning of events. For example, she was amazed there was so little cheating during test days despite ample opportunities; the teacher even left the room. Rather than take this occasion as an opportunity to locate and explore cultural boundaries—norms— she let the observation pass perhaps because she lacked sufficient time to pursue the question or because she did not recognize it as an issue worth exploring. The latter point is especially important and will be returned to shortly in "A Note to Teacher Educators and Students." Nikki comments that the geometry class "was harder to observe" than the algebra class. This, also, is a point that will be considered later. Here we should note only that on the surface, well-routinized classes and well-behaving students seem to offer to novice teachers little that is deemed worthy of attention; the landscape appears smooth, and nothing reaches out and grabs attention.

Mark's insight, that a contract had been negotiated between the teacher and students, offers one of several potential points from which to view and get a handle on an otherwise placid and too familiar classroom scene. Like Nikki when she observed the geometry classes, Mark is surprised that the eighth-graders he observed were so well-behaved. Apparently he had expected otherwise. Unlike Nikki, he wonders why this is so and he speculates about possible reasons. As he considers these reasons, it strikes him that Mrs. G. and the students have negotiated a particular kind of relationship that benefits both parties. He explored some aspects of the "contract," particularly observing that by working with Mrs. G. he would be expected to maintain it; the contract came with the territory. He would be *Mr.* Pendleton, not Mark, as he comments, because "the contract demands that I be a mister." He begins to uncover some of the ways in which culture constrains practice. Yet, he also notes—and in noting softens what otherwise seems an overly deterministic interpretation—that it is possible in the classroom to slip out of a role, with the result that teacher and pupils come to know one another differently, as people who are not only, and certainly more than, the roles they inhabit. Put differently, there is "wiggle room."

Mark has identified a set of questions that promises to be useful in the future as he considers the nature of the contract he will negotiate with his students when practice teaching: "What is at stake? What is being lost or gained [through the contract]?" What is being agreed to? Although Mark offers relatively little supporting evidence that would enable the reader to understand the source of his insight, it is clear that the concept of "social contract" has enabled him to think richly about his future relationship with students. His implicit ideal, of being able to see "eye to eye" with students, appears tempered by his increased understanding of the contextual demands placed on teachers.

Like Mark, Laura recognizes that teachers and students negotiate roles in the classroom. She is especially struck by how class norms seem to differ despite her cooperating teacher holding to a consistent set of expectations. It is the power of young people to shape classroom norms and influence teacher behavior that proves most striking to her. She observed that some students and student groupings were extremely influential and that the kind and quality of relationship that existed among student groupings had a profound impact on the type of learning environment that existed and on the culture of the classroom. In one class Laura concluded that competition among groups was the central factor in making it noisy. This insight could prove important once she begins working with that class in practice teaching.

The power of students to shape the classroom culture was not the only important insight that emerged for Laura and that helped her to make sense of classroom events. Wisely, she did not take her cooperating teacher's description of what he was doing as necessarily accurate. Instead, she checked his claims, not to criticize them, but to come to her own understanding of the norms operating within the classroom. What she discovered was contradictory. She observed, for instance, that despite the cooperating teacher's expressed desire to involve all students, he played favorites: Boys received more attention than girls. Although Laura did not seek reasons for why this was so— perhaps the boys acted out more frequently than girls—it was an important insight that may well influence her own classroom practice. Additionally, she checked to see what definitions of "good discipline" were played out in practice. Was good discipline what her cooperating teacher claimed it to be: the pleasant learning atmosphere that encourages student self-control and participation? As she explored this question, she concluded that student passivity and conformity masqueraded as self-control. Clearly, Laura was beginning to think about how she would handle discipline and management problems and to consider the implications of those decisions on student roles. She listened carefully to what the teacher had to say that might reveal the boundaries of his understanding of the teaching role. Several phrases stuck out, each prompting the conclusion that for her cooperating teacher, controlling information and dispensing it was the essence of teaching. To gain knowledge, students necessarily went through the teacher. Moreover, she asserts that in their dependency the students became a "we," a faceless collective, devoid of individuality. Students who accepted their place received benefits; those who did not, like the boy who was censored for engaging in behavior just like that of his "good student" female classmate, were punished.

The power of Mark's study comes from a single idea that enables him to think about his practice in new and interesting ways. Laura's study has similar virtues, but her insights are more eclectic and diverse. She poses many different questions of the context before her and tests a variety of interpretations—hypotheses—seeking ones that better explain what she sees. There is a tentativeness—even when making bold claims—about her conclusions that suggests hers is an ongoing and unfinished quest for understanding. One gets the feeling that better interpretations, ones more useful for thinking about and making sense of the teaching context, will be forthcoming with additional experience. It is this attitude, perhaps more than any other quality, that makes Laura's study worthy of careful consideration.

A Note to Teacher Educators and Students

There has been an explosion of interest in the study of school culture the past few years. The picture that has emerged is quite different from the one presented even twenty years ago, when researchers commonly assumed a uniform culture, particularly of teaching. This view is now untenable (Feiman-Nemser & Floden, 1986). School cultures differ, just as subgroups of teachers within the same school differ—the teachers in the science department compared to those in the English department. Despite this research finding, the tacit nature of cultural norms and their function as rules by which everyday life is made sensible and meaningful make it nearly impossible to imagine that practice might be organized differently (see Sarason, 1971). For beginning teachers this problem is especially acute not only because of their relatively low institutional status and vulnerability, expressed in the desire to fit in, but because they are too familiar with the culture. "Like anthropologists studying their own culture, they are apt to miss the underlying cultural knowledge organizing practice because it has become so familiar to them that it is, in fact, invisible" (Florio-Ruane, 1989:164).

Mark and Laura's studies illustrate how ethnographic inquiry can lead to making the familiar problematic. School and classroom life are, as these beginning teachers discovered, fraught with contradictions. The source of these contradictions is "the fact that teaching and learning have multiple and conflicting meanings that shift within our lived lives, with the theories produced and encountered, with the deep convictions and desires brought to and created in education, with the practices we negotiate, and with the identities we construct" (Britzman, 1991:10). The discovery of contradiction is fundamentally important. With the discovery comes the realization that alternative practices are possible, even for student teachers. This said, a caution is in order: "The fact is, to place student teachers in compulsory school settings and to expect them to act as if they have entered a neutral zone where they can single-handedly fashion it into places [*sic*] of learning sets them up for . . . self-blame" (Britzman, 1991:221).

Ethnography, then, holds the possibility of giving the beginning teacher access to what is transpiring in a classroom, and opens the door for considering what might be. Mark, for instance, recognizes that he is and is not "Mr. Pendleton," yet accepts that he will become a "Mr." Knowing that the context will push this role upon him and some of the ways in which the pushing will take place makes it possible for him to forge a different role, through adjusting classroom conditions as his teaching skill and understanding increase, one that is more nearly in line with his ideal of seeing "eye to eye." Here is wiggle room.

As a means for encouraging reflectivity, ethnography has found a place both within campus-based teacher education courses and in field experiences (see Gitlin & Teitelbaum, 1983; Zeichner & Liston, 1987). However, most of the work supporting its use is anecdotal. For example, after describing their own classroom practice, Teitelbaum and Britzman remark: "While we have no longitudinal empirical evidence to support us, we contend that our use of . . . ethnography with education students has been successful in promoting the goals of reflective teacher education" (1991:179). We echo their words: The ethnographies have encouraged our students to explore culture and begin to build a knowledge base about school life; they develop observational and interpretative skills that have long-term value; and they debate about how life in schools is structured and how it might be transformed.

Doing Ethnography

As noted previously, good ethnographies require a tremendous amount of time to produce. It is not only that time needs to be spent in the classroom, but also that time is needed to make sense of the data gathered. Since we are not conducting a class in educational anthropology, our expectations are relatively modest ones. We are more interested in having our students explore culture and test some tentative hypotheses than produce tightly argued and polished papers. Still, we want papers that have meaning for our students, that will generate useful insights. To this end, and in recognition of time constraints and the limitations associated with being novices to the study of teaching and culture, when we introduce the assignment we include, in addition to sharing sample studies, tips on note taking and on making sense of the notes taken. We also include a warning to avoid what Teitelbaum and Britzman dub the "rush to judgment" (1991:174) to which Mark may have fallen prey. Time constraints are a major factor behind the rush. One needs to slow down, suspend judgment, and in a sense, let the data speak.

Note Taking and Making Sense

Prior to conducting the ethnography, the students have not only formally interviewed their cooperating teacher but also spent a good deal of time with them and in their classroom. We urge our students to select a class for study that seems interesting, and one that they will most likely be teaching when practice teaching. We tell them to pick a location in the classroom that is unobtrusive but that allows them to see what is going on. And we urge them to review the assignment with their cooperating teacher to make certain they understand what is being done and why. At first we suggest that a running record of classroom events be kept, perhaps with time counts in the margins (e.g., "8:45 A.M., class begins when . . ."). As they record—as they learn to see—we encourage them to write "memos" to themselves, marginalia, when an event stands out as interesting, exceptional, or puzzling or when they have a flash of insight about the meaning of events. Later, but certainly sometime the same day of an observation, we urge them to review their notes. At first the purpose of the reviews is to flesh out gaps in the notes and especially to respond to and perhaps amplify the memos, which generally serve as the basis of the interpretations that will emerge. "What is going on?" is the question to be asked. Soon the purpose of the reviews shifts somewhat, and the quest begins for patterns. A second question is posed: "What is going on, and why?" Finally, the focus narrows and hypotheses are proposed to account for the patterns that are observed. Lastly, hypotheses—tentative interpretations—are tested through additional observation, adjusted, and sometimes rejected.

These phases of analysis, loose to be sure, are evident particularly in Mark and Laura's studies, although Mark rather quickly jumps to an interpretation—the social contract—and it is somewhat difficult to tell how he got there. Laura's study contains evidence not only of proposing hypotheses but also of testing them. For example, to test her hypothesis that lack of student participation in first period was due to the early hour of the day she observed other classes, at first through a fortuitous turn of events but later intentionally. By observing these additional classes, she began to better understand the nature of student power within the classroom, its operation, and its influence on her cooperating teacher's practice. Other better and more compelling hypotheses followed that most certainly will inform her understanding of classroom events come practice teaching.

In addition, we urge our students to test their tentative interpretations by checking them out with their cooperating teachers and the pupils. Sometimes surprising results follow. As Laura discovered, a teacher's perceptions of classroom events and those of an observer may be quite different. Depending on the nature of the beginning teacher and cooperating teacher relationship, these differences can provide the occasion for a rich and lively discussion of teaching. Unfortunately, such discussions are not always possible and interpretations must be kept to oneself. In any case, perceptions should be checked, for more complex and interesting understandings will often result. We should also note that when interpretations differ, the beginning teacher should not necessarily assume that his or her interpretation is incorrect. After all, reality comes in many forms!

Pupil interviews are a useful way of checking some interpretations. For instance, Laura could have relatively easily checked out her conclusion that competition among groups was a crucially important cultural element in one of the classes she observed. Time constraints and her interest in many other aspects of culture prevented her from doing so. Interviews are not the only means for obtaining pupil input, however. Some of our students have designed questionnaires to gather data and test hypotheses. A few have even conducted whole-class discussions, with cooperating teacher permission and without their presence. What is important is that data be gathered by means that will enable interpretations to be assessed.

On Making Interpretations

Nikki had difficulty moving beyond description in her study. She seemed nearly overwhelmed by all that was going on in the classroom and unable to find and frame a question or issue for exploration. Put differently, no events stood out or challenged her to ask, "Why? What is going on here?" Because discipline problems are readily apparent, many of our students who feel adrift grab hold and study them, and sometimes they prove to be a productive avenue for uncovering and exploring norms, but not always. But what does one do when no genuine discipline problems appear, as when Nikki observed the geometry classes?

It is for this reason, among others, that memos are of such importance. When observing, an idea or question will pop into one's head and, if not immediately recorded, quickly be lost. These flashes of insight, like Mark's uneasiness when being introduced as "Mr. Pendleton," often prove to be rich avenues for beginning to understand the meaning of events. For students who struggle to get an "angle," as some of them call it, discussions with other students or with you, the teacher educator, may prove helpful. If such meetings take place, it is important to remember that the purpose is to pose questions and nudge along understanding and not to impose an interpretation. One important way to further understanding and to help the students find an angle is to recommend readings that elaborate themes or patterns found in the ethnographic studies of schooling. While this can lead to imposition, the alternative of trying to remain neutral places the students in an intellectual vacuum that encourages surface or commonsensical explanations. We have approached this task in different ways. Sometimes we have required readings that help orient the students to the study of culture and help them frame questions for exploration, as noted by Mark when he mentioned *The Forgotten Dream* and *Jocks and Burnouts*. Other times we have suggested readings and had the students locate their own readings that speak to the issues that concern them. In either case, we encourage them, through open critique of the readings, to be wary of the conclusions of others. It is important that an angle be found, a beginning made, but it need not be one that we, or the authors of the ethnographic studies we have the students read, think is the central or most significant focal point. As we have seen from the studies presented, there are perhaps an infinite number of interesting angles awaiting exploration that will shed light on classroom norms and their operation.

Sharing Studies

As noted, the studies are discussed in class. When time permits, a good alternative is to group the students by subject area, school, or grade level and have them read and criticize one another's work. Within the groups they test interpretations, and the opportunity is given to write a postscript (see Teitelbaum & Britzman, 1991).

CHAPTER SEVEN

Textbook/Curriculum Analysis

The curriculum in a large percentage of American classrooms is the textbook. One estimate is that 75 percent of a student's classroom time and 90 percent of homework time is spent with textbook materials (Keith, 1981). Preservice teachers such as yourself are often highly critical of experienced teachers' heavy reliance on textbooks. Ironically, once in charge of your own classroom, you are likely to find yourselves similarly dependent. It is very important that you consider how textbooks should be used with students and for what purposes.

There is an intimate but generally ignored relationship between curriculum, textbooks, and the role of teachers (see Apple, 1979b; Apple, 1986; Zumwalt, 1989). Buried in textbooks and curriculum guides are preferred teacher roles, ways of working with young people, definitions of the disciplines, and even beliefs about the social world. Choosing to use a particular textbook is, therefore, inherently a political act. No wonder heated battles have been waged across America over textbook adoption (see Apple, 1986; Bullough, 1988, chapter six; Tanner, 1988; Woodward & Elliott, 1990).

The challenge for you is to become a critical consumer *and* producer of curricula and to learn to approach textbooks and curriculum guides with a skeptical eye, one sensitive to the assumptions about teaching, learning, and the nature of social life that are embedded within them. Some of these assumptions are hidden, and it requires a bit of detective work to reveal them. For example, the way a curriculum is organized—its "curricular form" (Apple, 1982)—tells a great deal about what the developers most valued. Frequently, curricula follow a technical form, where knowledge is broken up into discrete "bits" that are supposed to add up to something, like the ability to read or write, for example. To facilitate measurement, educational objectives are stated in behavioral terms, as skills to be mastered (see Mager, 1962). Such a curriculum form has the effect of prescribing teacher behavior and of elevating isolated bits of information to the status of knowledge (Bullough, Holt & Goldstein, 1984). When deciding to adopt one or another curriculum, it's important to carefully consider how a particular curriculum form might influence what you do in the classroom and the types of relationships you will have with students. It is also important to carefully consider the biases inherent in any materials and in relationship to your teaching goals. To be sure, like other teachers you will adjust and adapt the materials given to you to make them more compatible with your understanding of teaching, your students' abilities and interests, and even your assumptions about education (see McCutcheon, 1982). Our hope is that these adjustments and adaptations will be mindfully made and educationally justifiable.

To become increasingly critical consumers of curricula, our students conduct a textbook analysis. The questions presented are only suggestive: A good analysis does not necessarily address all these questions, and a good analysis may come from other questions. Thus, our questions provide a point of departure for the analysis.

Before turning to the actual writing, we should mention that prior to introducing the analysis we explore with our students four central curriculum concepts that are essential for focusing curriculum criticism: the explicit curriculum, the hidden or implicit curriculum, null curriculum, and the curriculum in use or implemented curriculum. The explicit curriculum is what the public is told young people will be taught. The explicit curriculum is contained in curriculum guides and textbooks. The hidden curriculum is "the tacit teaching to students of norms, values, and dispositions that goes on simply by their living in and coping with the institutional expectations and routines of schools day in and day out for a number of years" (Apple, 1979b:14). These are not all negative learnings; the "implicit curriculum of the school can teach a host of intellectual and social virtues" (Eisner, 1985:95). The null curriculum is "what the schools do not teach," what is missing (Eisner, 1985:97). When one stops to think about it, the most difficult curriculum issue of all is deciding what not to teach, since there is so much worth learning and so little schooltime available. The curriculum in use, or implemented curriculum, is what actually gets taught.

Both the hidden and null curriculum get at issues of bias, and implicitly raise questions about inclusion, an issue that has been most widely explored with history texts (see Wolf, 1992). What belongs in the biology, art, or health curriculum? Are there good reasons for excluding sex education from the health curriculum or should it be included? If included, whose values should inform the selection, organization, presentation, and study of the content?—the teacher's? one or another special interest group's? whose? Addressing these issues is not only important to becoming a critical consumer of curricula developed by others but is crucial to assuring that teachers' own curriculum work is educationally defensible and morally responsible. It forces us to attend to the politics of curriculum development *and* to the right of young people to encounter content that represents the best that is known and in ways likely to connect with and enrich their experience and background.

Recognizing that there is a difference between the explicit curriculum and the curriculum in use is important for two closely interrelated reasons. First, this distinction underscores the central role teachers play in remaking the explicit curriculum so that it better reflects their educational values and their students' needs. This is one of the sources of teachers' wiggle room discussed earlier. It is only at the teacher's bidding that the explicit curriculum enters the classroom door. Second, it also underscores that teaching, as we have argued in *Becoming a Student of Teaching*, is a moral and political enterprise, one that places a tremendous responsibility on the teacher. To meet this obligation requires that when teachers use textbooks, they consume them critically. It is toward this aim that the textbook analysis is addressed.

Writing

The following is the textbook or curriculum analysis assignment we present to our students.

> Obtain a copy of the textbook or curriculum guide used by your cooperating teacher or one that is commonly used in a local school. When analyzing the textbook consider the following questions: (1) Who wrote the text or guide? What part did teachers play in its production? (2) Is a rationale or statement of philosophy included? If so, is it academically, intellectually, and ethically defensible? Do you find it personally compelling? Explain and support your conclusion. (3) Are goals and objectives included? Are the goals worthy ones? Are some goals you deem worthy missing? Are some goals and objectives included that ought not be there? Why not? Explain and support your conclusion. (4) How is the text or guide organized (e.g., thematically, topically, chronologically, logically [an expert view of the discipline], psychologically [based on a conception of how people learn], or . . .)? Is the organization a sensible one? Is it intellectually defensible and consistent with how children learn? Does it facilitate teaching and learning? Why or why not? (5) Is the content adequate? Is it intellectually and socially defensible? Do you see signs of a hidden or null curriculum? If so, how so? (6) What are students supposed to be doing when they engage the content? What kind of student role is encouraged by the textbook or guide? (7) What is the teacher supposed to be doing when using the text? Is there a preferred teacher role? (8) Is provision made for evaluation? What kind of information is sought through evaluation and what is to be done with the information? Are some kinds of activities or types of knowledge excluded from consideration, others emphasized? If so, what are these? Is the evaluation linked to the goals/objectives/philosophy? If so, what kind of connection is made? (9) Is the text or guide usable, teachable? For textbooks only: (10) Is the text written at a level that makes it easily accessible for students? Is the writing engaging? *Note*: In your write-up, use *evidence*—quotes—to support your conclusions.

Two edited analyses follow. The first is of a junior high school mathematics textbook and is written by Irene Tomsic, who requested that her name be used. Irene demonstrates some of the power of using the concepts of hidden and null curricula as analytic tools. The second, written by Joshua, is of a text used in high school art classes. This critique is written by a beginning teacher who is a practicing artist. Through his analysis he discovers that the view of the content and purposes of art instruction presented in the text is quite different from, and in some respects contrary to, his own.

Irene: Teachers Are Stupid but . . . It's an Improvement

Review of *Mathematics—Applications and Connections* (a Glencoe book, published 1992). About the authors: The text is jointly written by twelve people. The authors are a fairly diverse group, comprising six females and six males, of which one was black and one Hispanic. Of the twelve, eleven were teachers; six were junior high school teachers and five were from the university level. One was a consultant. Approximately fifty other consultants were listed. Interestingly, one of the junior high school teachers had experience teaching in Ethiopia with the Peace Corps.

Rationale and Statement of Philosophy

The primary [purpose], according to the authors, is to answer two questions for students: "Why do I have to study this?" and "When are we ever going to use it?" It is the belief of the authors, based upon their research and the research of others, that students don't see math as having much to do with their every-day lives, and that they see little connection between math and other subjects studied.

I agree with this philosophy; I remember thinking the same thing when I was a student. I also hear this sentiment from students today. I think the reasons why a subject is being taught should be clearly conveyed to students. If they can be convinced of the need, their interest and participation should increase.

Stated Goals and Objectives

The development of the ability to solve problems is the overriding theme of [the text]. In order to meet this goal, there are sections in each chapter on problem-solving strategies, problem-solving hints, applications, connections with other math concepts, critical thinking exercises, decision-making lessons, and "make up a problem" sections. Other objectives include (1) incorporating technology into the classroom (calculator and computer lessons are included); (2) providing a multicultural perspective on math; (3) meeting individual needs; . . . (4) meeting NCTM (National Council of Teachers of Mathematics) standards. . . .

I believe that utilizing this text would provide the opportunity to meet the stated goals. I was particularly impressed by the fact that problem-solving strategies were discussed throughout [the text]. . . . Heavy emphasis is placed on analyzing information and deciding exactly what is being asked. From there, differing strategies and different techniques for solving problems are reviewed. For example, eight different ways to estimate solutions are covered. Students are also encouraged to use estimation techniques to see if their solutions to other problems seem realistic. Open-ended questions as well as problems which lack adequate information are included. I think this would encourage information analysis and critical thinking skills.

The problems are related to the lives of students, and generally involve real-life situations. They generally relate to teen life. I think more emphasis could be placed on situations and professions where math is used after graduation so that students could envision future use.

I find it beneficial that NCTM information is spread [throughout] the text. This could help reduce the need to disrupt the normal curriculum [to prepare for standardized tests].

Overall Text Organization

The chapters are organized topically and logically. . . . The order in which topics are presented should be considered, but at this point, I don't think I have the experience necessary to [judge it].

Chapter Organization

Each chapter is organized in the following way:

1. Chapter introduction, consisting of a two-page scenario that is intended to motivate or arouse interest in the topic that follows.

2. Objective statement [which] states what the . . . section seeks to accomplish. I really liked this feature, and felt it was well done. I think it is valuable to give students an overview of where you are heading . . . before embarking.

3. Body of the lesson, explaining the concept. Concepts were explained in simple, concise terms.

4. Examples. Often, only one or two examples were provided. More examples would be helpful.

5. Checking for understanding. This section provides an in-class review of the concept that has just been explained. In this section, students were generally required to explain a concept in their own words, without using symbols. I think this is a great idea. It helps students clarify ideas, and assists the instructor to evaluate understanding.

6. Exercises. Adequate, but more would have been [helpful].

7. Journal entry. Here students [are] to explain their feelings and thoughts about the topic. I suspect that you could get some real entertaining responses from junior high students in this section! Instead of explaining their [students'] feelings, [the authors would provide] a written explanation of the concepts covered.

8. Mid-chapter review.

9. Summary of chapter contents. I thought this was a great feature, and one that I've never encountered in a textbook. Good closure tool.

10. Chapter exam. Exams did test exactly what had been covered.

11. Vocabulary words listed in margins.

Adequacy of the Content

As far as I am qualified to judge, I felt that the topics covered were [consistent] with the stated requirements. The teacher's text indicates which topics, problems, and exercises are included in the NCTM standards. It is the authors' claim that all topics are covered.

The text also included other [useful] topics. . . . In general, the text touches lightly on subjects such as algebra, geometry, statistics . . . that will be encountered in future courses. I see this as useful [in that it prepares them for what is to come]. . . .

To improve upon the text, I would recommend providing more examples following each lesson body. I don't believe there were enough practice problems provided. I think that math ability is developed by practicing and working a greater number of problems than what [the book provides].

Socially Acceptable

It is the goal of the authors to provide a text that includes people of all races. They attempt to meet this goal in several ways. First, students and adults of all races are pictured in the text. Another technique is a section entitled "Cultural Kaleidoscope," where people of various races and their accomplishments are highlighted. Also available are optional booklets emphasizing multiracial accomplishments. . . . I was encouraged [by this]. Pictorially, the people shown in the text were a good mixture of people and students from all races. They did a good job here. On the other hand, the "Cultural Kaleidoscope" section could have been better. . . . For example, one person highlighted in the Kaleidoscope is Cesar Chavez. His contribution to the betterment of the working conditions of migrant farm workers is to be praised. Granted, Mr. Chavez's accomplishments were truly noble, but just what does this have to do with mathematics? I think the authors should have highlighted people of various cultures and races who made contributions to the field of mathematics. They missed an opportunity to show how our knowledge of math has been put together piece by piece by people from all over the globe. Of the six Kaleidoscopes in the book, only one was directly related to math contributions. . . .

The null curriculum [showed up] with gender [issues]. To be socially acceptable by my standards, I feel that it is vital that we stop portraying women as cooks, gardeners, seamstresses, and secretaries, and men as carpenters, business owners, realtors, plumbers, and sports jocks. In reviewing the word problems, the authors generally [presented] situations where people were in sexist roles.

[I noted signs of a] hidden curriculum in [the authors'] portrayal of American life. The authors seem to project the daily lives of Americans as being focused around excessive materialism, dieting, and sports. Many of the word problems focus on females shopping, males competing in sports, and both sexes dieting. They seem to embrace the idea that it's divine to be thin, affluent, and leisurely. On the positive side, there were a fair amount of examples involving community projects, such as fund-raisers.

Student Role

It is the goal of the authors to provide a student-centered text. A lot of effort is focused on making the text interesting to students. Through increased interest, the students are seen as active explorers of math topics. Working cooperatively in groups is included. [Various] tools [are used] to meet this goal: "Teen scene" provides little trivia factoids meant to capture the student's interests. I felt the "teen scene" section was there for the teen's entertainment only. Once again, there was too little connection to math. For example, one "teen scene" explains that

[when] the "first two-piece swimsuit was seen at the beach, it was named for the shock it caused. Bikini is the name of an island in the Pacific Ocean where the hydrogen bomb was first tested." This is nice, but I'm not so sure it would be of interest to pre-teens, and I'm confident it has no relationship to math. It seems to me that the authors could come up with better examples . . . related to math. For example, explain the correlation between the number of hours a teen spends watching television, and school performance!

[A second tool to capture student interest involves] the use of blocks titled "When am I ever going to use this?" These show the ways various professions utilize math principles. These tidbits were very informative and provided concrete examples of math applications. . . . As an example, the way photojournalists use math to estimate distances and calculate F-stops was explained. "Save Planet Earth" is [another attempt to gain student interest]. This section [presents] environmental issues and explains how students can make a difference. I think students would find this section interesting. They were well chosen, . . . and I agree with the intent of teaching social responsibility. However, I wonder if it wouldn't be more appropriate if these topics were discussed in a civics or science textbook rather than in a math book. . . .

Teacher's Role

The way teachers are viewed is an example of a hidden [value]. If I were to give [the authors'] view of teachers as a metaphor, I'd say they see the "teacher as a robot." The role of the teacher is to follow their step-by-step program, and all will be accomplished. . . . The information given in the margins of the teacher's manual gave me the first clue that these authors believe that teachers are stupid. For example, there are directions for "checking for understanding." Included in many of these blocks is the statement that "you should work through these exercises with your students and then monitor their work." Do they really believe that we wouldn't figure this out on our own without their instructions? Another example of "helpful" items found in the margin is the "error analysis" blocks. In the section that teaches inequalities, our error analysis tells us to "watch for students who use the symbols > and < incorrectly"!

The second reason I didn't care for their view of teachers is that this text attempts to fulfill our every need. There are twenty optional packages available which cover everything from lesson plans to transparencies. I got the impression that we were being handed a complete set of instructions on *how* to proceed. Obviously, these packets spell added sales and revenue, but I felt they were lacking in quality, and were written at a very elementary level (I had access to four of the twenty).

Evaluation

Overall, I was impressed with the evaluation process because it offered a variety of ways to assess understanding. . . . [But] too often the problems [used for evaluation] were stated in the exact same manner as the examples. Varying the way questions are posed should prevent students from developing the habit of plugging numbers into formulas without knowing what they are really doing. In the answer section at the back of the book, almost all solutions were given, instead of the traditional odd or even problems only. On the positive side, this could provide students with more feedback but would hamper the teacher's efforts in using part of the problems for homework.

Activities

Twenty activity pamphlets are available to complement the text. These included pamphlets covering topics [from] various cultures [to] technology. . . . These booklets were rather sparse, and seemed more of a frill than useful materials. Group activities as well as cooperative learning sections are found throughout the text, which I thought would be helpful. . . .

Writing

The book is written in a manner that is intended to tweak the interest and curiosity of the student. The level of writing seems appropriate for junior-high-age kids.

Overall Impression

. . . It seems that a lot of thought and effort went into the preparation [of this text]. . . . I see [it] as a sign of progress [in math textbook writing].

Joshua: Interesting, But I Can't Use It

The text I chose for review is *Art Fundamentals: Theory and Practice* by Ocvirk, Stinson, Wigg, and Bone from the School of Art, Bowling Green State University. In its sixth edition—first published twenty-seven years ago—the book came about through a synthesis of the authors' lecture notes and classroom experience. It was intended initially as a college book, but has been used successfully in high school art classes.

Implementation [of the curriculum] . . . is left up to the instructor and student. . . . The text . . . provides no student practice or involvement beyond reading and looking at the many art reproductions. Among "student-friendly" features . . . are vocabulary lists preceding each chapter. The lists increase the likelihood that terms used in the chapter are understood before reading.

The goal of *Art Fundamentals* is to build an understanding of the elements of artistic creation in order to serve the student in creating art and appreciating art. The book has a definite rationale behind it: "Art relationships are best understood, we think, through dissecting and analyzing constituent parts as assembled by the artist." Such a view seems consistent with the Aristotelian view which Albert Levi claimed is the established doctrine of artistic creation of our time. Such a view asserts that the creation of art is the "imposition of an idea upon matter."

This is in contrast to what Levi refers to as the "Platonic view"—creation through inspiration.

It follows that if the creation of art is the imposition of an idea upon matter, then dissecting and analyzing its constituent parts would be working backwards through a logical process. [This] rationale has its problems, however, dealing with the creation of certain types of works, such as those of the plein air painters or the abstract expressionists. Particular care would need to be taken in using this text in order that students were made aware of views [different from] the Aristotelian. In other words, its "okay" to be an artistic romantic and believe in art as inspired rather than logical.

Personally, I feel that both views are important, and not necessarily incompatible. Still, the danger of presenting the formal considerations of art is that the student's own sensitivity and response to things visual can be short-circuited; they learn how they are supposed to respond to certain visual cues rather than learn to feel and value their own responses. The authors also seem to sense this general danger in making a text about art, a subject they say is "hardly compatible with the scientific method." Even with this acknowledgement, however, the text is built upon certain assumptions [that need scrutinizing. One of these is] the component assembly model of art creation which would seem "neither here nor there" to many working artists.

As far as accomplishing the second part of the text's goal, to aid students in appreciating art, my concern is that art appreciation according to the book is built upon a framework of assumptions [that I have some difficulty with], including the necessity of art *intending* to express an idea: "An artist must begin with an idea. . . ." Such thinking is bound up in the [apparently] sequential world of [sciences]. Art can be created without a formal idea or plan worked out in advance of the undertaking. Likewise, visual art can be enjoyed in a purely visual sense without knowing how to name its constituent parts. This can be compared to being moved by a piece of music without being able to name its composer or key signature. Perhaps this kind of unfettered enjoyment is best of all, and possibly numbed by overemphasis on words and definitions. . . .

After reviewing this text, I have arrived at two major conclusions. First, for teaching what I value most in art education, the book is of no use. In my mind there is still a gulf between the . . . individual process of learning to draw or paint, and learning about dissected art "principles and elements" as presented in the text. I value the learning outcomes that result from learning real studio skills, such as drawing. Learning to draw is far more a product of learning to see and develop coordination than it is a product of understanding art principles or elements. Because of my belief in the value of learning studio art skills such as drawing, the teaching of the "principles and elements" of art is a secondary, though still important, consideration. . . .

Second, as far as teaching the principles and elements, this text is confusing, especially for high school students. Although the [chapters are] organized in a generally sensible way, confusion is created [because of the organization of content] within chapters. For example, in one chapter the "Principles of Organization" are listed as: "harmony, variety, balance, movement, proportion, dominance, economy, and space." Yet on the diagram to the right of the page, under "Principles of Organization," "space" is not included. Furthermore, the discussion of "space" follows the list immediately, and is not discussed under the heading of "Principles of Organization" that comes later in the chapter. The text might be useable if specific guidance were given in helping students [better] organize the information presented in the book. But, an introductory text on the principles and elements of art . . . should be more straightforward. . . .

Commentary

Irene finds much that she likes about *Mathematics—Applications and Connections*, but as she begins digging through the text she uncovers elements of it that are troubling, that suggest a hidden curriculum is at work. Two stand out: the presence of a significant amount of material that has nothing to do with mathematics but is included to grab student interest; and the implicit view of teachers as "stupid," a view communicated through the written text and its organization. It puzzles her why non-mathematics material would be included in the text when so much of interest connected to mathematics is available. Irene knows mathematics and assumes other math teachers do as well; she also assumes that other teachers have a measure of what she would consider common sense, that teachers know students need monitoring, for example. She rejects outright the possibility that some teachers might actually need such hints. Implicitly, Irene thinks of teachers as educated professionals capable of exercising judgment while it appears, at least to Irene, that the authors have a more limited view of their ability. This difference is a crucial one that would have a profound effect on how Irene would use the text. Returning to the concepts introduced earlier, because of her analysis the *implemented curriculum* of her classroom would likely be quite different from the *explicit curriculum* presented in the book.

Joshua is less concerned than is Irene about the social aspects of the hidden curriculum of his textbook. What commands his attention is the authors' views of the subject matter. He has read extensively and thought long and deeply about the purposes of teaching art, and is troubled by the approach taken in the text. From his perspective as an artist (underscoring the importance of biography in curriculum decision making), emphasizing art concepts and downplaying the expressive and emotive value of art shortchanges young people and, in effect, turns art into a subject like any other. Joshua has touched on a major debate currently surrounding art curriculum in the schools: is art like any other school subject— concept- and principle-based—or are it and its aims different in fundamental ways (see Bullough & Goldstein, 1984; Geahigan, 1992)?

Considering himself a subject matter expert, Joshua is anxious to engage in debate. So central is Joshua's disagreement with the authors' conception of art and art teaching that other questions and issues are pushed aside. His concern is to get and keep his purposes straight, first and foremost. Still, the nature of young people's encounters with art are at the center of his deliberation about purposes. There is danger, he thinks, that by overemphasizing the "formal considerations of art . . . the student's own sensitivity and response to things visual [will] be short-circuited" and that they will devalue their own feelings and responses to art as a result. Joshua is acutely sensitive to the student role encouraged by the curriculum and to the nature of the learning experience the authors most value. For Joshua, art is first and foremost about feeling, doing, enjoying and not primarily about "thinking."

Questions of whether Joshua is right or wrong in his views seem inappropriate when considering his analysis. He is engaged and thinking critically about the material in relationship to the kind of curriculum he wants to produce for his students. He links theory and practice. Looking ahead, we find ourselves wondering if he will be able to strike the balance he desires and whether, in his quest to help young people learn to "see," he will eventually find a place for works like *Art Fundamentals*.

Given Joshua's lively encounter with the text it is not surprising that small things, like the author's failure to include "space" in a diagram of "Principles of Organization," command his attention. We often find that once a student gets rolling, criticism generates energy and, as passion builds, it sometimes spills out in interesting ways revealing a myriad of author foibles, real and perhaps fanciful.

Unlike Joshua, for the most part Irene liked the way her textbook organized and approached the content of mathematics and, especially, its emphasis on practical applications. She checked the text carefully to see if it attended to the recent work of the National Council of Mathematics Teachers, and it did. It appears consistent with the best thinking in the field. Further, the topical organization also appealed to her understanding of mathematics. But she is cautious: "I don't think I have the experience necessary to [judge it]." With respect to these issues, Joshua's study is somewhat unusual. Most of our students take the organization and structure of their disciplines for granted, and generally accept how they are presented in textbooks. Irene questioned them; Joshua attacked them. Some students may quibble with the order of chapters, but few challenge the underlying views of the disciplines presented and the way in which the content is structured for presentation—the "curriculum form." Our students tend to view the disciplines as stable, expert-driven discourses, where the central issues are identified and widely accepted. Few have taken courses on the philosophy of history, or science, for example. Not surprisingly, we only occasionally receive papers that propose alternative conceptions of the disciplines, and Joshua's is one of these. Joshua understands that art, like other subject areas, is characterized by contending perspectives and that when he puts together a curriculum he must take a stand—curriculum development is a political act. Irene hints at a similar understanding.

While both Joshua and Irene's digging reveals a hidden curriculum, Irene finds it is not all negative. As Eisner commented—and this is easily forgotten—the hidden curriculum can teach positive values. For example, Irene singles out for praise the inclusion by the authors of "differing strategies and different techniques for solving problems. . . . [E]ight different ways to estimate solutions are covered." For the authors, mathematics is not so much a matter of memorizing [rules] but of learning to think. They recognize that there are various good ways to solve any given problem, even in mathematics.

Irene and Joshua's analyses share another characteristic: Although neither person has extensive teaching experience, both seek to get outside of themselves momentarily, to consider how students would engage the content. This needs underscoring: Effective teachers learn to see the world through children's eyes or, better phrased, through adult eyes sensitive to the problems and issues that inhibit children's efforts to learn. This is what teacher education researchers now often refer to as "pedagogical content knowledge" (Shulman, 1987). Such are the eyes of intelligent and critical consumers of curricula.

Both Irene and Joshua's studies illustrate an additional point worth mentioning: beginning teachers need not only questions but also concepts, like the "hidden curriculum," to help them analyze texts; otherwise, superficiality will inevitably result. But beginning teachers bring more than concepts to studies: Both Irene and Joshua brought to their analyses rich background knowledge and experience. By drawing on this knowledge, public and private theories of teaching interact.

A Note to Teacher Educators and Students

Additional Concepts

An additional cluster of concepts relating to the teacher role and teachers' conceptions of teaching undergird our work with the analyses, besides those associated with the explicit, hidden, null, and implemented curriculum and curriculum form. One of the sure signs of training is the commonly held view that teachers do not develop curriculum, someone else does; teachers instruct, "tell," but do not produce curriculum (Sardo-Brown, 1988). This is a serious problem not only because it represents a seriously constricted view of teachers' abilities (see Zumwalt, 1988), but because it places the burden of content development on experts who are generally little involved in classroom work. Teachers *are* experts, and their talent is desperately needed in curriculum development, an issue our first analysis question seeks to address.

Beginning teachers need assistance to understand that the commonly held view and form of curriculum, what Goodson dubs CAP (curriculum as prescription), brings with it a teacher role based upon the assumption that "we can dispassionately define the main ingredients of the course of study and then proceed to teach the various segments and sequences in systematic turn" (Goodson, 1991:168). This is the view that nonteacher curriculum developers often support; it runs throughout commercially produced texts and curriculum materials. It devalues teachers and teachers' work and emphasizes control of teacher behavior in order to achieve externally established outcomes. It is this approach that so troubled Joshua and Irene.

A good many beginning teachers feel compelled to come to terms with the role of teacher as "implementor of a predetermined body of knowledge" (Zumwalt, 1989:174) that comes with CAP. For beginning teachers struggling to define who they are as teachers, this can be a frustrating and discouraging experience.

> Not only must [the beginning teacher] implement a curriculum generally developed by others and with which they are unfamiliar but simultaneously they must negotiate a satisfying teaching role. At times the two demands are contradictory: The adopted curriculum prohibits establishing a satisfying role; and the desired role makes it difficult to implement the established curriculum. (Bullough, 1992:239)

Recognizing this problem and relationship is an important step toward addressing it. And it is an important reason for engaging in the critical analysis and reconstruction of curricula.

A Few Problems

A few of our students have had difficulty identifying a textbook or curriculum guide for study. We urge our students to analyze material that is in wide use and available and that they likely will teach. When a cooperating teacher uses more than one guide or text, we suggest the most frequently used one be analyzed.

A second problem has occasionally arisen: Some of our students resist being critical of the texts or guides. This problem is rooted in several sources. We will mention only two: Some of our students have had little experience in criticism and need a bit of help and encouragement. In a sense, they are victims of training's emphasis on "teaching as telling," which elevates the importance of public over private theory. Also, a few are hesitant to criticize because they do not feel they know the subject area well enough. Sadly, school content and university majors often have little in common. One of our students succinctly captured the problem when she said, "I don't know enough about the content to say whether or not what the book presents is any good." Under such conditions it is little wonder that so many beginning teachers find themselves depending on a textbook for much of the curriculum. With these students we suggest that in the textbook analysis they pay particular attention to those questions that address teacher and student role, and downplay those addressing content issues. A good analysis, as we have said, need not attend to all or even most of the questions we present. For these students a side benefit of the analysis is that by working carefully through the textbook, they learn a great deal about content.

Finally, we should note that what distinguishes a good analysis from a poor one is not length but the willingness of the beginning teacher to question the text seriously; to probe it for insights into authors' conceptions of teaching, learning, and content; and then to think carefully about the results of the probing in relationship to their own thinking and values.

Use of Analysis

Increased sensitivity to the central role teachers play in curriculum development has produced greater interest in curriculum analysis. This interest is not always driven by respect for teachers, however. Reflecting one or another political agenda, some groups are committed to curriculum censorship. There are also organizations, like the California Textbook League which publishes *The Textbook Letter: A National Report on Schoolbooks and Schoolbook Affairs*, that are concerned about the quality of content. Teachers, however, need to do their own thinking, their own analyses.

Even those who value teacher analyses sometimes neglect the important role teachers play in curriculum development. For example, George Posner, in a book appropriately entitled *Analyzing the Curriculum*, argues that the primary value of analysis is related to the need of teachers to select and adapt materials and not in creating them.

> Curriculum analysis is necessary by virtue of its centrality to two important tasks performed by teachers and administrators: curriculum selection and curriculum adaptation. When selecting or adapting a curriculum for use in a particular classroom, school, or school district, it is important to determine whether or not it is appropriate for the situation. This determination is not limited to an analysis of such matters as reading difficulty, the quality

of the graphics, the factual accuracy of the content, and the amount of math required. This examination also requires the ability to determine the extent to which the assumptions underlying the curriculum are valid for the particular class, school, or district. These assumptions consist of tacit beliefs about the central purposes of education, about the intended audience and the way people learn, about teachers and the best ways to teach, about the subject matter and how it should be organized, and about the community and what it values. (Posner, 1992:21)

Helping teachers become critical consumers of curricula is an aim we share with Posner. The insights and skills gained through this methodology also have value for creating curricula, however.

Unlike Posner, we do not have an entire quarter or semester to analyze curricula, just a short time in preparation for student teaching. Nevertheless, it is a crucially important activity that ought to be part of each teacher's ongoing effort to adjust, adapt, and create curricula to provide students an educationally and ethically responsible school experience.

Integrating Methodologies

CHAPTER EIGHT

Action Research

Introduction

By seeking to directly link theory and practice, Action Research differs from other types of research. Action and reflection occur in a cycle, as Stephen Corey, one of the pioneers of Action Research, states:

> Action Research . . . is a practice in which no distinction is made between the practice being researched and the process of researching it. That is, teaching is not one activity and inquiring into it another. The ultimate aim of inquiry is understanding, and understanding is the basis for improvement. (Corey, 1953, p. 3)

Approaches to Action Research differ. Writing in the wake of World War II, Kurt Lewin, for example, argued that Action Research is a means for diminishing the role of emotion in decision making and elevating the place of reason. To engage in Action Research was to think systematically about one's practice.

> And again, it is not an accident that the first act of modern Fascism in every country has been officially and vigorously to dethrone this goddess [reason] and instead to make emotions and obedience the all-ruling principles in education and life from kindergarten to death. (Lewin, 1948, p. 83)

More recent advocates—such as Carr and Kemmis (1983), Kemmis and McTaggart (1988), and Gore and Zeichner (1991)—endorse a more explicitly political approach, one that seeks to illuminate the values underlying seemingly technical teaching problems. For instance, within this view of Action Research, an examination of classroom management would raise questions concerning not only the effectiveness of a strategy or technique in keeping students on task, but also the desirability of the technique when viewed in light of its impact on the quality of teacher-student relationships and the kind of public world the teacher seeks to help create.

Still others, such as Stenhouse (1985) and Elliott (1991), view Action Research from a naturalistic perspective. These authors see the processes involved in Action Research as occurring naturally within the classroom as teachers grapple with the problems of teaching. The purpose of Action Research, then, is to make teaching, and the inquiry process that is part of it, explicit, which enables improvement. As Stenhouse writes:

> The effect [of Action Research] is not unlike that of making the transition from amateur to professional actor. Through self-monitoring the teacher becomes conscious artist. Through conscious art he is able to use himself as an instrument of his research. (pp. 15–16)

Because this approach seeks to make implicit processes explicit, it recognizes that teachers necessarily must determine the nature and focus of study when engaging in Action Research.

Primarily we draw on the naturalistic and more explicitly political approaches to Action Research. However, it is your practice, not ours, that is the focus of research and you may choose a different approach. Studying teaching, as we have argued, requires digging into and criticizing private and public theories about teaching. Nevertheless, while we encourage our students to engage such topics, in the final analysis you must decide the focus of your research if for no other reason than, as Stenhouse observes, "teachers are in charge of classrooms" (p. 15).

At this point, we need to broaden our discussion momentarily. One of the factors that influences what type of Action Research is undertaken is the structure or organization of the teacher education program within which you are enrolled. Full-time practice teaching for a single quarter, for instance, will limit the types of questions that can be asked and the rigor of the project itself. Even with a student teaching seminar, the pressures of teaching under such conditions seriously constrain what can be accomplished. Furthermore, the long-standing separation of preservice from in-service teacher education makes a continuing conversation about theories embedded in educational practice difficult. We mention this here because expectations for Action Research often run well beyond what can reasonably be expected of beginning teachers. Preservice teacher education should introduce you to the process of Action Research and provide you skills and understanding that will enable you to continue researching your practice once you assume a teaching position.

Action Research is an integrative methodology because it brings together inquiry about self and context. It is, after all, your concerns as they emerge in your classroom that are the focus of study. And it is an integrative methodology because it provides the opportunity to pull together and apply insights gained from each of the methodologies previously discussed in *Becoming a Student of Teaching*.

Writing

The Action Research assignment is laid out in three phases. In phase one a concern or issue is identified and written up, and data collected. In the light of the data gathered, the problem is reconsidered, perhaps reformulated, and a problem statement written. In phase two an action plan is written and implemented, and data gathered. In phase three the plan is assessed in the light of the data gathered and recommendations are made for future study and practice. We set due dates for each phase to nudge along the work and help with pacing. Pacing is important because the temptation is to let more immediate and obviously pressing teaching demands consume your energy.

This assignment has several parts:

Phase One

1. Describe in writing a concern or issue relating to some aspect of your teaching.

2. Gather data using one or a combination of the following methods:

   A. *Peer observation.* Choose one or two of your cohort colleagues to work with. Prior to being observed, discuss your concern or problem with your colleagues. Observation notes should focus on this issue, but other significant events should also be recorded. Observation notes should be shared in a postobservation conference and discussed.

   B. *Audiotaping.* Audiotaping is an easy and effective way to gather data. If you choose this option, make certain you tape relatively often, which will allow you to make comparisons. The difficulty with audiotaping is to make certain you set up a classroom situation and/or find an appropriate placement for the machine to make certain you record useful information. A trial run will be a good idea.

   C. *Videotaping.* Although sometimes distracting to students and to beginning teachers, videotaping can be a powerful means for gathering data. If you decide to videotape your classroom, a practice run to get you and your students accustomed to the camera might be helpful. Make certain you give explicit directions to the operator to make certain it is understood what, specifically, you want captured on tape. As with audiotaping, it is a good idea to do multiple tapings to allow for comparisons between lessons.

   D. *Student work/feedback.* You may wish to use student work of one kind or another as a source of data. More formally, you might want to conduct student interviews (or have someone in your cohort or your cooperating teacher conduct them), design a questionnaire, or have the students perform some task that will produce data useful for thinking about your problem or concern. If you design a questionnaire, have your cooperating teacher or

instructor review it before it is used, to avoid leading
questions and to make certain you will obtain useful
data. Be cautious in what you ask of students. Make
certain you do not put your students in the position
of betraying a confidence or of revealing information
that later might adversely affect their relationship
with you.

3. After gathering and reviewing your data, reconsider
   your initial written description of the concern or
   problem. Because other issues or concerns are likely to
   surface, you may need to reformulate the problem or
   make it more specific. Write a problem statement.

Phase Two

4. Write a plan for addressing or ameliorating your
   concern or issue.

5. Share your plan with your cooperating teacher, and if
   working with a peer group, your team. Based upon their
   feedback, revise the plan.

6. Implement the plan.

7. Gather data (see #2 above) to assess your plan. At this
   point you may wish to include your cooperating teacher
   in data gathering. If so, make certain he/she
   understands the purpose of the observations. All data
   gathered should be systematically gathered, and sharply
   focused on the issue or concern.

Phase Three

8. Review the data to determine the effect of your plan.
   With an eye toward your future work as a teacher, write
   up and share the results. Include recommendations for
   future practice.

9. Time permitting, engage in additional cycles of Action
   Research.

Before presenting two edited and much abbreviated
Action Research projects, it is important to place these projects in
context. Currently, the Action Research projects are conducted
during full-time practice teaching (happily, this will soon change
as the program is shifted to half-time teaching over two quarters

instead of one). Because of this contextual constraint, additional Research cycles are not possible. These projects, then, are best understood as signaling the start of what we hope will be an ongoing and systematic study of practice.

Although we refrain from determining what issues or concerns are identified for study, our students often need assistance in forming researchable questions. "I'm having a difficult time deciding what my problem statement will be, but I'm quite sure that it will be something related to discipline and learning." Frequently, issues like classroom management are identified at first. Such issues are too broad to study; they need redefining and sharpening to become manageable for study given program constraints: "What I would most . . . enjoy . . . solving is the problem that occurs when students show no desire for learning and no motivation." On the other extreme, some trivial problems are identified, the solution of which will have little impact on your development or understanding of teaching: "I use 'um' during transitions way too much. This gives an impression of being unsure on my part and the students get a little restless." Had this beginning teacher undertaken the study of his tendency to say "um," one wonders what, if anything, would have been learned about teaching.

It takes time to identify and usefully frame a problem for study. Be patient. Remember, the problems of teaching are interrelated, and no one can work on every problem or concern at once. What is important is that a beginning is made, recognizing that other concerns will emerge over time that will command attention in a continuous cycle of reflection and action.

The two edited and abbreviated studies that follow were written by two preservice teachers, Vicki Healy and Sonja. We use Vicki's name with her permission. Vicki's study was chosen in part because it represents an effort to link public theory—concepts studied in teacher education—with her teaching practice. The nature of her relationships with students is a primary concern. We should mention that both Sonja and Vicki taught English—and Vicki, low-level reading classes, what is called "developmental reading"—in an ethnically diverse working-class high school. Sonja, whose work is also included in the next chapter, addresses a range of issues common to beginning teachers, particularly those associated with establishing classroom authority, and engages in honest and open reflection. But what makes this study particularly interesting is that she initially poses a broad-value issue, "who she is as a teacher," which in the end is reduced to a set of technical concerns.

Vicki's Study: Building Referent Power

While studying classroom culture, attention was given within the program to various sources of teacher power or influence. Four sources were identified, and research relating to each was read: (1) Referent power is based on the teacher's personality, the connection that comes from knowing about and caring for one another; (2) expert power is tied to respect for a teacher's knowledge and expertise; (3) legitimate power flows from the teacher's position within the institution as teacher; (4) coercive power comes from a teacher's ability to punish and dispense rewards. Vicki was interested in increasing her referent power. What is significant about Vicki's problem statement is that she understands management as a relationship problem, and not merely as a problem arising because of the lack of skills. We include portions of Vicki's study that followed her reformulation of the problem statement (the last part of #3 above).

Problem Statement

"[I recruited] a fellow cohort member [to do] observations to help identify a problem. These observations did reveal some management concerns, and upon reflection I identified some students who seemed to be very alienated, others who were 'testing the limits,' and still others who seemed to be engaged very minimally if at all. I wanted to develop a plan which preferably would address all of these concerns.

"At this point in student teaching, I am concerned with building referent power in the classroom. Amazing as it may seem, not every one of my students has come to love and adore me. Although I can live with this (I admit with chagrin that I don't love and adore every one of them, either), I sincerely believe that the establishment of referent power in my classroom will go a very long way toward preventing and/or eliminating most management problems.

"I have arrived at the decision to concentrate on this issue after considerable thought and a review of [some of our class readings]. I still feel fairly confident in my ability to maintain expert power. I am a strong advocate of my content area and attempt in all my lesson plans to make the subject and content relevant to the students. I am less comfortable with resorting to legitimate power, and at this point completely reject the idea of resorting to coercive power [to influence students]. I believe that a combination of referent and expert power is the most desirable method for [creating the kind of classroom climate I want]."

The Plan

"One way that I plan to address the issue of referent power is through holding individual conferences with each student. Since I am experiencing what I would characterize as management problems most noticeably with my fourth-period . . . class, I plan to try the individual conference approach with this group first.

"In these conferences, I plan to discuss several matters with each student. . . . First, I will discuss their grade so far this quarter, congratulate them on successes, make suggestions for improvement, and ask for their input and ideas. . . . I also plan to discuss the book they are currently reading in class and the type of books they enjoy reading and, if they would like, offer suggestions for future reading selections. I would also like to take this opportunity to find out more about each student, their attitudes, and interests and, if necessary, discuss any management concerns I may have. . . . I hope through this process to establish a more personal relationship with each student, thus bolstering referent power in the classroom.

"I have discussed this idea with my cooperating teacher, and she agrees that it is a good strategy for addressing the issue of referent power. She feels that this method of discussing concerns individually would be very beneficial and that it would also avoid calling undesirable and/or negative attention to any student by making [him or her] feel singled out for such a discussion. She thinks that individual conferencing could be accomplished while the rest of the class is doing group work, silent reading, or individual seat work.

"I have also had another cohort member do some peer observations of my fourth-period class to assist me in framing this problem. I plan to continue peer observations, particularly during the conferencing process. . . .

"My hope is that this process will enhance my rapport with the students, decrease power struggles and management problems, and create a classroom climate more conducive to learning."

Final Report

"Early in the quarter I identified the building of referent power as an objective for two major reasons. First, the establishment of referent power as opposed to legitimate or coercive power in the classroom is consistent with my philosophy of teaching and therefore comfortable and desirable to me. Second, I felt that the establishment of referent power in my classroom would go a very long way toward preventing and/or eliminating most management problems.

"Although there were only two or three students in any given class whom I considered to be causing significant disruption in the classroom, the approach I decided upon to begin building referent power was to conduct individual conferences with each student. My hope was that this process would enhance my rapport with the students, decrease power struggles and management problems, and create a classroom climate more conducive to learning. . . .

"I had a fellow cohort member, my cooperating teacher, and one of my university supervisors do observations during the individual conferences in fourth period. All three observed that although many students seemed fairly nervous at the beginning of the conference, at some point in the conference most loosened up and seemed to realize that I was not just a 'teacher figure,' but a fellow human being who is genuinely interested in them, their concerns, and their interests. The observation notes which I received would seem to confirm this assessment. My own perception of the conferences was that each student with whom I had a conference at least left [it] with the impression that I sincerely wanted them to succeed in my class.

"I was generally pleased with the outcome of the conferences. I observed most noticeably that the teacher/student relationship was altered in significant ways during these one-on-one conferences. We were able to relate to each other on a more personal and informal basis, and I feel that this really helped to build a more cooperative relationship with some of these students.

"Other observations during the quarter noted a comfortable 'ambience' or 'atmosphere' in my class. To me, this constituted a major accomplishment and improvement from the way things were. . . . The environment in the class felt better to me, and this feeling seemed to 'rub off' on the students. I also noted that many management problems, particularly in the fourth and sixth periods, decreased.

"During my planning and teaching, I attempted to keep the objective of referent power in mind while planning activities. . . . I did not want to build a positive personal relationship with the students at the expense of learning and academics. Some observation comments I received indicated that I was on the right track. From my cooperating teacher: 'I like your writing topics! They are thoughtful and interesting.' 'Everyone seems to be comfortable with you! Hooray! I heard some good ideas being discussed.' 'I think this is a really fun idea. They seem to understand the concept very well!' and 'I like the way you are always so positive with everyone. They seem to feel comfortable with you and the things you ask them to do.'

"As a final phase of this project, I wanted to get some student feedback. I designed an evaluation form which I had students in fourth and sixth periods fill out anonymously. This was really an exciting and satisfying part of the project for me. The questions which I felt applied most directly to the issue of referent power were Question #3: 'The thing I liked best about Mrs. Healy's teaching was . . .'; Question #4: 'One thing I think

Mrs. Healy could do to be a better teacher is . . .'; and Question #6: 'The thing I will remember the most about class this quarter is . . .'

"Many of the responses I received to Question #3 are very gratifying and lead me to believe that I have in fact achieved some success in establishing referent power in these classes. Some [of the responses to Question 3 follow.]

"The thing I liked best about Mrs. Healy's teaching was:

- 'The way she taught that made it fun.'
- 'She makes reading class more fun.'
- 'Made me feel more comfortable.'
- 'She was so cool; she was kick[ed] back, but she had us get the work done.'
- 'She is so nice and she really likes to teach.'
- 'She was nice, she explained things well, she was patient.'
- 'She is very nice and is patient, to help you understand things better.'
- 'Cool, laid-back environment.'
- 'She seems to care about you and [is] willing to help you.'
- 'She is nice. She makes this class fun.'

"Although most of the responses I received to Question #4 (such as 'I think she's a good teacher' and 'Nothing,' 'She was the best,' and 'I hope she works at [this school] next year') were highly complimentary and positive, I did find some of the suggestions for improvement . . . enlightening.

"One thing I think Mrs. Healy could do to be a better teacher is:

- 'Get the kids [to be] more controlled.'
- 'Be more strict. (She's too nice!)'
- 'Be more strict and tell the kids they need to stay in their seats and do their assignment. Just be more *strict.*'
- 'Not be so lenient.'

- 'More stricter [sic].'

"These responses indicate to me that many students are more comfortable with [high] structure and limits. I do realize that referent power is not the whole picture and that it can only go so far in maintaining order in the classroom. I plan to take these comments to heart. . . .

"I was also very gratified by many of the responses I received to Question #6.

"The thing I will remember the most about class this quarter is:

- 'It would be Mrs. Healy. She is cool.'
- 'Mrs. Healy and my friends.'
- 'I had a great teacher this quarter, Mrs. Healy.'

"I provided a space for additional student comments. Some I received were:

- 'Mrs. Healy, I think you did a really good job. Thanks for being such a good teacher.'
- 'Mrs. Healy is an awesome teacher.'
- 'Mrs. Healy has been a great teacher. She made this class fun for me!'

"Needless to say, these comments made my day and did go a long way toward helping me see this project as a success. However, as mentioned above, I did not merely want to make . . . class a 'fun' experience for the students. My desire was also that they actually learn something. Therefore, I also carefully perused the evaluation forms for indications that some learning had taken place and perhaps made a difference to the students. I was particularly interested in the responses to Question #1, 'What has been the best thing [about class] this quarter?' and Question #6, 'The thing I will remember the most about class this quarter is . . .' Out of 31 evaluation forms I received, 25 of them listed an item which we had studied or something we had learned in their responses to one or both of these questions. Although I am of course delighted by the students who stated that they liked me and referred to the enjoyable atmosphere in the classroom, I am exceedingly pleased that the majority of them also chose to remember and refer to some of the learning activities. . . .

"I am very glad I conducted this project. It helped me to reflect on my teaching in a way I know I would not have done otherwise. Although I am pleased with the progress I have made in achieving referent power in the classroom, I feel I still have a long way to go. As some of the student comments revealed, I need to 'fine-tune' my management style and achieve more of a balance between 'laid-back' and 'strict.' I want to be able to indicate a genuine interest and friendship for the students without being seen as a pushover or a patsy. In my first year of teaching, I would like to set some specific goals and objectives for establishing and maintaining both order and a comfortable ambience in my classroom (promoting learning all the while, of course)."

Identity and Classroom Presence: Sonja's Study

Initial Problem Description

"As I have taught my junior and senior English classes, the one situation that continually concerns me is classroom management. I have learned many things already that have helped me to improve my management skills, such as better pacing . . . speaking loudly and clearly, waiting for students to quiet down, and adjusting the curriculum to keep the attention of the class. I find that even as I teach, I think of some new way to better the lesson. . . . Sometimes I leave [the classroom] frustrated, but I realize that I am going through a process and learning what will work. . . .

"In trying to combat management problems, I have sought the advice of my cooperating teachers [but] they are very different and have different philosophies on student discipline. I have found much of their advice very helpful and have applied some of it. However, I began to realize that I needed to find my own philosophy and my own way of dealing with management problems. . . . On the one hand, I feel that I need to be firm and show the students I will not put up with nonsense. On the other hand, I want to have a caring and friendly relationship with students."

This statement was read by one of the cohort leaders, and on it written: "Gee, Sonja, these are huge, broad, issues. Can you focus more sharply on just a piece . . . a small but crucial part of what troubles you?" A discussion followed to help Sonja begin to think through what a problem statement might be. She began to gather data that would help her focus her study. As a result of listening to audiotapes of her teaching and watching a videotape taken by her husband, and feedback from her cooperating and supervising teachers, Sonja reconsidered the problem. Management was not the central issue: Sonja was struggling with her identity as a teacher.

Revised Problem Statement and Plan of Action

"Although at times I am excited about my teaching, I am not completely the teacher I want to be. I feel that I am starting to find myself as a teacher. Before I started student teaching, I didn't realize how long it would take to develop an identity as a teacher. . . . Sometimes I have held back because I was afraid that if I demonstrated too many emotions or too much of a personality, the students would take advantage of me. I have also held back because I do not always know what type of [teacher] I want to be in front of the classroom.

"In order to allow my personality to develop, I need to put myself more into the classroom and become a presence. . . . I am trying to use my voice more. It is difficult sometimes for me to walk among the students and come out from behind the pulpit or from behind the table. It takes a conscious effort for me to walk among the students; sometimes I forget that I need to reach out to them physically. . . .

"In order to further develop my . . . presence in the classroom I have [made] a plan of action. . . . In order to make my presence felt in the beginning of class or during transitions, I [will] wait until I have every person's attention before I start to explain what is due or the lesson for the day. In each lesson, I [will] write, in bold letters, notes to remind me to move throughout the room and to better use my voice. I will continue practicing certain pieces of literature at home with expression before I [read] them in front of my class. . . . I will continue . . . recording [my classes] in order to better evaluate my voice [which is weak and uncertain]. I will also have my husband videotape me [again] in order to assess my movement [throughout the classroom]."

There is a great deal going on in Sonja's mind and in her classroom. She is uncertain who she is or wants to be. She feels uneasy with students, but is reluctant to engage them as a person. She recognizes that she is not seen by the students as an authority figure, nor does she see herself in that role. She observes that she acts differently depending on how the students respond to her. As she contemplates these discoveries and how she wants to address them, she determines that her first efforts must be directed toward engaging the students, toward becoming a "presence" in the classroom. She understood the issue technically, that what she needed to do was to move around the classroom, speak up, and better plan her transitions. These actions, she thought, would increase her authority in the classroom. The crucial issue of identity, of who Sonja is as teacher, is lost, at least for the time being.

Sonja implemented her plan and continued to gather and analyze data. A few days after student teaching ended, she turned in her final report.

Action Research Results

"My . . . project consisted of better using voice and movement in the classroom to establish a stronger teacher presence [in the classroom]. . . . I chose to use videotapes, feedback from students and my cooperating teachers . . . as data to assess where I was and how I was improving.

"The videotapes were especially revealing. . . . After watching the first videotape . . . I realized how unauthoritative and weak I sounded at times. I was too tentative when I gave an assignment or when I asked for students' attention. My voice became weaker sometimes when I was making a request, not stronger as it should [have been]. One weak point that I noticed in the video was when I told [a] student to be quiet. I did not sound firm. It seemed that I was almost afraid of telling him to quiet down. I have worked on this area as well, and I have become more firm.

"Frequently I did not wait for the class's full attention before I gave an assignment. Consequently I found myself constantly repeating directions for assignments. This wasted a great deal of time. . . .

"[After implementing my plan of action] I started waiting a little longer for the class to quiet down. I also began warning the class before I gave an assignment that I would only mention it once, and if they missed it, they would have to find out about it from someone else. Once they realized I was serious, they started to quiet down. I realize now that I cannot take responsibility for everything the student should do. If a student does not take the time to make up an assignment, I do not have the time to continually check with the student. I would help students in any way I could, but I feel by taking on the students' responsibilities, I only . . . make them more dependent on me. . . .

"From the video, I realized that I had another problem with voice. I repeated the word 'OK' a lot, which seemed to demonstrate that I was tentative about giving the lecture or the assignment. It definitely did not add to sounding more authoritative. I also paused several times in my speech adding an 'umm,' 'uh,' or such. This also gave the appearance of being unorganized although I had carefully planned the lesson.

"I also realized that I needed more movement in the classroom. I didn't realize how much I stayed to the front of the classroom or how isolated I looked until I watched the first videotape. I stayed in front of the classroom the entire time and frequently my back was to the students because I was writing on the board. I would talk while I was writing on the board, and it sounded a little mumbled. . . . I now realize how important eye contact is between the teacher and students. . . . As I viewed this tape I realized how important it is that when a student answers a question, I give feedback clearly by looking directly at the student and responding . . . promptly. This too, I now realize, is an important part of teacher presence. . . . By isolating myself at the front of the classroom, I was unaware of how much talking was going on while I was giving a lecture. I was stranded in front of the classroom because I had to write constantly on the board. . . . I was surprised how much extra talking the video showed was going on. I realized from watching it that there were times when I was competing with it. [Handouts helped.] . . .

"[Students] lost an increasingly large amount of interest in the subject matter because the lesson was too long. I should have broken the grammar down into chunks [and varied my instruction to increase interest]. I later did this and found more success in so doing.

"Before I had the students turn their papers in at midterm, I had them write an evaluation of their goals and things that we could do in class to help them. [This was part of the data I gathered]. I received a great deal of good feedback. One student said that she felt it would be better if I broke the period down into different lessons so she could better stay attentive. . . . Based on this evaluation . . . [I adjusted my plan].

"After trying to improve . . . my teacher presence by better using my voice and movement, I [was videotaped again]. After watching this video I could see a great deal of improvement. Immediately I realized how much stronger my voice was. . . . I sounded much more firm and authoritative. I noticed that in the first video it seemed that I felt embarrassed to walk among the students. I looked much more confident. . . . I moved a great deal more. . . . I saw more life in my face. [Wanting] to make the material come alive for the students [I varied my instruction]. . . . Overall, I was greatly improved.

"In this video there were several times when the students wanted to know about previous assignments that they had missed, but I quickly told them to speak with me after class, and I moved on with the lesson. This kept me from losing my train of thought. . . . I didn't have as many 'umms' and 'uhs' in my voice. I had more eye contact with students, and I picked on a variety of students rather than completely allowing only a few students to speak out. I made an effort to include all the class.

". . . [W]e read . . . together. Instead of allowing the students to volunteer, I picked on several of the students. Frequently I chose a student who was not paying attention. I also moved around the class as the students read and checked to see who was reading [along]. I noticed that as I walked by some students, they suddenly appeared more interested. I also saw myself wake up some students that were falling asleep. . . . I glanced several times around the room to see if the students were following along."

Commentary

Sonja's study illustrates how problem definitions evolve. She begins with a very general and common problem, classroom management. By gathering data she comes to see her management problems as associated with other problems, insecurity and lack of a clear teacher identity. Lack of identity is tied to a lack of classroom presence, and presence, in turn, is linked to her lack of enthusiasm, lack of movement in the classroom, and "weak voice." These latter issues are ones she can address directly, and the results of her efforts are quickly apparent.

The decision to gather data through videotaping proved crucial for Sonja. She could see her face, hear her voice, and witness herself hiding behind the desk and avoiding students. This data, along with the observations of her cooperating teachers, helped her focus her energies. Although it is not fully apparent in either Sonja's study or Vicki's, ongoing and extensive conversation about these issues was extremely important to understanding their problems and, ultimately, to how they addressed them.

Sonja's study also illustrates, however, how some very important issues can be lost if care is not taken. Sonja's concerns for identity and to build a philosophy of management are overwhelmed by the quest for means to gain greater classroom control. She appears frightened of the students, fearful of revealing herself to them. They may reject her. Rather than risk revealing who she is, Sonja explores techniques for being more "teacherlike." Questions of philosophy introduced in the initial problem statement, where she sought a balance between an approach to management that was "caring" and one that was "firm" and no-nonsense, are set aside for learning techniques of control, ways of getting students to, as she puts it, "quiet down." Firm wins out. Sonja wants to sound "authoritative" and this is her aim.

Sonja's concerns are legitimate ones. We would not want to discount the importance of various teaching skills to producing a productive learning climate. The issue, however, is one of purpose. The study illustrates that Sonja did become more of a "presence" in the classroom and, apparently, students were more respectful of her, but for what purpose? Classroom control and classroom management are not ends in and of themselves. And one wonders if the firm, no-nonsense presence Sonja began to create was one that represented an authentic expression of who she is as a person and wants to be as a teacher. Sonja needs to address these issues if Action Research is to be something more than a way to accommodate to institutional role demands.

Vicki's study presents an important contrast. She too is concerned about management, but management, as she conceives of it, is about relationships not control. Rather than seek to withdraw into a teacher presence, Vicki seeks means for breaking down barriers in the belief that the more she can relate to students as persons, the more likely learning will take place. The few students who want a "more stricter" Mrs. Healy illustrate the power of institutional roles to shape teacher and student behavior. Because Mrs. Healy does not fit the strict teacher role the students are used to, they encourage her to change, and perhaps she will adjust somewhat. But it is uncertain what the students actually mean when they request more strictness. This would need to be explored before any changes were undertaken. In the light of this additional information, Vicki would need to decide if she will or should change. However, the study does illustrate that Vicki desires a different role, one more consistent with her view of herself as a person. The tension Vicki feels is also felt by Sonja, but she seeks technical rather than interpersonal means for increasing her power. One wonders if, in the process of accommodating, she will form the authentic identity she wants.

The ultimate question for Sonja is who she will be as a teacher and whether or not the context of schooling will allow her to be that kind of teacher. Perhaps eventually she will be able to shape the context in ways necessary to achieve an authentic teaching self. Until this question is answered, the context of teaching will prove overpowering.

Both teachers honestly and openly explore their teaching. They seem committed to the ongoing study of their practice even though they realize that at times the struggle to improve will be painful and compromises necessary. Both studies contain strong evidence of increasing understanding about teaching, of a willingness to listen to and to learn from students and others, and of growing confidence about their ability to become effective teachers and direct their own development. This said, both realize that they are just beginning their professional journeys and that much remains to be learned. Sonja ended her study with these words: "I feel that I am making progress in my profession. . . . I realize, though, that I need to carry this self-analysis on when I have my own classroom. . . . I want to continue to be a student of my [practice]."

A Note to Teacher Educators and Students

Critics of Action Research have raised a wide range of issues. Goodson (1991), for example, observes that if teachers and teacher educators seek collaborative relationships, Action Research may disappoint. Goodson's concern is that by placing teacher practice at the center of action, Action Research "focuses on the maximum point of vulnerability" (1991:141). He suggests that "a more valuable and less vulnerable entry point would be to examine teachers' work in the context of teachers' lives" (1991:141). The point is a good one, as Sonja's project suggests, and underscores the importance of thinking about the methodologies presented in *Becoming a Student of Teaching* in relationship to one another and to in-service teacher education. Action Research comes after our students have engaged in a good deal of self and context study and after a reasonably good level of trust, a feeling of community, has been developed within the cohort group.

Gore and Zeichner (1991) raise other issues that deserve attention. There are comparatively few studies of the use of

Action Research in preservice teacher education. The results show that for the most part, Action Research helps beginning teachers be more thoughtful about their teaching, "aware of their own practices and of the gaps between their beliefs and their practices . . . and . . . of their pupils' thinking and learning" (Gore & Zeichner, 1991:131). These are very positive outcomes evident in the two studies we presented. However, and referring to their own work, there is a disappointing lack of evidence that Action Research addresses contextual, political, and ethical issues. Beginning teachers, like Sonja, are generally consumed with practical questions and only rarely address wider contextual issues. We generally agree, but some of our students, like Vicki, do consider wider issues. Student teachers in our program have studied the moral implications of teacher bias and favoritism: "I knew without a doubt that I tended to favor smart white girls, and was biased against loudmouthed boys of any race." Student power: "Who really runs the classroom?" Student dependency: "I felt the students were too dependent on my opinion of their work or progress on an art project. They are not talking to each other about art questions." The nature of evaluation: "For those of us raised in an industrialized society the tendency to apply ourselves to a simple standard of measure is overwhelming. We have been eager to buy unconditionally the economists' pitch that innovation and competition would solve our problems. . . . To serve the interests of the simple economic standard of productivity, we have been waging, and winning, a war against our own people and our own land. . . . I find myself all too easily succumbing to an all too simple standard of measure." Class size and student learning: "There seems to be an ongoing debate over the effects of class size on the classroom and student performance. . . . Teachers contend a class with fewer students is a better atmosphere for [teaching] and thus leads to better learning." These are among the many issues that reach beyond the more common technical issues and concerns of beginning teachers and in which contextual, political, and ethical questions are posed.

Issues: Beginning Teacher Frustration

Sometimes beginning teachers are put off by the word, *research* and are a bit threatened by the term *theory*. This uneasiness is not unusual, as Garth Boomer observes:

> We cannot remove the semantic dye into which "research" has been plunged. It is almost impossible to give it the "small *r*" meaning. It has accumulated connotations of validity, generalizability, objectivity, and control, which get in the way of those of us who want it simply to mean "finding out in order to act more effectively." (1987:7)

Additional difficulty, as we have noted, arises because of the pressures associated with practice teaching. Student teachers are tired, stressed, and often frustrated. Given these feelings, a good many resist the idea of formally studying their practice. They want to teach, and teaching is not about researching practice, or so some assume. *Becoming a Student of Teaching* is based on a different and contrary view, that teaching, as Stenhouse suggests, is researching.

Despite many of our students' initial resistance to Action Research, once the process gets underway their attitudes usually change. "Once again," one of our students wrote in her final Action Research report, "you have pushed me to do something I did not want to do, and I am grateful. Yes, student teaching is a lot of work [even] without having to [do] other projects, but I would have not learned as much [as I did]." Another initially disgruntled student wrote: "As I look forward to [my first year of] teaching next fall, I continue to have many concerns about my development as a teacher; the experience [of conducting an Action Research study] has helped me to see that I need to continually study . . . teaching. I need to think critically about how I prepare lessons and the effects [of my teaching] on students. I think it is necessary to continue gathering data on how I teach. If this assignment has done nothing else, it has taught me to view my [work] critically and to look for ways to improve daily."

Action Research *is* a lot of work, especially when it is understood as an addition to teaching and not integral to it. Yet, Action Research represents, formally, what reflective teachers or teacher researchers do informally, and that is study their practice. It is part of the quest to become self-conscious about teaching. Understood as a cyclical and ongoing process, as Elliott (1991) characterizes it, Action Research is a means for beginning teachers to more quickly escape the vicissitudes and frustrations attendant to trial-and-error approaches to learning to teach, to muddling through, that are commonly associated with the first years of teaching (Bullough, 1989).

Issues: Data Gathering

The data sources we listed could easily be expanded: Field notes, anecdotal records, diaries, logs, portfolios, photographs and slides, and cooperating teacher observations are all useful sources depending on the problems being addressed. Whatever sources of data are identified, it is crucially important that ethical issues about data gathering be addressed beforehand and that careful consideration be given to potential dangers inherent in some sources of data and their use. In addition, some sources of data are intrusive and potentially disruptive. Already we have mentioned that videotaping is sometimes disruptive to a class, but also to a teacher.

> I chose [to] videotape my teaching, and I can assure you it was frightening! I am glad [I did it], as it was very interesting and helpful; however, I feel that the experience was somewhat negative because of the affect of the camera in the classroom. I felt slightly intimidated by the camera, as did the students such that normal classroom behavior was altered, and the "natural" rapport between the students and myself "stiffened."

Videotaping is a rich source of data, but students and teachers need to get used to the camera's presence.

Issues: Plan Implementation

Once a plan is made, some of our students have difficulty implementing it. Again, the pressures of practice teaching get in the way.

> I would like to speak of a major difficulty I have encountered with [my study]. . . . The difficulty is that once I [made my plan] of self-examination, it [was] extraordinarily difficult to remember to [implement] it. I would begin class . . . and, typically, within about 20 seconds I would have forgotten to do it. It is absolutely extraordinary what little willpower I have. . . . Indeed, the realization of just how unconscious I am of what I am [doing] is shocking. This explains the "video effect" that occurs when one sees a videotape of oneself and exclaims, "Who is that?"

For some of our students, more careful planning has helped ameliorate this difficulty, including written reminders, like Sonja's, of what actions are supposed to be undertaken. For others, cooperating teachers have been invaluable sources for making certain the plans get implemented and that habits are set aside. Half-time practice teaching also helps.

Issues: Sharing Results

It is crucially important that time be made available, perhaps in the student teaching seminar, for sharing the studies as they unfold and not just the results. Assuming a reasonably good level of trust, sharing is a means for helping identify and usefully frame problems for study, for exploring issues associated with data gathering and use, for reconsidering initial hunches and results, and for strengthening community. Our experience has been that, generally speaking, beginning teacher concerns are more common than not and that much can be learned by openly and honestly exploring them. Minimally, beginning teachers are reminded that they are not alone, as they sometimes may feel, that they are not the only ones struggling, and that others can and will help.

CHAPTER NINE

Creating a Personal Teaching Text

Introduction

Through *Becoming a Student of Teaching* we have sought to provide an alternative to training views of teacher education and development. The methodologies described have the potential to enhance beginning teacher reflectivity and the development of a professional community. This potential, however, will be lost if the methodologies are viewed as disconnected and discrete techniques to be laid out sequentially, side by side, like a row of hurdles. Instead, they need to be connected, and closure needs to be provided at crucial transitional points in the program. As Buchmann and Floden (1992) remind us, teacher education is unlikely to have much impact on beginning teacher development if it lacks coherence and remains fragmented.

The cohort organization, where students stay together in a group, is an important but partial step toward overcoming fragmentation and providing program coherence. This administrative arrangement, which puts beginning teachers and teacher educators together for extended periods of time, must be complemented with changes in the form and content of the teacher education curriculum. Clearly, unless content is carefully integrated and efforts are made to provide closure, fragmentation will remain a problem despite the cohort organization.

The creation and use of a personal teaching text (PTT) has proven to be a powerful means for addressing this problem and for helping beginners to reflect on their experience (Bullough, 1993). The PTT builds on a number of innovations currently being explored in teacher education, including portfolios and student journals. Like portfolios, PTTs encourage beginning teachers to put together an array of products that in some fashion illuminate their teacher education experience. However, PTTs differ because portfolios are typically created for the purpose of demonstrating to some external body, like a certification agency or board, that a standard of one kind or another has been met. In contrast, we are interested in teacher development and in helping beginners "hear the voice of their own experiences" (Munby & Russell, 1993:11), not external evaluation. It is this difference, a fundamental and largely incompatible difference in purpose, that distinguishes PTTs from portfolios.

Conceptually, PTTs also draw on the use of student journals as a means for encouraging writing and thinking about one's experience within teacher education (Berry et al., 1991). The aim of student journals is usually to further development of some kind by identifying and describing significant events on a somewhat regular basis. In this sense, they have much in common with PTTs. However, the writing contained in journals is often narrowly introspective and unfocused, and seldom are attempts made to critically consider the relationship of one entry to another. Furthermore, as Knowles (1991) observes, beginning teachers often find the time demands of journal keeping prohibitive. Our acute awareness of these problems prompted consideration of alternatives. A third source of insight came from the use of cases in other fields, especially medicine. Nurses, for example, are taught to construct case records of their patients, histories of treatment and of patient response to treatment, that enable decision making. But in nursing, those who gather the material and assess it are different from those whose records or materials are included in the record; again we encounter the problem of external evaluation. In contrast, personal teaching texts require those gathering the data to assess it.

All written assignments generated by the methodologies presented in the preservice section of *Becoming a Student of Teaching,* along with any additional written work deemed appropriate, are placed chronologically in a binder which forms a case record (Yin, 1984), a text, of each student's development over the course of our program. Throughout the year the students are encouraged to read the materials contained in the PTT and consider what they have written and where they are in their development and thinking about teaching. They write reviews of the PTT generally near the end of each quarter, and at year's end. The reviews are occasions to critically examine one's development as a teacher, to celebrate accomplishments, to identify areas of concern that need attention, and to plan for the future.

Writing

One of the recent end-of-year review assignments read as follows:

> Reread the contents of your personal teaching text for the entire year. Based upon this reading, assess your development as a teacher. Are you pleased with what you have accomplished this year? Any disappointments? Has your resolve to become a teacher strengthened or weakened? Why? Has your view of yourself as a teacher changed during the course of the year? If so, what has prompted the change? If not, why not? Are you on course for becoming the kind of teacher you imagine yourself capable of becoming? Be specific, and give examples.

Each review encourages the beginning teacher to think carefully about his or her professional development—past, present, and future. Comparing reviews enables beginning teachers to see the progress many of them make over the year.

Three edited and abbreviated reviews follow. Each was written by the same beginning English teacher, Sonja, whose work was included in the previous chapter. These reviews were chosen for inclusion in *Becoming a Student of Teaching* for three reasons primarily: Sonja addresses a range of issues common to beginning teachers; they show a beginning teacher seriously examining her experience during the program; and they indicate growth and change in thinking, but uncertainty remains.

We should note that some beginning teachers choose to organize their reviews around specific program activities and their impact, while others organize them around the specific questions asked. Capturing the spirit of the task, still others write essays that focus on questions and issues of concern that range rather widely, reaching beyond the PTT entries. Regardless of the approach selected, the purpose of the reviews is to reflect on one's experience in relationship to one's personal and professional teaching ideals.

First Review: Fading Innocence

[December 10, at the end of the first quarter:] As I review my personal teaching text and the experiences I have had as I have studied to become a teacher, I realize that I have developed and changed my philosophy [about] what type of teacher I am going to be. I have seen some approaches [to teaching] work and many approaches I thought would work, fail. I have become aware of many negative aspects of teaching which would have been very discouraging if I had not also [encountered many] positive aspects [of teaching] that overshadowed the negative.

[The] life history . . . was an important assignment for me because I was able to reflect on the reasons why I have chosen to become a teacher. Prior to this paper I had reminisced about my life history, and reflected on how certain events had changed my life, but I had never pieced together several episodes in my life in order to assess why I had chosen [this] particular path. Once I started writing my life history, the words flowed. I felt such emotion that I even started to cry as I wrote about some of the events of my life. Sometimes memories dim, but through writing them down I was able to recapture how I felt. . . .

[My] life history was what inspired me to choose my teaching metaphor. I started to reflect on the times when I had no one to turn to and no one to defend me from the cruelties of other students. I chose the metaphor of "defender." As I visited the classrooms of my cooperating teachers, I began to realize that I could not simply sit with a stick in my hand and ward off every attacker. . . . I realized that I would have to teach them to defend each other. After doing my classroom ethnography . . . I realized that in order to teach them to help each other, they first must learn to defend and value themselves. I added the metaphor of "nurturer" to that of defender. I now realize that I must fill my classroom with caring in order to nurture the students. I am beginning to understand how carefully I need to construct not only the intellectual and emotional characteristics of the classroom, but the physical environment as well. I noticed in my ethnography how the physical appearance of the classroom had been altered to provide a nurturing atmosphere. I feel that I am obligated to help the students by providing ways for them to develop self-esteem and self-motivation. Once students are empowered with these qualities, they will be more prepared to defend and protect others.

As I considered seriously becoming a teacher, I thought that I would take the role of a friend to the students, an equal, someone who understood what they were going through. I could see myself joking with them and being a part of their groups. Because I was close to the age of the students, not long out of high school myself, and because I had siblings their ages, I felt that I could treat them as equals. After observing . . . classes for the ethnography . . . and watching videos of other [beginning teachers], I realized that if I tried to be too friendly I would soon lose control of the classroom. When I substituted for [my cooperating teacher] on December 1 (this was part of an assignment), I realized that I could not have a "peer" relationship with the students. As I substituted . . . I had to constantly monitor the students in order to keep them on task. I had previously assumed they would work hard for me because I could relate to them as a "peer." I was surprised at how obstinate one particular girl was. . . . When I walked up to her and asked if she was working on the assignment, she said she had completed it. I told her [that the teacher's] instructions were that they were supposed to [keep working on the text]. She replied that she was tired of doing it. I told her she had better work on it. I was surprised by the resentful, almost hateful look she gave me. I didn't anticipate this kind of reaction when I had fantasized about myself as a teacher or when I had observed other classrooms. I think I partially developed this notion of being a "peer" to the students because several times when I had done observations I had been mistaken for a student by other students and some adults. I felt like I was one of them. Also, as a student myself, I could relate to [them].

When I did my Shadow Study, I picked an honors student. She was much more mature than many other students, and I was able to relate to her more on an adult level. She reminded me of myself and the type of people I formed relationships with in high school. . . . [She] felt I was "one of them." Contrary to these assumptions . . . I found that it was quite a different feeling to be up in front of the class. Once in front of the class, the students treated me differently. . . .

While preparing to become a teacher, I encountered some disappointments. . . . I found pessimism and skepticism in some of the teachers I interviewed. Some teachers were burned out with teaching. . . . I realized that some students were antagonistic towards school, but I had the impression that these teachers felt that the majority of students did not enjoy learning in school, and that they constantly had to "force feed" them. During my teacher interview with [one of my cooperating teachers] I was dismayed when I learned how she felt about some aspects of teaching. Her question to me was troubling: "Can I do this for the next 25 years of my life?" I was fearful of developing [a negative attitude] as a beginning teacher. I dreamed of walking out of the classroom each day [after teaching] feeling rewarded for the things that I had accomplished and knowing the students appreciated my efforts. Instead, in my interview, I confronted a teacher who told me that the students would take advantage of me whenever they had the opportunity. . . .

My other cooperating teacher . . . told me that the only way he could survive teaching and the stress that goes with it was to have fun. When I did my ethnography . . . I began to understand what he meant. . . . He would make jokes with [students] and talk to them about their lives. This alleviated stress for the students because they felt more relaxed and thus opened up; it also alleviated the stress on [him] because he was able to develop a relationship with the students based on humor which allowed him to shape and guide the students without the tensions and rebellions that [usually] follow. . . . I have always wanted to have a sense of humor while interacting with students. I feel that because I am younger [than most beginning teachers], it may be more difficult for the students to take me seriously and therefore I need to be firm and control the relationship that I have with them. I am concerned about finding a balance between establishing a firm classroom and creating a relaxed climate in which students feel they can participate openly and freely.

I am pleased with the progress I have made towards becoming . . . a good teacher. Although some of my idealism has been [lost], I feel that some of the more negative responses I have heard about the "reality of teaching" are only realities in the minds of those who speak them. I feel that I am capable of being a good teacher. As I watch the videotapes of former student teachers, I realize that the purpose of [teacher education] is to discover new ways and objectives of teaching, improve what I already know, and change that which I feel is detrimental to myself and my students. I feel that as I have probed my past, reflected on my present state, and projected myself into the future, I have become more secure in what type of teacher I want to be. . . . I know that I am on the right track for becoming the kind of teacher that I want to be, I just need to go through a few more towns.

Second Review: Getting to Know Students

[March 11, following the "short course" (a three-week unit taught to a single class during winter term):] After reading through my personal teaching text, it is as if it has been several years since I first wrote my educational life history. I have changed so much. As I read through the work from fall quarter to the present, I realized that I see my role as a teacher from a "real" perspective versus an "artificial" perspective. I see myself less idealistic and more practical, although I feel even more excited to delve into teaching.

After reading my writings before [the] short course, I found myself wanting to make comments in the margins of my own papers and express to myself all that I had learned.

Everything that I had put in my papers to that point was merely observations of an outsider. Now I really am starting to feel that I am a real teacher, and I feel that I have a right to consider myself part of the teaching profession.

As I read through my life history I realized that I did not always see in each of my students a reflection of myself during the short course. A couple of the girls I had were "jocks." This type of student has always bothered me throughout my own educational experience, and I found myself judging [such] girls through my experience. . . . I didn't have much patience with them, although I never voiced this. . . . I didn't realize before how difficult it can be not to be judgmental and compare these students to others who were troublesome to me in my secondary school years. On the other hand, there was another student for whom I felt a great deal of compassion. I think I felt this way mainly because he was so shy. I was a very shy student. He never gave me any problems. Throughout the course I found myself really wanting him to succeed. . . . I wanted all of my students to succeed, but I felt more compassion for him. His image haunted me. . . .

I am really beginning to see the reality of what [my cooperating teacher said in my interview with her]. I remember her talking about her relationships with her students. I feel a bond with the students I taught even though I only taught them for three weeks. I also remember [her] talking about the more negative aspects of teaching. She said she was tired of the games the students played and how they would try to take advantage of her. I did find this to be true, even in the short time I taught. . . . [Still,] I am very anxious to go back into the classroom and teach them. . . .

After reading through my other assignments such as the mundane models [where we described how our cooperating teachers accomplished the mundane tasks of teaching, like collecting homework and handling late papers], I realized how little I really understood the realities of paperwork. . . . I didn't realize how makeup work could become such a problem. In my short course it seems I had more makeup work than the actual work I had assigned. . . . When I read about the distractions that teachers often face in the classroom, I had no idea how irritating they could be. . . . I was interrupted several times by people pulling students out, announcements, late students, and students who had to be excused from class for one reason or another. Each time I would lose my train of thought and my lesson would suffer. . . .

I am pleased with what I have accomplished. I now know that I can stand in front of a class and teach a lesson and that I can do it competently. I am pleased about the relationship that I have been able to develop with my students. I am excited about developing my sense of humor and presence in the classroom. Before, when I only read about these concepts, I really didn't understand what it meant to have a "presence" in the classroom. With each day of teaching I developed that presence more. I am realizing that although I have not changed my initial personality, I am also developing another aspect of my personality, one that is only revealed in the classroom. I am pleased with this personality so far, although I realize that I need to develop more discipline and management [skills].

My biggest disappointment came from students who did not do the homework and who tried to cheat or get away with doing as little as possible. . . .

My initial teaching metaphor has not necessarily changed, but I have expanded it. I feel that a teacher is many things. When I first wrote about metaphors, I saw myself as a defender [of students]. I think a great deal of this stemmed from my experiences in education and my review of those experiences in my life history. I did not have anyone to defend me in some of my darkest times during my junior high school experience, and I really felt that I needed to be there for my students. As the quarter progressed, I started to see myself as a nurturer. As I observed the teachers and the way they nurtured their students through joking with them and helping them to feel important, I realized that in order to defend my students and to teach them to defend others, they would have to be nurtured first. As I began winter quarter and began working with my cooperating teachers, I realized that a [student] could not benefit from nurturing if he or she was not motivated to accept the nurturing. Finally, after my short course my perspective changed because I became a part of the students' environment, not just an observer of that environment. I developed a feeling of concern for my students and also a responsibility for teaching them that they are important. My metaphor then expanded to include the roles of "caretaker" and "self-esteem lifter." . . . As I look back on my experience now, I also see other metaphors emerging. Although I am not a parent, I think that the way I feel about my students is similar to the feeling of a parent [for his or her] children: although I was often disappointed because I knew they could do better, I still was concerned about them and felt responsible to help them succeed. I didn't expect to get attached to them so quickly. . . . During the . . . short course, I ran into students on two different occasions outside of class. It was kind of neat to see them outside of class. . . .

I think my greatest concern right now is putting together a policy for classroom management [for student teaching] that I can give to the students. I have an idea of how I will do it already. . . .

Third Review: Teaching Is Difficult

[Saturday, June 5, a day after completing practice teaching:] After reviewing my personal teaching text for the year and reflecting on my experience, I have realized that I have really changed and developed throughout the . . . year. . . . I have undergone a complete transformation. . . .

My ideas of what a teacher was and what a teacher did when I first stepped into the program were very naive compared to what I now know. Of course, I realize that when I read [these words] after a few years of teaching, I will think of this writing as only [preliminary and incomplete].

[A]t the beginning of the [program] I felt that with the help of other future teachers like myself, I could transform the nation. Although I still feel that I would like to be part of improving our nation through teaching, I now see it [differently]. I hope that many students will find new insights from my teaching, but I also realize that many will not be significantly changed by being in my class, because they are unwilling to [change]. Throughout my student teaching I felt so much responsibility for the students. I felt responsible to entertain, uplift, and inspire them. I felt that if they missed any assignments, it was my responsibility to see that they made them up. . . .

During my student teaching, I began to realize that . . . I could not be responsible for [seeing that every student does every assignment]. I spent hours grading and talking to the students about what assignments they were missing. I soon found that the time I spent trying to help some students with their grades was wasted by the student arguing about his/her grade and not about what he/she could do to improve it. These students wanted me to be responsible for [their performance]. . . . Earlier in my grading practices description (an assignment that required them to meet with their cooperating teacher and discuss grading and then write a description of how their cooperating teachers graded student work), I decided that I would follow a portfolio format [as a way] to deal with late and makeup work. I felt that much of this problem would be eliminated by the portfolio format. I decided, however, that I needed to have the students turn in the portfolios more frequently in order to assess their [work]. During student teaching I found that I no sooner had the students turn in the folders for midterm [grading], [than] it was time to turn them in again for finals. . . .

I realize that in order to become a better teacher and further develop myself, I need to learn to adapt to each situation. Sometimes this adaptation requires developing a defense mechanism so as not to allow students to destroy the identity that the teacher has created. . . . In the beginning, I identified my first personal teaching metaphor as that of a defender. . . . [Since then] I found that I had to defend myself against the games and tactics of the students. Certain students would continually attack my curriculum. I had one girl in particular who would whine at everything. When I had the class do a unit on short story writing, she complained continually. One day she walked up to me before class and asked me why we were writing in this English class. I told her that it was an English class and that writing was important because it would help her in all aspects of her life. She said that she had never had to write in class, that she only had read. . . . Although I feel that many students benefitted [from what we did], this girl still continued to complain about everything. When I finally gave out grades, she complained that she was getting a "D." She felt that if she simply turned everything in, she would receive a high grade. I explained that the quality was important and that if the assignment was half-done, it was not going to receive the full points.

At times I wondered if my expectations were too high. . . . Sometimes I allowed myself to believe that the rest of the class felt the same way [as she did], and that I was [overly] strict and defensive [as a result]. [Learning] what the other students felt [helped] me to overcome this feeling. . . . I had them write evaluations of the class [as part of my Action Research project]. . . . Many of the students gave critical but positive feedback about things that I could do that would help, such as doing several activities during the long period rather than one the entire [time]. After reading [their comments], I sat down with the class one day and talked about the problems we were having and [shared] what I expected from them and what I would try to do to better the situation. From that point on, I found that I had the support of several of the students. In fact, when the one girl continually whined about the assignments, other students would tell her to be quiet. . . .

I am a perfectionist, and I always felt that everything had to be very precise in my grading practices. I still feel that [I must keep track of] everything. . . . But I realize that I need to learn shortcuts and time-saving techniques. My cooperating teacher told me not to stress so much over the little things. I think that with time I will be able to define what the little things are and what the big things are. I have improved in this area. During my short course I felt that I had to keep track of who was absent each day and personally give the student the assignment. Toward the end of student teaching, I had copies of the assignments and passed them out to those missing them. When I begin teaching, I will have folders that will have each assignment for each day, and the student will only need to go to that folder to find what he/she is missing. Many of the improvements I will make will be in the area of [getting better organized]. . . . I feel that part of my organization problem was not feeling that I really owned the classroom and not feeling that I could organize my things in the classroom. Toward the end of my student teaching I created a space for a box in which to turn in makeup work and extra credit. I realize now the importance of the ethnography assignment. [A classroom has a culture] and it is important [for me] to take ownership of the classroom, [to take responsibility for setting] the atmosphere. . . .

With [better] organization and understanding, which I will continually develop, I will be able to attend to the needs of my students. I simply found myself so tied up in . . . management [problems] and [the] whining of a few students that I felt that to some degree I neglected the needs of other students. [I did little nurturing]. . . .

I didn't realize how difficult it would be to motivate students. I felt that if I had enthusiasm for the subject matter, the students would also be motivated. . . . I often had a difficult time maintaining enthusiasm because I felt so run-down from . . . disciplining [students] and dealing with problems. My fifth-period class was wonderful, and so I tended to allow myself to relax too much. . . . Just because they were quiet and well-behaved did not mean that they were motivated to learn the subject matter, [I discovered]. I began to realize that although I didn't have management problems with [this class, unlike the others], I [still] had to motivate them because they often weren't paying attention when they appeared to be.

One problem that really concerned me was the difficulty of relating to the students. I realized that there were "jocks" and "burnouts," and intellectually, when I read the book earlier in the year about them, I felt that I would be able to respond to and help each group. However, this was a difficult matter. . . . I sometimes had a difficult time understanding the personalities of the other students. Some were very aggressive and mouthy. Although I related to the quiet students, I found myself giving more attention to the aggressive students at times. I feel that this happens quite frequently and that, unfortunately, some of these quiet students slip through the cracks. The more aggressive students were always hovering around my desk demanding to know about their grades or wanting an explanation of everything. Toward the end of student teaching, I started to spend less time with these students. . . . In the future I will make an attempt to give equal time to all, including those who do not demand it. . . .

I made many mistakes. I have learned from those mistakes and now have the knowledge to start building my own career. . . . Earlier in the year I thought about teaching students, but I never realized how much more was involved [in teaching]. . . . Both of my cooperating teachers frequently told me that they are continually changing and trying new ways to do things. I think that this is one of the most exciting things about the teaching profession: there are endless possibilities for bettering the situation and learning. I feel that the greatest thing perhaps that I have learned this year is that the best teacher is the best student of his or her [teaching]. . . .

Commentary

After having read a good many reviews over the past few years, one gets a sense that there is a rhythm or pattern to the certification year. The problems that demand attention in the first review are often not of concern later. This is important for beginning teachers to keep in mind. The pattern also reflects an increasing sophistication about teaching and appreciation for the complexity of teaching. Naive conceptions of teaching, and particularly about students' and teachers' work, begin to be replaced by more sophisticated conceptions (Bullough, with Stokes, 1994). The talk is about the loss of idealism, but a more accurate description is a loss of innocence. Beginners like Sonja commonly talk about facing "reality," and of struggling from time to time to avoid discouragement particularly because of management problems or difficulty establishing authority within the classroom as they move from one side of the desk to the other. But typically, our students end the year on a cautiously optimistic note. This said, how Sonja and many other beginning teachers use the word *reality* is disturbing. At times it seems she assumes that there is a fixed world of teaching and that her charge is to fit into it regardless of the personal costs; she is powerless in the face of the "realities" of teaching, and ideals such as the desire to care and nurture students are set aside.

Sonja does not always talk this way, however. Other times she writes as though she can shape the context of teaching and make it more educable for herself and the students. She talks of "realities" when she is most discouraged; the danger is that discouragement will get the better of her. As we have suggested in *Becoming a Student of Teaching*, a key to overcoming discouragement is to reach out to other teachers and become actively engaged in building a professional community.

Sonja's reviews well illustrate why we consider the personal teaching texts an integrating methodology. Taken together, the reviews present snapshots of Sonja's story of becoming a teacher. In them she links activities to one another and applies public theory learned in class to practice and to her private theory. She links, for example, her written life history with the tendency to prejudge students and her desire to reach out to quiet, shy students. She is troubled by her impatience with and bias against the "jocks," and hopes to be responsive to all students. Similarly, her initial teaching metaphors come directly from her life history. Drawing on her "darkest times" during junior high, she concluded that some students needed defending and it was her job to be a "defender." Additionally, she uses concepts taught in the cohort, like "presence" and even "jocks," as a means for thinking about teaching and tests specific strategies and techniques like "checking for understanding." Presence, a concern noted in the second review, featured prominently in her Action Research project.

Like the Action Research project, the personal teaching text brings self and teaching context together, and the reviews enable their exploration. That this is so is well illustrated by Sonja's ongoing exploration of teaching metaphors and her struggle to realize these metaphors in the light of contextual constraints like paperwork and worrisome students. Generally, she likes the job of teaching, but the work of teachers sometimes gets frustrating. She discovers that her future as a teacher may well rest on her ability to manage the mundane and technical concerns of teaching before they become consuming. We sense in Sonja's criticism of the conditions under which teachers work the beginnings of a cultural and structural critique of schooling.

From the first to the last review we see Sonja's understanding of teaching becoming increasingly complex. She adds metaphors indicating recognition of additional teaching responsibilities. Responsibilities proliferate until she seems to stagger under the burden, finally concluding that there are limitations on what a teacher can and should do. She cannot "transform the nation," nor can she get every student motivated to do her assignments. What, then, is her responsibility as teacher? She is uncertain but wants to give all types of students "equal time" and nurture and care for them, but she cannot.

Sonja does not settle into a fitting and authentic teaching role. Not all beginning teachers do. This may come later with additional experience, but maybe not. Given the culture of teaching that is present in many schools and that leads to teacher isolation, she may not get it. That this danger exists underscores the importance of linking preservice with in-service teacher education, as we have argued in *Becoming a Student of Teaching*.

Among the themes of Sonja's reviews, two require special attention. During much of practice teaching Sonja's relationship with students was the most crucial factor in her feelings of success or failure, not their learning. Like many other beginning teachers she desperately wanted to be liked; she wanted to be one of them even though in her first review she claims otherwise. This was a source of her initial problem with identity and authority that figures so prominently in her Action Research study. Over the course of the year she discovered that she could not be one of them no matter how young she looked or felt. Still, Sonja's sense of self-worth was heavily dependent on their views of her as a person. Criticism was personalized, and she had difficulty distinguishing important from unimportant events. Complaints about the curriculum, for example, were personal attacks. Feeling defensive, she was strict and distant yet still in need of student affection. Finally, unhappy with her relationship with students and frustrated with management problems, Sonja had the students give her written feedback on her teaching and invited one class to help her create a more positive climate. This was a risk that paid off handsomely. She begins to think of the students in less adversarial terms. They can and will help her create a positive learning climate if she provides the means for their involvement; the class is, after all, theirs too. Potentially, this is a very significant development, one that may eventually lead to insights that will fundamentally alter her views about teaching and further deepen her already lively sense of the ethical responsibilities of teachers.

Central to this theme is Sonja's struggle to get to know young people who were different from what she was like as a high school student, ones outside of her experience. Issues of social class and class antagonisms rear up. At the conclusion of practice teaching Sonja accepts that her experience is limited as a means for understanding the experience of others. She realizes she must transcend her background if she is to connect with students in productive ways and create a setting that facilitates learning. Sonja's difficulty well illustrates the limitations of private theories and the need for openly testing them.

From the first to the third review there is a subtle shift in Sonja's relationship with her cooperating teachers that bears mention. Concern for negativism gives way to understanding of the frustrations of teachers. She also becomes frustrated. One would hope that these feelings would be taken as occasions to engage other teachers in open and honest explorations of teaching with the aim of altering work conditions. Too often they only lead to withdrawal and disillusionment. What was striking about Sonja's relationship with her cooperating teachers was that both expressed appreciation for being able to work with her and to talk about their work. It was for this reason, in part, that her relationships with them deepened and became more caring. Each cooperating teacher profoundly influenced how Sonja thought about teaching, and through them she comes to see herself as connected to the wider profession even while she struggles to establish herself in the classroom. She also positively influenced them. Through experiences shared with other teachers in the school, particularly her cooperating teachers, Sonja concludes that the key to becoming a great teacher is to continually study one's own practice and, we believe she would add, reach out to other teachers.

A Note to Teacher Educators and Students

As we have worked with the personal teaching text, a somewhat unanticipated benefit has emerged. We have seen some beginning teachers make dramatic progress over the course of the certification year, and yet in follow-up studies some of these same students seemed little aware of the role teacher education played in producing the change (Bullough, 1989). Such a conclusion has been widely reported in the literature. When considering this disturbing outcome, we have realized that part of the difficulty may be that, swamped by the many and varied demands of the first year or two of teaching, many beginning teachers forget what they were able and not able to understand and do prior to entering their teacher education programs. The personal teaching text has proven a helpful means for assisting beginning teachers to be more aware of their development as teachers not only for the sake of teacher educator self-esteem, but also so they might better direct it.

Planning Ahead

As noted previously, if the personal teaching text and the reviews are to have the desired results of increasing program coherence and of enhancing student reflectivity in particular, careful planning is required. Students need to be encouraged to organize their PTTs carefully, as one recently observed in a year-end review:

> I really didn't know if I wanted/could teach. Anyone who picks up my personal teaching text could probably see this. It was poorly organized. Papers were thrown in haphazardly. There was no rhyme or reason to its order. . . . I kept the text because I was expected to. My attitude toward my text was, "I'll keep these papers stuffed in this folder in case I ever do teach." The folder was a source of irritation because it was always in a place where I needed to dust. [But now, after student teaching], I'm proud of my text. It symbolizes more than activities that have taken place over the last year. It serves as a

> reminder of all the doubts I had about myself. . . . Yet it
> also serves as a source of confirmation: "Yes, I can teach
> and do a pretty decent job of it."

Careful plans need to be made for when and how students will return to them for analysis. As a form of guided inquiry, you may discover that the questions we use may or may not be the ones you will find most beneficial. Different contexts may require different questions. We have found that some questions—for example, "Are you on course for becoming the kind of teacher you imagine yourself capable of becoming?"— are good ones to include in each review. We mention this because including some of the same questions in each review facilitates comparison and helps tie content and activities together. In addition, we try to balance our questions so that each beginning teacher will be encouraged to identify and celebrate accomplishments while simultaneously uncovering areas of weakness. Celebration and criticism ought to go hand in hand.

A Source of Feedback

Reading the reviews has proven very helpful to us as we think ahead about the program and about our personal relationships with students. Strong, caring relationships between teacher educators, cooperating teachers, and students are essential to program continuity. Occasionally problems will emerge with a beginning teacher's relationship with a cooperating teacher. The negativism of one of Sonja's cooperating teachers, for example, was a worry, and a conversation with the teacher followed. When concerns raised in the reviews have been shared by more than a few students, we have addressed them in class. The reviews, generally speaking, are relatively good barometers for gauging program success.

Program Coherence

Finally, an additional word should be said about the relationship between program coherence and the PTTs. Coherence, that sense of wholeness that one hopes to provide beginning teachers, comes only partially from having clear purposes, stable and caring relationships, and well-sequenced activities and assignments. In reality coherence represents an achievement of each beginning teacher who makes the program more or less meaningful in his or her own way. Ultimately, coherence arises out of the flow and direction, the feeling of purposefulness, of each beginning teacher's individual and idiosyncratic story of professional development and its resonance with one's life story. The reviews are crucial to achieving cohesiveness and to bringing about a sense of closure. The reviews present occasions to stop and think about who one is and what one is becoming as a teacher and to consider alternative endings to the story. In interviews and through questionnaires our students consistently support this conclusion and add, as Sonja's reviews indicate, that they are a valuable means for reflecting on their professional development for the purpose of better directing it (Bullough, 1993).

PART TWO

In-Service Teacher Education

To this point, the methodologies presented in *Becoming a Student of Teaching* provide a set of experiences that can challenge a training approach to teacher education. From the perspective of teacher development, their success depends, in part, on creating bridges between preservice and in-service teacher education. Without bridges, the view that learning to teach is a continuous process of development is lost and the values of training become dominant. The chapter that follows presents a methodology for enabling beginning and experienced teachers to carry on the process of becoming students of teaching. It is included not only to show how preservice and in-service activities might be linked, but to encourage teacher educators to think about their curriculum in more expansive ways. At the same time, we want to encourage you to continue your study of teaching. Even though your work context might discourage this sort of inquiry, there are nonetheless significant opportunities to engage in the study of teaching. Our hope is that teacher educators and beginning teachers, such as yourself, will work together to find and create opportunities to make your professional relationships more educative.

CHAPTER TEN

Educative Research

Introduction

We shift now from preservice to in-service education. This shift reflects one of our basic assumptions about teacher education: that preservice and in-service efforts should be part of a continuous, long-term approach to teacher development. In-service education enables the types of inquiry described in *Becoming a Student of Teaching* to become part of teaching. In-service education provides opportunities to engage in an analysis of self and context that are unavailable in a preservice program. Most importantly, you now have your own classroom! With your own classroom you can shape the curriculum and your interactions with students without wondering how your decisions will fit a cooperating teacher's philosophy or affect your final evaluation. Furthermore, where preservice education places you in a temporary community that you likely will leave, in-service education takes place within a relatively stable community of educators. Participation in this community puts you in a position to shape not only the quality of life found in your classroom but also the school in which you work. In-service education takes place in a context that allows you to actively participate in teacher and school development. This is important because as Fullan and Stiegelbauer note, "you cannot have one without the other" (1991:289).

In this chapter we build on the approaches already presented in *Becoming a Student of Teaching* by describing an integrative methodology, Educative Research (see Gitlin et al., 1992), explicitly developed for in-service teacher education. This methodology should further your efforts to become a student of teaching—to pose questions about your work, act on those queries, and increase your participation in the educational conversation taking place in your school.

As an integrative methodology, Educative Research draws on the use of autobiographies to explore issues of self, and on school histories to examine the school context. To this mix is added a form of peer assessment, horizontal evaluation, that can enable the examination of classroom practices and their relation to your intentions (see Gitlin & Smyth, 1989). Educative Research places these methodologies within a unifying framework. This framework reflects the need both to make research and schooling *educative* and to have teachers become "critical actors" who speak out about the way school context and teachers' actions constrain the type of education offered to students.

The word *educative* is used to describe this approach to research because all those who participate in the research process should learn and benefit from the process. Traditional approaches to research usually divide the research process between those who pose the questions, analyze the results, and write up the reports and those who are studied—the subjects. Researchers set the agenda, learn from the experience, state their opinions, and seek to influence public theories. Subjects, who are often teachers, have little or no say in what is researched, tend to be shut out from the learning process that is part of systematic inquiry, and have little or no opportunity to influence public theories. Educative Research challenges this view by placing teachers at the center of the research process. This said, the aim of Educative Research is not just to turn teachers into researchers who study classroom and the school contexts. Rather, the aim is to have teachers participate in the development of the school as they are developing as teachers. Again, self needs to be understood in relation to context, as we have argued throughout *Becoming a Student of Teaching*.

"Voice," as a form of protest, is a metaphor for the way teachers can make a difference. Because teachers have been largely excluded from debates on public theories and practice, strengthening their say in these matters is a way to enable practitioners such as yourself to use experiential knowledge and the knowledge produced through systemic inquiry to link private and public theories and to reshape the public theories that currently dominate the field. Being critical of what is taken for granted, and acting on what is seen to be unjust, will go a long way toward achieving this aim.

Horizontal Evaluation

Because we have described autobiographies and school histories previously (see chapters two and four), we move now to the peer assessment model we use as part of the Educative Research process: horizontal evaluation. Horizontal evaluation occurs in three phases: preconference, observation, and postconference. In the preconference all those involved in the evaluation process clarify their intentions—what is it that they want to accomplish for a lesson, unit, and more generally for the long-term good of the students. At this point intentions are not questioned; rather, discussion centers on making them clear to the observer. For example, if your long-term intention is to develop intrinsic motivation among students, it is important for the teacher who will be observing your class to know what you mean by "intrinsic motivation." Typically, no more than three intentions should be stated at any one time to assure that the process does not become overly complicated. The observation phase of the process involves collecting two types of data: those relating to interactions which support and/or conflict with the stated intentions, and those about the significant events which seem to shape the lesson in important ways. Clear, detailed notes should be taken that describe observed interactions and events. The postconference brings participants together to examine the relation between stated intentions and what is observed. When successful, this examination should lead to a consideration of alternative practices and, in some instances, a rethinking of stated intentions.

The discussion of intentions and practices can be enhanced by using three strategies: communication analysis, historical perspective, and challenge statements which illuminate the values underlying what you want to accomplish and what you do in the classroom.

Communication Analysis

Communication analysis helps participants to understand how the prejudgments they hold about teaching encourage them to act on certain problems while ignoring others. For example, if a teacher regards chaotic student behavior as being caused by the "low" abilities of the students, the question "What do you mean by 'low abilities'?" could be posed. By doing so, some of the implicit values that lie behind statements and practices like this can be made explicit and examined. Examining the underlying values, in turn, should influence how teachers act in their classes and in the school. If teachers realize, for example, that the labeling they use is inappropriate because it speaks directly to the socioeconomic status of the students more than to their abilities as students, then classroom structures and pedagogy may be reorganized to reflect a less biased and more egalitarian view of the ways students should be treated.

Historical Perspective

Historical perspective enables participants to see how current practices and public and private theories are related to past discussions and events taking place both inside and outside the school. Adopting a historical perspective allows teachers to see apparently commonsense notions and actions not as natural and immutable but rather as choices which are part of a historical and biographical tradition. For instance, if a teacher regards teaching as a process of depositing information in the heads of students, adopting a historical perspective can encourage discussion about what factors have historically encouraged this kind of pedagogy. The interests embedded within such a view can then be more fully analyzed. The school histories and autobiographies that you already have produced are important resources for developing this type of analysis.

Challenge Statements

Sometimes discussion between a teacher and colleague about an in-class activity becomes stilted or bogged down and cannot go beyond clarifying values and prejudgments. At such times, either participant in the evaluation process may initiate a "challenge statement" designed to get discussion moving again. For example, if a teacher holds to the view that students should obey her classroom rules in all circumstances, questions can be raised about students' and teachers' rights, and about the role and purpose of adult authority. The resulting conversation might seek to investigate the legitimacy of adult authority or the implications of holding such a view for the education of students in a democracy.

Alternatives

In addition to these strategies, horizontal evaluation encourages participants to link the insights gained through dialogue to the realization of alternative teaching practices. Making a difference in the classroom becomes part of a continuous process of reflection and action. In this sense personal development—constant reflection on teaching—is linked to school development, as least in terms of classroom change. When the discussion concludes with a suggested alternative, this alternative can then become a starting point for further reflection on teaching.

Practicing Educative Research

Educative Research involves bringing together horizontal evaluation with methodologies that focus on self and context. To do so, we suggest the following: Since you have already produced an autobiography, take it from your personal teaching text and early in your first year of teaching give it a careful read. There is no need (and there will be too little time) to do much rewriting, but it is helpful to look at the themes that run through this exploration of self and consider new insights. If you have managed to begin a conversation with other teachers, the next step is to produce a collective school history. This history helps focus the group and allows those who are new to the school to learn with those who have a more in-depth understanding of the work context. It may be difficult to find the time to write a complete history of the school, but what you can do is put together a series of meeting minutes which reflect the discussion of the group as the school history is explored. This text, along with the autobiography, may be put aside for the moment.

Efforts should be made to observe in one another's classrooms. Any peer assessment approach can be used. If you feel comfortable with horizontal evaluation, use this approach with other members of the group. After the observations are conducted, the peer evaluation teams should audiotape the discussion that follows. Transcribing these tapes is desirable, but much can be gained simply by listening to the tapes and jotting down key insights.

With the three texts in mind—the autobiography, school history, and the assessment of your teaching—you now have gained some understanding of context, self, and the relation between intentions and practice. Based on your analysis of these texts, it is time to raise a question or two about your teaching. However, maintain some flexibility because the questions you pose may change. At this point, you have at least two options: You can begin to collect data, using the Action Research cycle described in chapter eight, or delay that process until you have looked at what the literature says about your query. In either case, once you have collected some data, you should go back to your initial question. This is because a preliminary examination of the data often suggests a slight shift in the question that needs to be asked. The "new" question, when one is required, should help you redirect the data collection process and, ultimately, your teaching. The final step of the Educative Research process is to share the insights gained with other members of your group and, if possible, others in the wider educational community. Sharing is an essential part of community building, and can encourage collective actions that challenge the school structures that have been identified as limiting the type of education offered students. If successful, personal development will go hand in hand with school development.

Support is essential to the success of Educative Research. In the example of Educative Research that follows, support came in the form of a cooperative master's program that allowed teachers to earn university credit. As will be mentioned in our note to teacher educators and students, programs such as this one have the potential to link preservice and in-service teacher education and make it possible for teacher educators to provide support for teachers to write school histories, write autobiographies, and do classroom observations. We strongly recommend that you seek graduate programs that provide the means for engaging in an ongoing conversation with other teachers, and provide support for inquiry and school change.

What follows are three texts produced by Johanna, a veteran elementary school teacher in the cooperative master's program, as she worked with Educative Research. Her autobiography, school history (which was written with one other teacher), and a report of a peer assessment experience are included. This section concludes with a consideration of how the examination of self, context, and the theory/practice relation enabled Johanna to pose a question and introduce new pedagogies into her classroom.

An Example of Educative Research

Autobiography

To consider issues of self, including the private theories that teachers hold, we began the cooperative master's program with the writing of an autobiography. (These teachers had not participated in our preservice program.) To facilitate this process we looked at other autobiographies written by teachers and examined them in terms of form and what they said about teachers and teaching.

As Johanna started to write her autobiography, she had an uneasy feeling about her teaching but she was unsure of its origins. In her writing she explored what made her views about teaching so passionate, and the relation between these views and her actions as a teacher. What follows recounts her attempt to describe and interpret past experiences, including her relationship with her father. This relationship had an important influence on Johanna's attitudes toward education, and on how she addressed educational issues. To advance the interpretive part of the autobiography, Johanna has incorporated published articles and books which she selected as part of her work in the cooperative master's program.

Johanna's Story

"My epitaph is going to read, 'Life with Elena was like living in a *Monty Python* sketch.' I have always known that normality is somewhere nearby, but I have thus far managed to avoid it. . . . I take great pride in eccentricity. I respect the rebel, admire the revolutionary, and hold the 'gods of conformity' in contempt. The rebel is not silent, the revolutionary does not fear freedom. They fight conformity at every opportunity. This is the way I once believed myself to be. I have come recently, though, to know that I too have been 'silenced.' . . .

"Much of the way I am today is a reaction to my father's history. Dad had a tempestuous career in and out of politics and academia, offending many in positions of power over him. He knew his opinions would cost, and yet he was unable to refrain from voicing them. . . . We were with him when he would energetically blow into each new situation like a tornado. He was determined to change things for the better—teach students to 'question authority in all forms,' stir up the power structure, and make them think. And we were with him when he quietly left after being informed that they were not 'renewing his contract' or were 'abolishing his position.' We tackled each new situation with vigor and passion, and left them all with no regrets.

"Those experiences have taught me to question, but they also taught me never to trust. I became fearful of self-expression in the public forum because I saw my father suffer so much. We were always encouraged to discuss our views at home, and we always did. But upon entering the outside world, those of us who were witness to my father's plight became 'closed.' We never let anyone see the real person behind the false front. We believed people could not be trusted with our deepest thoughts and feelings. We shouldn't openly disagree with or fight against injustice because something 'bad' would happen—we might lose our jobs or be ousted from the community. . . .

"This inability to trust others has led me to an impasse. It has created a fear of self-expression—and yet I believe in it so strongly! Paulo Freire states:

> Fear of freedom, of which its possessor is not necessarily aware, makes him see ghosts. Such an individual is actually taking refuge in an attempt to achieve security, which he or she prefers to the risks of liberty. (1993:18)

"I pretended to be a defender of freedom while, at the same time, fearing to exercise it myself. I saw myself as a true humanist fighting oppression. And yet now I question all of that. Freire believes that it is necessary for a humanist to trust:

> They talk about the people, but they do not trust them; and trusting the people is the indispensable precondition for revolutionary change. A real humanist can be identified more by his trust in the people, which engages him in their struggle, than by a thousand actions in their favor without that trust. (1993:42)

"I seek a free exchange of ideas and fear it at the same time. But I truly want to express myself and listen to others express themselves without fear of repercussions. I believe, like my father before me, that this is the one way to make a better life for all of us.

"Much has been written on self-expression and the free exchange of ideas. Beyer calls it 'moral discourse' and defines it as

> the expression of divergent points of view[. S]uch a context must also include participants challenging and defending their positions. In the process, judgments must necessarily be made about the range of alternative positions discussed, so that the possibility of enlightened action may be realized. Within these processes of

expression, challenge and defense of positions, the
importance of communal traditions will be apparent, as
tensions between stated positions and received traditions
come to the fore. (1988:230)

"During my college years I was actively engaged in moral
discourse with a group of fellow students who were majoring in
my chosen field of political science. We conducted informal
debates and panel discussions regarding the Vietnam War and
other issues of interest to the group. A bachelor's degree in
political science will get you a job on someone's political
campaign on Guam, but politicians did not interest me. They
were untrustworthy and deceitful. So, I chose education,
believing that the testing ground for new thought was in the
classroom.

"I was right. My first year of teaching was one of the most
rewarding years of my life, and each year of teaching after that
was even more rewarding. I was constantly learning new things.
My students and I wrote to political leaders and received
answers. We visited local government meetings and made our
presence known with pertinent questions. We backed up our
questions with research and followed our convictions with
action. We conducted debates on the Constitution and current
events. Teaching was exciting, and the moral discourse in the
classroom was the best thing of all.

"Over the years my initial excitement persevered until a
few years ago when, quite unexpectedly, my integrity as a
person and a teacher was questioned. An accusation was made
that I had disciplined a student on the basis of race. I was
shocked and appalled! How could anyone believe this of me? I
had a history of teaching minority students to speak out and
working with minority youth to verbalize. Suddenly I was
effectively silenced. . . . I was no longer welcome at lunch with
the principal. I was not permitted to take an active role in
curriculum design any longer because those making the
curriculum decisions were in the 'favorite' group and I needed to
be punished. . . . Because of my fears of repercussion I also
silenced myself. The kind of teacher I want to be is more of a
reflection of the kind of person I am at home. . . . I have not felt
free to be myself in the classroom. I have not felt free to conduct

debates on prayer in the public schools, which is something I would really like to do. I have not felt free to allow my students to choose a topic of personal interest and research it. I have not felt free to allow controversial subjects to be discussed in an open forum. I am insisting that my students 'play the game' I play. When outside the classroom, be seen but don't be heard. . . .

"I have to ask myself if I am teaching my students to hide their newborn thoughts from the world. I want to be a teacher who 'help[s] students deliver their words to the world, and to use their own knowledge to enter into conversation with other[s] . . . in the culture' (Belenky et al., 1986:219).

"This is really what I thought I was doing all these years. But in reality I was teaching my students to fear the freedom I encouraged them to seek. I was asking them to live two separate lives, just as I had done—one enriched by moral discourse, and one oppressed by silence.

"I can live this dual life no longer. I need to strive to build a pedagogy that encourages the free exchange of ideas in the classroom and in our lives. I need to become a teacher who does not fear oppression, but rather is dedicated to fighting it."

School History

The writing of school histories followed the completion of the autobiographies. To begin this process, the teachers in the master's cooperative formed groups by school affiliation. Some teachers worked alone, but most worked in groups of two or three. In the school history that follows, Johanna is working primarily with one other teacher in her school. While doing some preliminary observations and interviews, Johanna and her colleague decided to focus on teacher dissatisfaction, a topic that was of great interest to Johanna given her recent disenfranchisement from the informal school decision-making group described in her autobiography. After giving out a survey which asked teachers to reflect on their job satisfaction, Johanna focused her efforts on understanding how issues of social class formation might help explain teacher dissatisfaction. Her colleague focused on the possibilities of using a team approach to overcome teacher dissatisfaction. This school history includes both the descriptive data coming from the teacher survey and the teachers' attempt to make sense of the data, including relevant literature on the topics discussed.

Northlake Elementary

"The total number of students attending Northlake Elementary school is 820. Our minority student population is 70 students, or approximately 8% of the total. We have 42 children who have been labeled 'at risk' in grades K–3. No 'at risk' category has been defined for the upper grades. . . .

"The area in which we teach is home to several low-income housing projects and low-income apartments. Approximately 30% of our students come from homes with only one wage earner. The majority of families are white, low wage earners who experience life as a day-to-day struggle to make ends meet in a declining economy.

"In the search for a framework through which we could analyze the school history of Northlake Elementary, a recurring theme materialized: teacher dissatisfaction. To better assess the extent of the dissatisfaction, we designed a survey and distributed it to the faculty. Our questions were open-ended to better facilitate the free expression of feelings and ideas.

"Many of the survey forms that were returned identified 'lack of parental involvement' and 'disruptive student behavior and lack of self-discipline' as main sources of frustration in the teachers' work. Teachers are disheartened, and remain teaching in this area because of many rather superficial reasons, such as 'location of building—close to stores, banks, cleaners, etc.' and 'windows to see out of.' A few state, however, that the association with the staff has been a benefit.

"The survey revealed that teachers felt that in order for them to remain in their current situation, some things would need to change. 'The faculty needs to be more united,' 'The principal needs to approach discipline in a more aggressive manner and support teachers more,' and 'Funding for materials is critical' were some of the statements made. Several survey forms reflected a despondent attitude on the part of the participants, in that comments were made indicating that change in the situation would never occur, so why try? Participants said, 'I no longer expect change—it hasn't come when it was available/possible,' 'difficult clientele—which cannot be changed,' and 'I am learning to accept what I cannot change.'

"In the final analysis, the survey indicated that teacher dissatisfaction is a recurring theme at Northlake Elementary. We will consider the relationship of the class position of the students to teacher discontent. Then we will examine the possibilities of teamwork in overcoming dissatisfaction."

Analysis: The Influence of Class

"The class structure in our society is characterized by four classes of people. Hunt and Sherman have offered a framework for the analysis of this structure: the class of capitalists (those who own the means of production and whose ownership is significant enough to allow them sufficient income to live in luxury and have great economic and political power), the class of independent craftspersons or professionals (those who own their own business or lawyers, doctors, etc.), the class of workers or wage earners (those who work for a weekly or monthly salary and are considered necessary to maintain the capitalist class in its position), and the poverty-stricken class (those who own little or no property and cannot work, for a variety of reasons (1986:73–75).

"Educators, then, appear to fit uncomfortably into the range between two opposing class positions. Objectively, teachers earn a wage or salary, and are therefore considered part of the working class. Subjectively, many of them identify with the professionals. Erik O. Wright has described teachers as fitting into a 'contradictory class location,' and states:

> Today there are still categories of employees who have a certain degree of control over their own immediate conditions of work, over their immediate labour process. . . . In their immediate work environment they maintain the work process of the independent artisan while still being employed by capital as wage labourers. (1978:79–81)

"This contradictory class location may explain, in part, why teachers seem to experience a philosophical conflict between what they believe *is just and moral* and what they *feel is their responsibility to teach*. Their conscious intentions are not to foster types of personal development compatible with the relationships of subordination and domination in society. Their aim is not the creation of a surplus of skilled labor, which provides employers with weapons with which they may discipline labor. In any faculty room across the nation teachers can be heard to express concern that 'Johnny isn't doing his work, and what kind of life will he have if he doesn't learn to read?' Comments are made that reflect concern that 'Jane is never in school. Her attendance is so poor. What kind of job will she ever be able to hold down?' Teachers inevitably want a happy and fulfilling life for the students they teach, and they see themselves as able to help their students (given the appropriate time, materials, and cooperation) acquire a better life and make a better world. And yet everything teachers do seems to strengthen a system that is inherently unjust.

"In the survey of the teachers of Northlake Elementary, several teachers made comments regarding the lack of concern of parents and students. And yet teachers also commented that Northlake had a large amount of 'latchkey children' and 'children who put up with a lot of garbage.'

"In conclusion, teacher discontent may be a direct result of the conflicting class positions in which we find ourselves. It may also lie in the basic contradiction between our desire to teach students to build a more just and equitable society (and our ability to see that this is not happening) and our 'duty' to perpetuate a system of inequities."

A Possible Solution: Teamwork

"One of the common, ongoing 'truths' of the teaching profession is that if you want to get really melancholy, go to the faculty room. The conversation is generally about what went wrong today, why the students are so 'off the wall,' and the latest 'crazy Mom.' When we talk of our jobs, our profession, we often talk of the problems. This is true in most parts of life—we see the symptoms of our problems. In education this seems to be more overt. Perhaps it is the result of the constant media coverage; the yearly, very public legislative struggle for funding; or the national perception that the schools (and teachers) are failing the nation's children. For whatever reason, teacher morale is low. . . . In a revealing study conducted by Rebecca R. Turner in a national poll (1987:57), she found that of the teachers interviewed, 40 percent reported that they would not choose a teaching career again, 42 percent would stay because the benefits outweighed the disadvantages, 17 percent were not sure. That, to me, is the most troubling statistic. How can you meet the needs of the student if you are not sure you want to be in the classroom? An even more telling set of data was documented in the same report. Of the teachers 58 percent reported that they would not encourage their own children to enter the profession. Some of these teachers even reported that 'I'd refuse to pay my son's college expenses if he wanted to be a teacher.'

"In our survey, two teachers reported that the best thing about teaching at our school was the feeling that they made a difference and a love of the students and teaching. Friendship and staff were given as the most positive aspect of the school in the greatest number of responses. This is ironic because of the items listed as problems, faculty cliques, administration favoritism, teacher conflicts, and judgmental behavior of teachers were frequently mentioned as the worst things about the school. Teachers' perceptions of how they work as a unit seem to determine to a large extent their satisfaction with their work position. This coincides with several research studies findings that the ability of staffs to interact in a positive way, to approach problem solving as a team activity rather than struggling on alone, is the single greatest factor in the school's success (see Csaslovka, 1992:27). Jane Bluestone (1986) wrote an article, 'Are Your Colleagues Driving You Crazy?' In it she writes, 'With all the attention students require, it's easy to lose sight of how much relationships with other adults can affect you. Yet conflicts with other staff can interfere with a teacher's ability to function. Too often, teacher stress is rooted in interactions with adults' (1986:41).

"At Northlake, there is an open separation between the 'lower'- and 'upper'-grade faculty. Part of the problem is the physical arrangement of the building; however, in part teachers have also chosen to remain isolated. Little cooperation is generally exhibited between these two groups. Individual teachers make connections, but as a group, there is an understanding of divided turf. There have been a few attempts at team configurations; however, none has survived the lack of support. Their demise might be characterized as a 'failure to thrive.' I believe that the isolation, be it self-imposed or institutionally imposed, is a major cause of discontent within our school. When only two teachers indicate that they feel needed and important and love to teach, change is needed.

"School after school that was examined to determine the reason for their success cited school teamwork. Ernest Boyer, president of the Carnegie Foundation for the Advancement of Teaching and former U.S. Commissioner of Education, was quoted as saying:

> In the end, the more the school is a community—not just a place of isolated successes in classrooms—the more it will succeed. To build a community of learning that has a sense of reinforcing vitality for the individual, yet teachers should be engaged in defining who they think makes a good teacher. . . . If there is no involvement, then teachers feel fragmented. (1987:289–90)

"The question is, can faculties that have a history of not valuing teamwork change? Will they perceive the need to change? . . . Is it an issue of isolation, disappointment, or wrong career choice or a combination of these that made change so difficult? . . . Wouldn't it be great to walk into the faculty room and be met with eager talk about the successes and excitement of people truly happy in their work."

Horizontal Evaluation

After the teachers in the master's cooperative finished their autobiographies and school histories, they put them aside for a while and focused directly on their practice. Using the horizontal evaluation model, they formed groups of two or three teachers and observed each other teaching. After all members of the team had been observed, they had a joint postconference. Once they had gone through at least two rounds of this process, they were asked to write a short paper which summarized what they had learned about their teaching. What follows is Johanna's description of her work with Heidi, another teacher in the master's cooperative.

Reflections on Horizontal Evaluation

When Heidi came in to visit my classroom the first time, my students were engaged in filming a comedy version of *Romeo and Juliet* that they had written. I felt that I had allowed a great deal of personal expression in the filming of the play. Some of the students ad-libbed their lines. The students directed and filmed the play, as well.

"I wanted Heidi to observe this activity because I felt I encouraged freedom of movement and nonconformity in my classroom. However, I noticed that when Heidi left that day, I began to catch myself saying, 'Wouldn't it be better if we did this with that scene?' and 'How about trying this?' My students cooperated with me because, I guess, they are used to doing that. That is how I *control* them. I make them think it is their own idea to do what I want.

"I have found myself, since then, acting this way many times. They really want to please me, and I know that. I have wondered if I am squelching their thoughts and creativity because I don't believe I have ever made it clear that they can disagree with me. We tease each other and we all get along, but I wonder how many times they feel like they just better not disagree today.

"Before Heidi's second visit I asked her to look for this behavior (gaining control through cooperation); she did, and she has issued me a challenge statement: 'Are you going to allow more freedom of decision making for your students as it concerns the curriculum? Are you going to try to draw out their personal philosophies and beliefs?'

"I really do want them to understand that I believe their feelings and opinions hold as much validity as any other person's in our society, regardless of the position they hold. I want my classroom to have a democratic atmosphere wherein equal access to educational opportunity is provided and diversity is respected. But I have not achieved this goal."

Question Posing

Johanna's autobiography indicated that she may be teaching her students to hide their thoughts in the same way that she had been socialized not to speak her mind in public. The school history shows that some teachers feel dissatisfied. In trying to understand this dissatisfaction, Johanna comes to the conclusion that it is related to the conflict between what teachers believe to be morally right and just and what they feel are their responsibilities as teachers. Observations of Johanna's classroom indicated that even when she thought she was encouraging freedom and nonconformity, part of her hidden curriculum was based on maintaining control over students. When these three texts were reviewed, it became apparent that Johanna's aim to have students speak out and deal with issues that were not bounded by narrow views of conformity conflicted in part with her practices. The question she posed tried to address this conflict. She describes her plans this way:

> I intend to implement an activist form of teaching in my classroom. Trips to the city council meetings in the area and to the legislature may help to foster a greater understanding of the processes at work in our society. Students will be encouraged to write letters to representatives in government and editors of local newspapers. Projects that seem to create a desire for political action may be taken on by the group at large. Debates on controversial issues chosen by students from readings in newspapers and magazines will be scheduled. Multicultural education that teaches the value of diversity as opposed to the assimilation of minorities will be instituted.

With this plan in mind Johanna expected to collect data through student interviews and observations, to determine the influence of her activist pedagogy. Space limitations make the description of the Action Research part of the project impossible.

Commentary

Johanna's experience with Educative Research shows how analyses of self, context, and intentions and practice can come together to illuminate a hidden aspect of teaching which becomes a focal point for reflection and action. One of the strengths of her focus is that it takes into account personal development, in the sense that Johanna needs to rethink her pedagogy. Another strength is that it attends to school development, in that historically the school has neither encouraged the type of activist pedagogy she wants to create nor rewarded pedagogical change. Put in terms of the aims of Educative Research, Johanna has taken a significant event, accusations about her treatment of minority students, and used this event to protest her part in furthering a hidden curriculum where students are reluctant to express their views. She also has protested some of the contextual factors that limit change, not the least of which are the divisions between faculty, their general dissatisfaction, and their lack of confidence in reform efforts.

Understanding the need to link personal change and school change also reveals some potential obstacles to Johanna's approach to reconstructing her classroom pedagogy. Specifically, Johanna must find ways to change the context to be more supportive of her classroom efforts while the faculty is, for the most part, despondent and disengaged when teaching. While writing a collective school history can help foster the type of collegial relationships required to change the school context, by itself it is unlikely to challenge teacher isolation. Further, because Johanna no longer has a direct communication line with the administration—she is not part of the "favorite group"—her community-building efforts might be interpreted as arising from a trouble maker. Put simply, while school development is essential for the changes Johanna wants to achieve, those changes are unlikely to have a lasting impact on the quality of education offered to students without an emergent community where teachers work together to restructure the curriculum. The challenge for Johanna is to work at developing a school community at the same time as she changes her classroom pedagogy.

Through studying her teaching, Johanna realized that her classroom practice at times contradicted her aim to establish a moral discourse with students. Because this tension was made explicit, she put herself in a position to consider alternatives (in this case, an activist pedagogy where students learn through community involvement) that may resolve the conflict between her intentions and practice.

There are many difficulties ahead, however, if Johanna is to enter into a continuous process of reflection and action, which scholars such as Fullan and Steigelbauer (1991) argue is essential for school change. Is she going to put into place an activist curriculum and then use it in the years to come as a new orthodoxy, or will she continuously assess the curriculum? Put differently, has Johanna become a student of teaching? Will Johanna receive the type of collegial support and resources she needs to assess her new curriculum when the cooperative master's program ends? Will teachers have some collective say in school decision making? And if Johanna is forced to struggle alone, is the most likely result teacher burnout? These questions suggest that while the Educative Research experience has pushed Johanna to articulate tensions between her theory and practice and pose questions about her work, there is much that is uncertain about the relation between the research process and significant school change.

Looking more specifically at the autobiography and school history that are a part of Educative Research, it is evident that Johanna has found a way to link public and private theories—an important aspect of becoming a student of teaching. She has clearly expressed her views on teaching and assessed them in relation to those of others who have also looked at similar issues. One of the strongest examples of this linkage of public and private theories occurred in her discussion of the importance of trust. A lack of trust has caused Johanna to "never let anyone see the real person behind the false front." While justified, in a certain sense, it is also the case that this self-imposed silence has created an impasse. By looking at the work of Freire, Johanna sees that the strategy of silencing herself may achieve security at the cost of freedom. And because freedom is central to Johanna's aims as a teacher, this insight encourages change in her relationships not only with other teachers but also with her students.

It is also apparent that in writing the school history and autobiography, Johanna has considered both teaching means and ends. She has escaped, if only temporarily, the powerful grip of a training orientation to teaching. In her autobiography, for example, Johanna views the need for a moral discourse in relation to practice. When she does so, she is able to see a tension between what she does in the classroom and what she desires for students. What is most interesting about this contradiction is that Johanna's feelings about what is possible ("I don't feel free to conduct discussions about prayer in the school"), rather than the context of schooling, constrain her ability to implement a moral discourse. However, once aware of this self-imposed boundary, she decides to give such activities as discussion of prayer in schools a try. Development of this kind arises from insights unlikely to occur in a training model of teacher education, where supposed outside experts give recommendations for classroom practice without paying attention to teacher histories.

Much the same can be said about the school history. One central theme in Johanna's history is that "teachers seem to experience a philosophical conflict between what they believe is just and moral and what they feel is their responsibility to teach." This theme links beliefs, what teachers want to do, with what they perceive they have to do. By framing her history in this way, Johanna is able to identify an underlying tension in the school and in her own past and begin to explore ways to alleviate the conflict. This important insight would be hidden if the focus were solely on the means of education, as is the case in training.

A Note to Teacher Educators and Students

Because they have a significant degree of autonomy in the classroom, teachers are uniquely positioned to participate in processes like Educative Research. (It should be noted, however, that experienced teachers likely have more opportunities than first-year teachers.) This is so because common school structures, such as the self-contained classroom, make direct forms of control over teachers' work difficult, if not impossible, to implement and maintain. On the other hand, teacher autonomy is bounded because activities, such as observing another teacher's classroom or systematically reflecting on practice, are usually not rewarded and must be added onto a teacher's already busy schedule. Further, while the self-contained classroom allows teachers to close their door and gain some control over events and their relationships with students, it also isolates teachers. Isolation, in turn, limits the likelihood of the type of collective action needed to further school change. Moreover, teacher development and school development take time, and with an ever increasing set of demands placed on teachers, finding time and energy to engage in such activities is often difficult.

While boundaries on teacher autonomy are part of traditional school culture, they can be modified and, in some cases, overcome. Teacher educators can play an important role in this regard both by furthering the type of teacher relationships needed to encourage school change and by providing time for teachers to reflect on teaching and enter into policy debates.

The cooperative master's program provides a context for such efforts. This program, as organized at the University of Utah, enrolls twenty-five teachers from a single school district. The classes for the "coop," as it is called, are held at one of the schools in the district, and the curriculum is based in part on teacher input. In this context, theory can be linked to practice, and the course work can be directed toward a homogenous group: practicing teachers. In essence, the coop provides an exchange between the university teacher educators and practicing teachers. Teachers increase their salaries by getting a master's degree, and have opportunities to reflect on their work, articulate their positions, and observe other teachers. Support for travel to conferences, where teachers share their ideas with others, can also be obtained by combining university and district resources. University teacher educators, on the other hand, have an opportunity to learn *with and from* teachers and more directly influence teacher and school development.

However, even in the case where it is impossible to begin a cooperative-master's-type program, there are other ways teacher educators can support practicing teachers. One way is to do collaborative research with teachers, so that they not only get to learn from the process but also benefit from any funds that may come from doing research. And even when collaborative research is not possible, teacher educators can involve others in the process by sharing results and working with the teachers being studied to better understand schooling. Some teacher educators write with practicing teachers (Bullough & Baughman, 1993; Gitlin et al., 1992), and increasingly preservice teacher education is seen as a collaborative responsibility between university professors and teachers.

In sum, if preservice and in-service teacher education is to represent a continuous process of teacher development, then it is important that teacher educators, such as yourself, get involved in schools. Just visiting a school to do some sort of research is not what we have in mind. Rather, teacher educators must work *with* practitioners to further their development and our own, and to challenge school structures that narrowly define education. By making this link, the important work you have accomplished in preservice teacher education will carry forward, and ongoing relationships can be established that are foundational to the emergence of an educational community—a community that sees teacher and university interests as complementary not oppositional.

Postscript

Becoming a Student of Teaching is the result of an ongoing conversation about teacher education. The methodologies presented are not prescriptions of what to do in a certification program, but rather represent our current thinking on teacher education. Inevitably, the methodologies will need modification to fit your particular context and will require revision over time. If we are to be students of our own teaching, we constantly need to examine our practice. Therefore, as we conclude this text, we invite those of you who share our vision of a professional community to be more than consumers of our work and to help us remake it. We welcome criticism of the text and would like to know about your struggle to build teacher education programs that attempt to move beyond the confines of training. In turn, we will try to be responsive and keep the conversation going. You can contact us at:

Robert V. Bullough, Jr., and Andrew Gitlin
University of Utah
Educational Studies
307 MBH
Salt Lake City, Utah 84112

Bibliography

Agar, M. (1980). *The professional stranger: An informal introduction to ethnography*. New York: Academic Press.

Apple, M.W. (1979a). What correspondence theories of the hidden curriculum miss. *Review of Education 5*(2), 101–112.

Apple, M.W. (1979b). *Ideology and curriculum*. London: Routledge & Kegan Paul.

Apple, M.W. (1982). Curricular form and the logic of technical control; Building the possessive individual. In M.W. Apple (Ed.), *Cultural and economic reproduction in education: Essays on class, ideology and the state*, pp. 247–74. London: Routledge & Kegan Paul.

Apple, M.W. (1986). *Teachers & texts: A political economy of class & gender relations in education*. London: Routledge & Kegan Paul.

Ball, S.J. & Goodson, I.F. (1985). *Teachers' lives and careers*. London: Falmer Press.

Belenky, M.F., Blythe, M.C., Goldberger, N.R. & Tarule, J.M. (1986). *Women's ways of knowing: The development of self, voice, and mind*. New York: Basic Books.

Berger, P.L. & Luckmann, T. (1966). *The social construction of reality*. Garden City, N.Y: Anchor Books, Doubleday.

Berry, D.M., Kisch, J.A., Ryan, C.W. & Uphoff, J.K. (1991). The process and product of portfolio construction. Paper presented at the American Educational Research Association Conference, Chicago, April.

Beyer, L. (1988). Schooling for the culture of democracy. In L. Beyer & M. Apple (Eds.), *The curriculum: Problems, politics, and possibilities*, pp. 219–240. New York: State University of New York Press.

Beyer, L. & Apple, M. (1988). *The curriculum: Problems, politics, and possibilities*. New York: State University of New York Press.

251

Bluestone, J. (1986). Are your colleagues driving you crazy? *Instructor*, November/December, pp. 35–41.

Bode, B.H. (1937). *Democracy as a way of life*. New York: Macmillan.

Boomer, G. (1987). Addressing the problem of elsewhereness: A case for action research in schools. In D. Goswami & P.R. Stillman (Eds.), *Reclaiming the classroom: Teacher research as an agency for change,* pp. 4–13. Upper Montclair, N.J.: Boynton/Cook Publishers, Inc.

Boyer, E. (1987). Why teachers are the real power behind school reform. *Instructor*, October, pp. 28–31.

Britzman, D.P. (1991). *Practice makes practice: A critical study of learning to teach*. Albany, New York: State University of New York Press.

Bruner, J. (1990). *Acts of meaning*. Cambridge, Mass.: Harvard University Press.

Buchmann, M. & Floden, R.E. (1992). Coherence, the rebel angel. *Educational Researcher 21*(9), December, 4–9.

Bullough, R.V., Jr. (1987). Accommodation and tension: Teachers, teacher role, and the culture of teaching. In J. Smyth (Ed.), *Educating teachers: Changing the nature of pedagogical knowledge,* pp. 83–94. London: Falmer Press.

Bullough, R.V., Jr. (1988). *The forgotten dream of American public education.* Ames, Iowa: Iowa State University Press.

Bullough, R.V., Jr. (1989). *First year teacher: A case study*. New York: Teachers College Press.

Bullough, R.V., Jr. (1991). Exploring personal teaching metaphors in preservice teacher education. *Journal of Teacher Education 42*(1), 43–51.

Bullough, R.V., Jr. (1992). Beginning teacher curriculum decision making, personal teaching metaphors, and teacher education. *Teaching & Teacher Education 8*(3), 239–252.

Bullough, R.V., Jr. (1993). Case records as personal teaching texts for study in preservice teacher education. *Teaching and Teacher Education 9*(4), 385–396.

Bullough, R.V., Jr. (1994). Personal history and teaching metaphors: A self-study of teaching as conversation. *Teacher Education Quarterly 21*(1). 107–120.

Bullough, R.V., Jr. & Baughman, K. (1993). Continuity and change in teacher development: First year teacher after five years. *Journal of Teacher Education 44*(2), 86–95.

Bullough, R.V., Jr. & Gitlin, A. (1985). Beyond control: Rethinking teacher resistance. *Education and Society 3*(1), 65–73.

Bullough, R.V., Jr. & Gitlin, A. (1989). Toward educative communities: Teacher education and the quest for the reflective practitioner. *Qualitative Studies in Education 2*(4), 285–298.

Bullough, R.V., Jr., Goldstein, S.L & Gitlin, A. (1984). Ideology, teacher role, and resistance. *Teachers College Record 86*(2), 339–58.

Bullough, R.V., Jr. & Goldstein, S.L. (1984). Technical curriculum form and American elementary school art education. *Journal of Curriculum Studies 16*(2), 143–154.

Bullough, R.V., Jr., Holt, L. & Goldstein, S.L. (1984). *Human interests in the curriculum: Teaching and learning in a technological society.* New York: Teachers College Press.

Bullough, R.V., Jr., Knowles, J.G. & Crow, N.A. (1992). *Emerging as a teacher.* London: Routledge.

Bullough, R.V., Jr. with Stokes, D.K. (1994). Analyzing personal teaching metaphors in preservice teacher education as a means for encouraging professional development. *American Educational Research Journal,* pp. 197–224.

Calderhead, J. & Robson, M. (1991). Images of teaching: Student teachers' early conceptions of classroom practice. *Teaching and Teacher Education 7,* 1–8.

Carr, W. & Kemmis, S. (1983). *Becoming critical: Knowing through action research.* Geelong: Deakin University Press.

Clark, C.M. (1988). Asking the right questions about teacher preparation: Contributions of research on teacher thinking. *Educational Researcher 17*(2), 5–12.

Clift, R.T., Houston, W.R. & Pugach, M.C. (Eds.). (1991). *Encouraging reflective practice in education.* New York: Teachers College Press.

Cole, A.L. (1990). Personal theories of teaching: Development in the formative years. *Alberta Journal of Educational Research 36*(3), 203–222.

Collins, E.C. & Green, J.L. (1990). Metaphors: The construction of a perspective. *Theory into Practice 29*(2), 71–77.

Connelly, F.M. & Clandinin, D.J. (1988). *Teachers as curriculum planners: Narratives of experience.* New York: Teachers College Press.

Corey, S.M. (1953). *Action research to improve school practices.* New York: Teachers College, Columbia University.

Csaslovka, A. (1992). Teachers tell the truth about school change. *Instructor,* January, pp. 24–34.

Diamond, C.T.P. (1991). *Teacher education as transformation.* Milton Keynes: Open University Press.

Dickmeyer, N. (1989). Metaphor, model, and theory in education research. *Teachers College Record 91*(2), 151–160.

Eckert, P. (1989). *Jocks and burnouts: Social categories and identity in the high school.* New York: Teachers College Press.

Eisner, E.W. (1985). *The educational imagination: On the design and evaluation of school programs,* second edition. New York: Macmillan Publishing Company.

Elbaz, F. (1983). *Teacher thinking: A study of practical knowledge.* London and Canberra: Croom Helm.

Elliott, J. (1987). Educational theory, practice philosophy and action research. *British Journal of Educational Studies 35*(2), 149–169.

Elliott, J. (1991). *Action research for educational change.* Milton Keynes: Open University Press.

Feiman-Nemser, S. & Floden, R.E. (1986). The cultures of teaching. In M.C. Wittrock (Ed.), *Handbook of Research on Teaching* (third edition), pp. 505–526. New York: Macmillan.

Florio-Ruane, S. (1989). Social organization of classes and schools. In M.C. Reynolds (Ed.), *Knowledge base for the beginning teacher,* pp. 163–172. New York: Pergamon Press.

Freire, P. (1993). *Pedagogy of the oppressed.* New York: Continuum.

Fullan, M. & Steigelbauer, S. (1991). *The new meaning of educational change,* second edition. New York: Teachers College Press.

Geahigan, G. (1992). The arts in education: A historical perspective. In B. Reimer & R.A. Smith (Eds.), *The arts, education, and aesthetic knowing,* ninety-first yearbook of the National Society for the Study of Education, Part II, pp. 1–19. Chicago: National Society for the Study of Education.

Gergen, K. (1991). *The saturated self: Dilemmas of identity in contemporary life.* New York: Basic Books.

Gitlin, A. (1983). School structure, teachers' work and reproduction. In M.W. Apple and L. Weiss (Eds.), *Ideology and practice in education,* pp. 193–221. Philadelphia: Temple University Press.

Gitlin, A. (1987). Common school structures and teacher behavior. In J. Smyth (Ed.), *Educating teacher: Changing the nature of pedagogical knowledge,* pp. 107–120. London: Falmer Press.

Gitlin, A. (1990). Educative research, voice and school change. *Harvard Educational Review 60*(4), 443–466.

Gitlin, A., Bringhurst, K., Burns, M., Cooley, V., Myers, B., Price, K., Russell, R. & Tiess, P. (1992). *Teachers' voices for school change: An introduction to educative research.* London: Routledge.

Gitlin, A. & Smyth, J. (1989). *Teacher evaluation: Educative alternatives.* London: Falmer Press.

Gitlin, A. & Teitelbaum, K. (1983). Linking theory and practice: The use of ethnographic methodology by prospective teachers. *Journal of Education for Teaching 9*(3), 225–234.

Goodlad, J.I. (1991). Why we need a complete redesign of teacher education. *Educational Leadership,* November, 4–10.

Goodson, I.F. (1981). Life histories and the study of schooling. *Interchange 11*(4), 62–76.

Goodson, I.F. (1991). Teachers' lives and educational research. In I.F. Goodson & R. Walker (Eds.), *Biography, identity & schooling: Episodes in educational research,* pp. 137–149. London: Falmer Press.

Goodson, I.F. (1991). Studying curriculum: A social constructivist perspective. In I.F. Goodson & R. Walker (Eds.), *Biography, identity & schooling: Episodes in educational research,* pp. 168–181. London: Falmer Press.

Goodson, I.F. (Ed.). (1992). *Studying teachers' lives.* New York: Routledge.

Goodson, I.F. & Walker, R. (1991). *Biography, identity & schooling: Episodes in educational research.* London: Falmer Press.

Gore, J.M. & Zeichner, K.M. (1991). Action research and reflective teaching in preservice teacher education: A case study from the United States. *Teaching and Teacher Education 7*(2), 119–136.

Griffiths, M. & Tann, S. (1992). Using reflective practice to link personal and public theories. *Journal of Education for Teaching 18*(1), 69–84.

Grimmett, P.P. & MacKinnon, A.M. (1992). Craft knowledge and the education of teachers. In G. Grant (Ed.), *Review of research in education,* pp. 385–456. Washington, D.C.: American Educational Research Association.

Habermas, J. (1971). *Knowledge and human interests.* Boston: Beacon Press.

Habermas, J. (1975). *Legitimation crisis.* Boston: Beacon Press.

Hargreaves, A. & Fullan, M.G. (Eds.) (1992). *Understanding teacher development.* New York: Teachers College Press.

Holmes Group. (1986). *Tomorrow's teachers: A report of the Holmes Group.* East Lansing, Mich.: Author.

Holmes Group. (1990). *Tomorrow's schools: A report of the Holmes Group.* East Lansing, Mich.: Author.

Hunt, E.K. & Sherman, H.J. (1986). *Economics: An introduction to traditional and radical views.* New York: Harper and Row Publishers.

Johnston, S. (1991). Images: A way of understanding the practical knowledge of student teachers. *Teaching and Teacher Education* *8*(2), 123–136.

Keith, S. (1981). *Politics of textbook selection.* NIE Project Report No. 81–A7, April.

Kemmis, S. & McTaggart, R. (1988). *The action research planner,* third edition. Victoria, Australia: Deakin University.

Kierkegaard, S. (1956). *Purity of heart is to will one thing.* New York: Harper & Row.

Knowles, J.G. (1991). Journal use in preservice teacher education: A personal and reflexive response to comparisons and criticisms. Paper presented at the annual meeting of the Association of Teacher Educators, New Orleans, February.

Knowles, J.G. (1992). Models for understanding preservice and beginning teachers' biographies: Illustrations from case studies. In I.F. Goodson (Ed.), *Studying teachers' life,* pp. 99–152. New York: Routledge.

Knowles, J.G., Cole, A.L. with Presswood, C.S. (1994). *Through preservice teachers' eyes: Exploring field experiences through narrative and inquiry.* New York: Merrill.

Kyvig, D. & Marty, M. (1986). *Nearby histories.* Nashville: The American Association for State and Local History.

Lacey, C. (1977). *The socialization of teachers.* London: Methuen.

Lakoff, G. & Johnson, M. (1980). *Metaphors we live by.* Chicago: The University of Chicago Press.

Lewin, K. (1948). *Resolving social conflict: Selected papers on group dynamics.* G.W. Lewin (Ed.). New York: Harper and Brothers.

Liston, D.P. & Zeichner, K.M. (1987). Reflective teacher education and moral deliberation. *Journal of Teacher Education 38*(6), 2–8.

Lortie, D. (1975). *School-teacher: A sociological study.* Chicago: University of Chicago Press.

Mager, R.R. (1962). *Preparing instructional objectives.* Palo Alto, Cal.: Fearon Publishers.

McCarthy, T. (1991). *Ideals and illusions.* Cambridge, Mass.: The MIT Press.

McCutcheon, G. (1982). How do elementary school teachers plan? The nature of planning and influences on it. In W. Doyle & T.L. Good (Eds.), *Focus on teaching: Readings from the Elementary School Journal.* Chicago: University of Chicago Press.

Measor, L. (1985). Critical incidents in the classroom: Identities, choices and careers. In S.J. Ball and I.F. Goodson (Eds.), *Teachers' lives and careers,* pp. 61–77. London: Falmer Press.

Munby, H. & Russell, T. (1993). The authority of experience in learning to teach: Messages from a physics methods class. Paper presented at the Annual meeting of the American Educational Research Association, Atlanta, April.

Nias, J. (1989). *Primary teachers talking: A study of teaching as work.* London: Routledge.

Norton, C.S. (1989). *Life metaphors: Stories of ordinary survival.* Carbondale and Edwardsville, Ill.: Southern Illinois Press.

Oakes, J. (1985). *Keeping track: How schools structure inequality.* New Haven: Yale University Press.

Olney, J. (1972). *Metaphors of self: The meaning of autobiography.* Princeton, N.J.: Princeton University Press.

Pateman, C. (1970). *Participation and democratic theory.* Cambridge: Cambridge University Press.

Pinar, W. (1980). Life history and educational experience. *The Journal of Curriculum Theorizing* 2(2), 159–212.

Pinar, W. (1981). Life history and educational experience: Part two. *The Journal of Curriculum Theorizing* 3(1), 259–286.

Plato (1966). *Plato's Republic.* Cambridge: Cambridge University Press.

Posner, G. (1992). *Analyzing the curriculum.* New York: McGraw-Hill, Inc.

Presidential Task Force on Psychology in Education, American Psychological Association (January, 1993). Learner-centered psychological principles: Guidelines for school redesign and reform. Washington, D.C.: American Psychological Association and Mid-continent Regional Educational Laboratory.

Pullias, E. & Young, J. (1968). *A teacher is many things.* Bloomington and London: Indiana University Press.

Raymond, D., Butt, R. & Townsend, D. (1992). Contexts for teacher development: Insights from teachers' stories. In A. Hargreaves & M.G. Fullan (Eds.), *Understanding teacher development*, pp. 143–161. New York: Teachers College Press.

Rhodenbaugh, S. (1992). One heart's canon. *The American Scholar 61*(3), 389–398.

Riordan, T. (1973). A view of self in the teaching-learning process: Self development as an approach to the education of teachers. Unpublished doctoral dissertation, The Ohio State University, Columbus, Ohio.

Riseborough, G.F. (1985). Pupils, teachers' careers and schooling: An empirical study. In S.J. Ball and I.F. Goodson (Eds.), *Teachers' lives and careers*, pp. 202–265. London: Falmer Press.

Rosenholtz, S.J. (1989). Workplace conditions that affect teacher quality and commitment: Implications for teacher induction programs. *Elementary School Journal 89*(4), 421–439.

Sarason, S.B. (1971). *The culture of the school and the problem of change.* Boston: Allyn & Bacon.

Sardo-Brown, D. (1988). Twelve middle-school teachers' planning. *Elementary School Journal 89*(1), 69–87.

Schon, D.A. (1987). *Educating the reflective practitioner: Toward a new design for teaching and learning in the professions.* San Francisco: Jossey-Bass.

Shulman, L. (1987). Knowledge and teaching: Foundations of the new reform. *Harvard Educational Review 57*(1), 1–22.

Sikes, P.J., Measor, L. & Woods, P. (1985). *Teacher careers: Crises and continuities.* London: Falmer Press.

Spradley, J.P. (1980). *Participant observation.* New York: Holt, Rinehart and Winston.

Spradley, J.P. & McCurdy, D.W. (1972). *The cultural experience: Ethnography in complex society.* Chicago: SRA Associates.

Stenhouse, L. (1985). *Research as a basis for teaching: Readings on the work of Lawrence Stenhouse.* J. Rudduck & D. Hopkins (Eds.). London: Heinemann Educational Books.

Sternberg, R.J. & Martin, M. (1988). When teaching thinking does not work, what goes wrong? *Teachers College Record 89*(4), 555–578.

Tanner, D. (1988). The textbook controversies. In L.N. Tanner (Ed.), *Critical issues in curriculum,* eighty-seventh yearbook of the

National Society for the Study of Education, Part I, pp. 122–147. Chicago: National Society for the Study of Education.

Taylor, W. (1984). Metaphors of educational discourse. In W. Taylor (Ed.), *Metaphors in education*, pp. 4–20. London: Heinemann Educational Books.

Teitelbaum, K. & Britzman, D.P. (1991). Reading and doing ethnography: Teacher education and reflective practice. In R.B. Tabachnick & K. Zeichner (Eds.), *Issues and practice in inquiry-oriented teacher education*, pp 166–185. London: Falmer Press.

Turner, R. (1987). To teach or not to teach. *Learning*, October, pp. 57–60.

Willis, P. (1977). *Learning to labour: How working class kids get working class jobs*. Farnborough: Saxon House.

Witherell, C. (1991). The self in narrative: A journey into paradox. In C. Witherell & N. Noddings (Eds.), *Stories lives tell: Narrative and dialogue in education*, pp. 83–95. New York: Teachers College Press.

Wolf, A. (1992). Minorities in U.S. history textbooks, 1945–1985. *The Clearing House 65*(5), 291–297.

Woodward, A. & Elliott, D.L. (1990). Textbooks: Consensus and controversy. In D.L. Elliott & A. Woodward (Eds.), *Textbooks and schooling in the United States*, eighty-ninth yearbook of the National Society for the Study of Education, Part I, pp. 146–161. Chicago: National Society for the Study of Education.

Wright, E.O. (1978). *Class, crisis and the state.* London: Lowe and Brydone Printers.

Yin, R.K. (1984). *Case study research: Design and methods.* Beverly Hills: Sage Publications

Zeichner, K.M. & Liston, D.P. (1987). Teaching student teachers to reflect. *Harvard Educational Review 57*(1), 23–48.

Zeichner, K.M. & Liston, D.P. (1990). Traditions of reform in U.S. teacher education. *Journal of Teacher Education 41*(2), 3–20.

Zeichner, K.M. & Tabachnick, B.R. (1981). Are the effects of university teacher education "washed out" by school experience? *Journal of Teacher Education 32*(3), 7–11.

Zumwalt, K. (1988). Are we improving or undermining teaching? In L.N. Tanner (Ed.), *Critical issue in curriculum*, eighty-seventh yearbook of the National Society for the Study of Education, Part I, pp. 148–174. Chicago: National Society for the Study of Education.

Zumwalt, K. (1989). Beginning professional teachers: The need for a
    curricular vision of teaching. In M.C. Reynolds (Ed.), *Knowledge
    base for the beginning teacher*, pp. 173–184. Oxford: Pergamon
    Press.

Index